What's Wrong with Children's Rights

What's Wrong with Children's Rights

Martin Guggenheim

HARVARD UNIVERSITY PRESS

Cambridge, Massachusetts, and London, England 2005

Library of Congress Cataloging-in-Publication Data

Guggenheim, Martin.
   What's wrong with children's rights / Martin Guggenheim.
      p.   cm.
   Includes bibliographical references and index.
   ISBN 0-674-01721-8 (cloth : alk. paper)
   1. Children's rights.   2. Children—Legal status, laws, etc.—United States.
   3. Parent and child (law)—United States.   I. Title.

HQ789.G78 2005
323.3′52′0973—dc22   2004060792

For Jamie, Courtney, and Lesley,
the most important children in my world

Contents

Preface

I AM a product of the 1960s. The various ways in which that decade has influenced my life are unworthy of an entire book. But in one particular sense the social upheavals of that remarkable decade had a profound and lasting impact on me: as soon as I graduated from law school in 1971, I joined a new field of practice very much still being invented. I became a children's rights lawyer.

Children's rights lawyers came into being only a few years earlier because of a landmark Supreme Court case holding that children accused of being juvenile delinquents in juvenile court have a constitutional right to free court-assigned counsel if their parents are too poor to hire a lawyer themselves. Until then, juvenile court, an invention of the early twentieth century, eschewed lawyers for children because they were regarded as an obstacle to furthering a child's best interests. *In re Gault* changed this in one dramatic decision and, as a consequence, created the need for thousands of lawyers to work in a previously nonexistent field.

I began my professional life working in the largest office devoted to representing children in the United States, a legal services office for children in New York City. Two years after beginning my first job, I was fortunate to be asked to create and teach the Juvenile Rights Clinic at New York University School of Law. Working under my supervision, students in the clinic represented children in delinquency and other legal matters in New York's Family Court. In the mid 1970s, I also worked at a national project devoted to furthering the rights of children.

By the mid 1980s, I, or students working directly under my supervision, had represented many hundreds of children in a wide variety of legal proceedings in New York and throughout the United States in state and federal court, including a number of cases in the U.S. Supreme Court. The various kinds of cases on which I worked included juvenile delinquency, child protection, foster care, termination of parental rights, and custody disputes arising from divorce-related cases. By this time, I enjoyed a reputation as a nationally known expert in children's rights and was known in professional circles as a leading advocate for children's rights. I have continued to work in the field of children's rights ever since, as a scholar, litigator, and teacher of scores of students who have gone on to make their own careers in fields connected to children.

And yet, something rather odd was going on almost from the beginning. As advocates for children continued to press for changes in the laws affecting children, it became increasingly clear that these advocates sought things to which I was diametrically opposed. The more engaged I became in advocating for changes in law or policy affecting children, the more I began realizing that my fiercest disagreements were with others also wearing the mantle of children's rights advocate.

What began as a journey defending children against prosecution by state officials became a growing internal fight among children's rights advocates. Within a decade I even reached the (what still seems to many) remarkable conclusion that providing children with lawyers in a whole variety of legal matters was antithetical to children's interests.

As deeply as I've always thought of myself as a children's advocate, much of what I read and hear being advocated in furtherance of children's rights seems to me misguided. And yet, I continue to identify myself as a children's advocate while rejecting much of what falls under the rubric of children's rights. This book is, in part, an effort to make sense of how this could be so.

Because the concept of children's rights entered the legal field at about the same time I did, I have had the fascinating benefit of watching it develop in its earliest stages. Beyond the excitement of the new, this vantage point invites a critical perspective: nothing is yet set in stone when the foundational steps in a field of law are just being laid. It is easier to see that we have choices about the political and legal values we are adopting when it comes to children's rights than with respect to more developed areas of law. We are not yet committed to any particular path. Thus we have the privilege, and the responsibility, of making these choices consciously.

Broadly speaking, the children's rights movement since the 1960s has focused on two sometimes intertwined but often completely separate matters. One concerns the rights of children with respect to the exercise of state power; the other, the rights of children with respect to the exercise of parental authority. Because these two situations are theoretically and practically distinct, they are best treated separately.

Children's rights as protection against the exercise of state power is an important subject involving the arrest and prosecution of young people and the rights of students in schools, among many other topics. In an era in which children are being permanently excluded from public schools because of "zero tolerance" policies, and young people are being charged in adult criminal court and are receiving adult-like sentences, including life imprisonment, in record numbers, there is little doubt that children need rights to constrain state officials in the exercise of their official duties. Except in passing, however, this book does not address this subject.

Instead, this book is concerned primarily with the way in which the children's rights movement has been invoked when it comes to the family and, particularly, parental rights. In this area, I am far less confident that children need rights or that speaking in terms of "rights" is even good for children.

Within the context of child-parent relations, this book will explore the subject of "children's rights" as a phenomenon: how the rhetoric of children's rights is used, by whom, and to whose advantage. It will describe how the children's rights movement began and what became its fashionable choice of language. We will come to see that the subject is considerably more complicated than is sometimes appreciated.

"Children's rights" is both deeper and more shallow than is often recognized. It has less substantive content and is less coherent than many would suppose. It has provided very little by way of a useful analytic tool for resolving knotty social problems. One of its shibboleths, for example, is its call for "child-centeredness." But this attractive phrase tells us nothing about how to use it or what are its sensible limits. It surely calls for too much to examine matters affecting children exclusively from the child's perspective. There are countless ways American society would change were children the only consideration. Certainly we would outlaw cigarette smoking, alcohol consumption, toxic pollutants, and war, for starters. But we have all of these things despite a consensus that they are not particularly good for children. And that is because there are other perspectives apart from a child's that we rightly take into account even when we talk about children's rights and needs. Children are, to be sure, a precious part of our world, but they are only a part.

Nor could child-centeredness be a manifesto to do things children themselves want at the time. Our society is premised on the opposite concept. Adults decide what the rules are for children based on what adults believe is good for them. When this manifesto dictates only that we should do what is good for them, the problem becomes, of course, gaining consensus.

But there is also much more to children's rights than is apparent. It has staying power because it serves adults too. Adults gain in a number of important ways by presenting themselves as caring about children. Across a very wide range of areas, including disputes between adoptive parents and unwed fathers, between biological parents and others who act as parents but lack legally enforceable rights, between grandparent and parents, between divorcing parents, between child welfare agencies and parents, and between parents and state officials over details of childrearing, the rhetoric of children's rights works well for adults on a number of levels.

Sometimes, it serves as a useful subterfuge for the adult's actual motives. It can be an effective diverter of attention, shifting the focus to a more sympathetic party than the adult. Other times, it is used to assuage guilt for the adult's bad behavior or intentions. Children's rights can be useful for masking selfishness by invoking a language of altruism. It can also provide a legal basis to achieve a result that would be difficult to achieve otherwise. Time and again we will see the frequency with which the concept of children's rights is used by adults to try to gain some advantage in their struggles with other adults.

This phenomenon is hardly unfamiliar to Americans, even those who have had no contact with legal arguments. "Children's rights" has become a mantra invoked by adults to help them in their own fights with other adults in all sorts of contexts. This happens at a national level every four years when we have a presidential campaign. Both the Republicans and Democrats fight furiously with each other, trying to win the mantle of being more child-friendly and child-focused than the other side. But winning that battle only occasionally (and incidentally) proves to be any kind of victory for children.

There is no question that the phrase has the rhetorical advantage of being difficult to challenge head on: who would be comfortable being anti–children's rights? But whether we should be for or against them must, of course, depend on what that phrase is used to mean and how its consequences affect people's lives. In the *Gault* Court's famous words, it is time to "candidly appraise" whether children's rights serve children's interests.

1

A Brief History of Children's Rights
in the United States

THERE never was a golden age for children's issues in the United States. Although the subject of what is best for children has long been the focus of political discussion, struggles to improve the lives of children invariably have been fierce. There have been two principal children's movements in American history. The first, led by the Progressives, ran from a decade or more at the end of the nineteenth century through the first two decades of the twentieth. The second, a product of the 1960s, is commonly known as the children's rights movement.

Though there are a number of important similarities between then and now, there is one preeminent difference. Before, debates about children were framed in terms of what was good for them. Now, we are much more likely to hear about children's rights. This chapter explains how this shift took place, setting the stage for the chapters that follow.

During the Progressive era, social activists included the welfare of children in their long list of required social reforms to make the United States a more humane and sensibly ordered society. The Progressives insisted that children's needs receive the attention of the state, and they focused on those needs that deserved the most compelling attention. As a direct result of the advocacy of Grace Abbott, Jane Addams, John Dewey, and Florence Kelley, to name only a few, American society shifted its understanding of children's well-being as a natural parental responsibility to an issue that government and those who forged official policy had a responsibility to address.

The laissez-faire mentality that dominated much of American life well into the twentieth century gave adults far greater leeway to use children as they wished than we can imagine today. Before the Progressive successes, children could be required to work in unregulated industries for as long as their parents deemed appropriate. Protecting children from harm was not a public responsibility. Nor was education. Whether or not children went to school was entirely the "choice" of their parents, with the full understanding that many poor families needed their children to contribute to the family income.

The Progressives changed all of this, and more. "Progressives," according to Joseph Hawes, "believed that they had found the means to reshape society: improve conditions for the children of today and the world of the future will be automatically transformed."[1] It is not an overstatement to suggest that they succeeded in transforming American society's understanding of its responsibility for children's well-being. Today, we take it for granted that children should be protected from being obliged to work at an early age. It is also ingrained in our understanding of basic principles of society that government owes children a free and appropriate education. And modern society recognizes its responsibilities to protect vulnerable children from abuse, even when that abuse is inflicted by their parents.

These things are so accepted today, it is even easy to fail to appreciate that it ever could have been otherwise, let alone just how hard won the battles were. Many opposed to proposed legislation regulating child labor and establishing compulsory education spoke in the voice of the parent, arguing both that the laws would impermissibly intrude on a parent's childrearing prerogatives and that they would be bad for children. The passage of such laws, it was asserted, would destroy "[t]he immemorial right of the parent to train his child in useful tasks" and "[t]he obligation of the child to contribute."[2] This position was hardly limited to a fringe group. In

1924, Columbia University's president condemned pending child labor bills in Congress, observing they "would empower Congress to invade the rights of parents and to shape family life to its liking."[3]

Proponents of these laws, for their part, were quite bold in their use of counter rhetoric. According to Viviana Zelizer, Progressives branded anyone "who defend[ed] the child labor that violates the personalities of children" as "unchristian." Parents opposed to these laws were condemned as selfish exploiters of their children's labors: "Those who are fighting for the rights of the children," in the words of a supporter of child labor legislation in 1917, "almost invariably, find their stoutest foes in the fathers and mothers, who coin shameful dollars from bodies and souls of their own flesh and blood."[4]

As perceived by those fighting the battle, the struggle was critically important. For some, children had the right to have their character shaped by hard work. Being relegated to a long period of hanging out with nothing productive to do, where play would become the predominant activity after school, was worse than unfair. It belittled children. Not only were they to be denied the "privilege to work," they were to be "forced [] to do nothing more of drudgery than is necessitated by playing on a ball team after school hours."[5] On the other side, adults fought to secure for children some space to grow up without the burdens of adulthood, free from exploitation, and with optimal opportunities to become happy and productive adults.

Of course, the battles were always about more than the children themselves. Even more important, they almost certainly would not have ended as they did, had child labor restrictions not been perceived as serving adults' interests as well as children's. As the immigrant population in the United States increased in the beginning of the twentieth century, opposition to child labor laws from industry weakened because another form of cheap labor appeared. Because others saw children taking jobs from adults who needed them, support for child labor laws increased.[6]

Looming behind every issue concerning children is an even

broader debate about the role of government. Thus, the child labor movement was dealt its first major blow by the Supreme Court in its 1918 decision in *Hammer v. Dagenhart* declaring unconstitutional the first major child labor restriction law ever enacted by Congress. At the time, the Court was at its height of power in rejecting social legislation enacted by Congress with which the justices personally disagreed. This was part of a struggle between the Court and Congress over which would have the final say in altering the social and legal landscape of the United States, a disagreement that lasted into the 1930s.

Twenty years later, when this fight over constitutional democracy was resolved in Congress's favor, the Court upheld the 1938 Fair Labor Standards Act, which broadly regulated child labor. In the throes of the Great Depression, the country faced its most serious constitutional crisis when President Franklin Roosevelt threatened to "pack" the Court with enough justices to uphold the New Deal laws that the Court was declaring unconstitutional. When the Court finally affirmed Congress's power to regulate child labor, little had changed about adults' perception of children or their needs. What had changed was our sense of which institutions should decide these matters.

Among the Progressives' successes was creating a process for keeping children's interests in the national spotlight. It is no accident that in 1909 Theodore Roosevelt was the first president to create the White House Conference on Children, a tradition that was continued approximately every ten years throughout the century.

But perhaps the Progressives' greatest achievement was the creation of juvenile court. Recoiling from a criminal justice system that was single-mindedly concerned with punishing criminals, the Progressives saw a richer and more humane purpose for a justice system. To the Progressives, a child's criminal behavior is an indicator of something being wrong. They believed the state's best role is to find out what is wrong and try to fix it.

Accordingly, juvenile court was broadly conceived as a helping institution whose principal goal was to make the young people who came before it better, happier, and more productive than they had been before they got into trouble with the law. The Progressives believed that child-friendly courts should seek to understand the whole of the child and not narrowly focus on the child's misbehavior. They believed official inquiry into *why* the child acted as he or she did was even more important than spending considerable efforts to determine *what* the child did.

The 1960s and the Beginning of the Modern Children's Rights Movement

The current world of children's rights was born in the 1960s, a period of remarkable protest and activism. More important movements thrived in that decade, of course. The civil rights and feminist movements became powerful influences in American culture and political life and have continued through today to transform society.

The sixties awakened in many Americans a sensitivity to oppression and subordination, two of the characteristics at the heart of the struggle of the civil rights and feminist movements. The sixties also inspired people to reconsider old ways and not to assume that just because a particular practice was venerable it was right or worthy of maintaining. The youth of the sixties took this idea to its extreme. Beyond a willingness to consider that the old ways may be wrong, many activists took seriously the injunction "don't trust anyone over thirty." The message, of course, was that anything that the older generation was doing was presumptively misguided.

Thus, the modern version of the children's rights movement was born in an era of deep generational conflict and was fueled by rhetoric grounded in demands for freedom and equality. For this reason, it is unsurprising that the writers who first took up the modern cause of children's rights employed a deeply radical tone. One of the leading children's rights books from the 1970s (an era characterized by an excess of rhetorical flourish) was entitled: *The Children's Rights Movement: Overcoming the Oppression of Young People.*[7]

Richard Farson, writing in the beginning of the 1970s, asserted that treating children differently from adults is a classic form of discrimination that denies children "their right to full humanity."[8] He asserted that "childhood" is merely a social construct created to facilitate adults' needs. John Holt's *Escape from Childhood,* published in the same year as Farson's book, sought to liberate children from virtually all disabilities the law imposed on them.[9]

But apart from children's rights, the sixties was a time of general upheaval. The success of the previous generation of children's advocates was mostly lost on young professionals coming of age in that decade. By the 1960s, an entire generation had grown up in an American society deeply influenced by Progressive values. But this generation had never been exposed to the conditions against which the Progressives fought. Instead, this new generation reacted to the institutions it knew. Of these, juvenile court was considered to be the epitome of unfairness. The modern children's rights activist cut his or her teeth challenging the very institution (deemed a state-sponsored exercise of paternalism) that was allowed to come into being only because of the tireless efforts of the previous generation's children's rights advocates.

In a world in which adults were doing too little to protect children from the conditions of the free market, child advocates were understandably focused on advancing children's protection. This explains the Progressives and their place in American history. By the 1960s, the world looked rather different. Children everywhere were required to go to school; they were protected against excessive exploitation through work. And they were part of an expansive juvenile justice system. In such a world, the 1960s activist argued, adults interfered too much in children's lives, and children's advocates sought autonomy and personal freedom for children.

The Progressives became, in the eyes of the 1960s children's advocates, the "Regressives." To these advocates, it was the Progressives who were responsible for the oppression of youth. This change in perspective led Anthony Platt, among others, to condemn not just the way in which juvenile court came to control children's lives but even the motives of the Progressives. In his view, they were motivated by the desire to control the lives of children rather than to improve them.[10]

None took up the call to liberate children from the disabilities of childhood more seriously and in a more sustained manner than lawyers. Indeed, one of the significant distinctions between the historical effort to advance the lives of children and the modern children's rights movement is the degree to which the modern movement is led by and disproportionately made up of lawyers. The modern children's rights movement scored an early and transforming victory in 1967 when the Supreme Court decided what still remains as the most important children's rights case in history. Through *In re Gault,* the Supreme Court declared many of the practices of juvenile court to be unconstitutional. Specifically, the Court held that juveniles accused of being delinquent have a constitutional right to several core procedural rights in the federal constitution (including the right to court-assigned counsel, the right to remain silent, and the right to cross-examine witnesses). But the significance of that decision goes well beyond what it held.

In the process of recognizing a young person's right to these procedural safeguards, the Court attacked juvenile court as an institution established to help children but which rarely met its lofty purposes. *Gault* thus fit nicely with the spirit of the times—which may be characterized as "what-have-you-done-for-me-lately"—preferring that greater attention be paid to results than to intentions. *Gault* insisted that institutions affecting the lives of children be "candidly appraised." No longer would special rules affecting children be evaluated solely on the motives of those who created them. This set into motion over the next decades efforts by children's advocates to challenge the institutions affecting children's lives, including juvenile court and public schools.

Another of *Gault's* legacies is the proliferation of lawyers for children in court proceedings. Before the 1960s, children's representation in court proceedings was virtually unknown. If children were represented, their parents retained a lawyer and the lawyer represented the parents, not the child. *Gault* explicitly changed that in juvenile delinquency cases. But its reach hardly stopped there. In 1974, Congress enacted a law calling for some kind of separate representation for children in neglect and abuse cases. Today there are thousands of lawyers representing children in a large array of legal proceedings.

Gault's most important legacy is the elevation of the prominence of lawyers in leading the modern children's rights movement. Earlier efforts to advance children's interests were led by professionals from many ranks, almost none of whom were lawyers. Since the 1960s, however, the movement has been characterized by three related components: It is dominated by lawyers; it looks to the courts for relief; and it is based on a rhetoric of rights. This is perhaps simply a longer way of stating the same thing. Lawyers are preternaturally inclined to look to courts for relief and to speak in the language of rights. This shift from "needs" to "rights" was even manifested in the language of the 1970 White House Conference on Children. This was the first conference, according to Rochelle Beck, to transform claims for children's "developmental, health, and educational 'needs' . . . into their 'right.'"[11]

What is a child's right, as the coming chapters will make clear, is often in the eyes of the beholder. Some children's rights advocates continue to draw upon the excess of rhetoric of the early days of the modern movement. Thus, a current leading children's rights advocate and law professor, Kathleen Federle, advocates for overcoming children's "subordination" and "oppression," connecting the way Americans treated slaves with the way the law limits the freedom of children. According to Federle, just as the "infantilization of African Americans was nothing more than an attempt to control and oppress an entire race," "[t]heories which cannot accommodate the rights of children perpetuate these traditions of power and dominance."[12] Federle is only one of many current writers who have likened the legal status of children to that of slaves.[13] One philosopher, writing in 2002, called the status of children in American law "a sort of moral nightmare" and "an evil and morally hideous" position.[14]

This has had unfortunate consequences for the children's rights movement. The call for freedom and an end to oppression, as applied to children, is received by many Americans as overheated nonsense. And for good reason. Most adults are unpersuaded that children, like other minorities, are an oppressed group, and that laws discriminating against them should be measured against a heightened standard to ensure children's rights are protected by the majority. Such arguments, in the words of the philosopher Onora O'Neill, have "neither theoretical nor political advantages."[15]

There is no denying that law insists that children be subordinate to adults and subject to adult authority. But this subordination has virtually nothing to do with the oppression experienced by racial minorities or by women. It is false to suggest that adults are oppressing children by developing laws that restrict the liberties of children. In many contexts, children are in the control of adults for unassailable reasons. As most of us recognize, childhood is a stage of life that normally ends through the natural course of development. More pertinently, the rules created by adults for children are designed with the idea that children will emerge from childhood and enter adulthood.

This does not mean, of course, that everything adults do in the exercise of their control over children is appropriate. But it is not the condition of control that is wrong. It is the way it is being exercised. Adults may err in the design of special rules concerning children. Certainly I do not want to be understood to be an unabashed supporter of all of the rules and laws currently in place regarding children. But the question currently being considered is not the wisdom of various laws or rules; it is the motivation of the adults who make them. For the most part, "[t]hose with power over children's lives usually have some interest in ending childish dependence."[16]

Many sensibly believe, along with the Progressives, that it is a child's right not to be deemed capable of making certain decisions. Providing children with immunities that the law would not apply to adults and limiting children's privileges and rights differentially from adults are, for many who care deeply about children, prominent examples of honoring and caring about children. Thus, many adults would deny that children gain something that is good for them by being able to do what the law permits adults to do. This is, of course, a core point about children's rights. In a famous phrase in the legal literature, this is akin to "abandoning children to their rights."[17]

It is worse than misguided to speak of highly dependent children, such as newborns and toddlers, as needing or lacking "freedom." They need the opposite. Children need caring adults to ensure they will live and grow into independent adults. Children, at least for an important period of their lives, are dependent on adults for their very existence. In the language of an early nineteenth-century court, it would be an act of cruelty to deny (very young) children custody.[18]

Many adults quite reasonably reject arguments grounded in eliminating oppression. As Onora O'Neill argues, although proponents of freedom "have repudiated the justice of familial analogies which liken kings to fathers, see colonial powers as mother countries, women and underdeveloped peoples as childlike, and social relations as patriarchal," the same arguments do not work as applied to children if only because "it is no mere analogy when we speak of mothers and fathers as parents, and children are not just metaphorically child-like."[19]

Thus, claims for children's rights based on a sense of oppression or subordination are unlikely to generate much support. This is true both inside and outside of the law. Such claims are framed in terms of equal protection within the courts. But, as applied to children, equal protection claims are highly problematic.

American law and policy today either flatly forbid differential treatment of persons on the basis of their national origin, race, religion, or gender or place a high burden on those who seek to use such characteristics as the basis for discrimination. Indeed, this was the signal victory achieved by the civil rights and feminist movements. Whether through modern definitions of the Equal Protection Clause of the Fourteenth Amendment or federal and state legislation guaranteeing freedom from discrimination in the use of public accommodations, the workplace, schools and the like, law has gone a very long way toward respecting equality of treatment of diverse Americans.

This form of "freedom" makes almost no sense when applied to children, however. Some children's rights claims straightforwardly assert that children are denied the constitutional guarantee of equal protection of the laws when children are denied rights adults have. The Supreme Court has handled this claim very simply. It has consistently held that equal protection claims based on age are the weakest form of constitutional challenge. Laws that discriminate based on age will be upheld so long as they are rational, the easiest test to meet when defending a law. Because children *are* different from adults in significant ways, courts almost uniformly dismiss equal protection claims based on unequal treatment of children as compared with adults.

The Supreme Court has also consistently held that it is rational to treat children as a group based on characteristics most children share (even if some children do not share them) such as immaturity and the lack of intellectual and experiential capacity. States are free to lump children into a broad category of "minors" and declare them incompetent to make a whole range of decisions for themselves that adults have the right to make without allowing individual children to demonstrate that they are capable or mature.

For these reasons, the claim that laws that discriminate against children based on their age are illegal because they violate the principal of equality is an incomplete or doomed argument. Thus, a challenge to compulsory education laws as a violation of a child's right to be treated the same as an adult (who is not required to attend school) would be instantly rejected by a court.

If the law were to be struck down, it would have to be for a reason other than that it treats children differently from adults. The *way* in which it treats them differently would have to be challenged as irrational or otherwise unfair. A law, for example, that forbade children from entering video parlors with "violent" video games might be successfully challenged as irrationally denying children the right to engage in a safe activity.[20] Although the law might also be challenged on equal protection grounds (claiming that permitting adults, but not children, to enter video parlors is itself illegal), such a challenge is much weaker and less likely to prevail.

Rejecting the argument that children ought to have the same rights as adults is hardly anti-child. Nor does it mean that children lack rights simply because it is permissible to treat them differently from adults. What it does mean is that advocates for children have to work hard to develop persuasive arguments that advance children's lives because the traditional rights-rhetoric upon which other groups have relied rarely applies to children.

It quickly becomes plain that the children's rights movement needs an original vocabulary and cannot afford to echo the language of other movements seeking to advance the freedom and rights of others. Children are different from adults and sound laws and policy will want to reflect those differences.

If the first call by liberationists started the modern movement on the wrong foot, the second contingent stumbled backward. In 1972, Henry Foster and Doris Jonas Freed (a law professor and lawyer, respectively) in their "Bill of Rights for Children" asserted that children have the right to "receive parental love and affection, discipline and guidance."[21] Foster and Freed's error was in confusing the meaning of rights by naming certain things that are good for children, such as being raised in a loving environment, as among their rights. These unenforceable claims did little to advance children's place in the world.

Between the liberationists and the advocates who lost their way in figuring out what rights are, the children's rights movement has been a confused and often ridiculed one. The internal incoherence in developing children's rights claims plainly has had an impact on the way our culture treats the subject of children's rights.

Nearly forty years after the movement began, it has made very little progress developing a cogent conceptual position. At the very beginning of the movement, a then-recent law graduate, Hillary Rodham, famously observed that children's rights was "a slogan in search of a definition."[22] The same could be written today. But the difference between then and now is that many meanings of children's rights have emerged. Unfortunately, some are totally incompatible with others. Modern children's advocates include those who insist that children be given adultlike rights and those stressing that adults must do more to help children. As Joseph Hawes describes it, "Both kinds of advocates speak in terms of children's rights, and both can claim to be a part of the children's rights movement."[23] Or, as Martha Minow noted, by the end of the 1980s, "It remained possible to argue that young people deserve the same treatment as adults, that young people deserve special legal protections differing from the law of adults, and that law should refrain from intruding on the ordinary practices of adults responsible for children."[24]

Compounding this extraordinarily complicated set of claims, the modern children's advocate is likely to advance claims for children that are based on a fatally flawed premise. As rights have entered center stage, many children's claims are advanced on the basis of the child's individual personhood. Again, lawyers are especially responsible for this focus, which falsely suggests the possibility and, even worse, the desirability of isolating children from the larger fabric of the society into which they have been born and are being raised.

Regrettably, a leading characteristic of the children's rights movement is its propensity to separate children's interests from their parents'. It is also its most egregious error. The effort has created a struggle within the movement, almost completely invisible to the public, over who is permitted to be called a "children's advocate." Within this struggle, the label "parent's advocate" frequently takes on a pejorative meaning. Even "family advocate" is often sloughed off by children's advocates as a nice try, not quite stout enough to earn the title "children's advocate."

Children are inherently dependent for much of the time they remain in the category of "child." For this reason, it is highly problematic to discuss the rights of children in a wide variety of contexts without simultaneously considering the rights of the people on whom they are dependent. In our culture, this means their parents. Attempting to consider the rights and needs of (very young) children without simultaneously taking into account the rights and needs of their parents is akin to attempting to isolate someone's arm from the rest of their body.

Finally, there is a deeply ironic quality to the modern movement's achievements. Because so many children's advocates are distrustful of parents' treatment of their children, the judgments and decisions of parents are subject to an unprecedented degree of review by judges. As a result, the degree to which children's lives were subject to the control of the state because of the Progressives' efforts pales compared with what goes on today.

In another significant sense, it is futile to separate children and their rights from the rest of society. To state the obvious, children live in the world of adults. As a result, most changes in law concerning children will impact adults (and vice versa). Rules concerning children simultaneously are rules concerning adults. The inverse sometimes, but not as often, is true: Rules concerning adults often are also rules concerning children.

Virtually everything about children's rights must be understood within the larger culture into which children are born. Even the language commonly used to advance children's rights must be understood within the familiar taxonomy of American society. In the United States, rights tend to be "negative" (freedom from government oppression). Many countries have a dramatically broader conception of rights that incorporates "positive" rights (obligations owed to them by government). The international community is far more likely to regard rights as including positive claims than is the United States. Indeed, the signal characteristic of the International Human Rights Movement that is distinctly out of step with American constitutional principles is the positive nature of the rights secured by the International Law.

Thus, it is unsurprising that many children's rights advocates expend considerable energy relying on International Law to advance children's rights, such as the United Nations' Declaration of Human Rights and its Convention of the Rights of the Child which, among other things, establish minimum standards for economic, legal, and political rights for children throughout the world.[25] Many of these advocates also support a wide variety of government programs that guarantee all people, adult and children alike, services and protections such as adequate housing, medical care, and income, for the simple reason that they form the core of human rights.

For this reason, it is equally unsurprising that many oppose reliance on international norms even as applied to children for reasons having little to do with children directly. For some, the Convention on the Rights of the Child is regarded as the camel's nose in the tent. They do not wish to contribute to establishing precedents that may lead to a dramatic transformation of government's role in society.

In this way, fights over children's rights frequently implicate deeper, and unrelated, disagreements among adults. Children's rights advocates seem to score points proving that the United States is anti-child because we are the only nation in the world not to have ratified the convention.[26] Yet this country's refusal to sign the convention has very little to do with children's rights, and certainly is no proof of their repudiation.

Instead, it is a variant on a much larger theme that has long been a central dispute among adults about the principles on which American society is built. One need not join in this debate to agree that it is about more important things than children's rights. And, particularly when the adults fighting over whether or not to ratify the convention see the debate in these larger terms, it is not only misleading but false to suggest that its defeat in this country is evidence of an uncaring attitude toward children.

The consequences of the inseparability of children and their interests from the rest of society's interests also has deeper implications. Virtually anything can be said to affect children. When the list ranges from minimum wage requirements; driving while intoxicated; same-sex marriages; resource fights over allocating money for defense, space exploration, health care, education, and child care; it is clear that an adult can credibly invoke children's rights into almost any debate of national import.

This makes the scope of this book potentially boundless. But its boundaries will be delineated by the most common efforts to invoke the name of children's rights currently in vogue in the United States.

What rights do children acquire at birth? What should be the rights of toddlers and young children? Does it even make sense to speak of rights for them? These, and other questions, form the core inquiry of Chapter 2.

The next chapter will suggest that the American policy of giving parents superior rights to the care and custody of their children over all others is the opposite of the denial of children's humanity. Instead, it should be seen as an affirmation of a sensible goal of providing children with their best chance to grow and be supported within a family, with an edifice of significant barriers to state control and intervention.

2

The Rights of Parents

THIS chapter introduces the subject of children's rights by setting forth the legal and political justification for the most important rule concerning the rights of children: the rights of parents. Simply stated, the bulk of laws affecting children and the law in the United States are interwoven with the laws of parental authority. One can fully grasp the complete scope of children's rights under American law only by knowing the rights of their parents.

For better or worse, the law's treatment of children began from the bottom up, starting with infants and young children. To be a young child means to be completely dependent upon another for the most basic needs of survival. For this reason, young children and their caregivers are inextricably connected. A young person's rights ultimately are inseparable from the duties, responsibilities and, as we shall soon see, rights of the adults upon whom they rely.

The leading children's rights issues over the past thirty years can be grouped into two broad categories. The first is an ongoing challenge to the laws that cede to birth parents the right to have the care and custody of their biological children and the primary authority to control the details of a child's upbringing. This challenge seeks to wrest from parents some of the control they have under current law and shift power either to another adult (usually some state official such as a judge, school administrator or teacher, or to someone who cared for a child in a parentlike relationship but who, under current law, is not defined as a parent) or to the child him- or herself. The second is an effort to gain rights for children that adults have.

Both of these challenges necessarily engage the law of parental rights. The first does so explicitly. But even the second intrudes into parental rights since one of the conspicuous characteristics of the law's differential treatment of children from adults is the dependent status of children in relation to their parents.

The subject of parental rights has been profoundly shaped by the Constitution of the United States, even though neither the word "parent" nor "child" appears anywhere in it. Nonetheless, the Supreme Court of the United States has consistently and vigorously protected parental rights through the application of constitutional principles. The Court considers "the interest of parents in the care, custody, and control of their children" to be "perhaps the oldest of the fundamental liberty interests recognized by this Court." Indeed, it has characterized the rights to conceive and to raise one's children as "essential," "basic civil rights of man," and "rights far more precious . . . than property rights." In the Court's language, a parent's legal interest in his or her child is "established beyond debate as an enduring American tradition."[1]

Why has American law developed this fierce protection of parental rights, often known as the "parental rights doctrine"? The parental rights doctrine may be usefully subdivided into two separate categories. The first addresses why parents, as opposed to others, have rights in and to their children. The second explores the details of a parent's rights (once the law recognizes the status of "parent.") Later in this chapter we will consider the details of a parent's rights to raise his or her child. But we begin by examining why the law privileges biology as the presumed basis for conferring legally recognized parenthood.

To some readers, defending a birth parent's rights will seem unnecessary since parents "naturally" have the right to the care and custody of their children. But the inquiry is considerably more complicated than that. An examination into the justification for parental authority as the "natural" default takes us on a short journey into philosophy and the law.

Imagine that we were assigned the task of developing the rules and laws for our society, unencumbered by history. Our task is to determine who should be assigned the responsibility, duties, and rights to raise children. One possibility would be to create a state agency that is responsible for maintaining a list of all persons interested in becoming parents. The agency would conduct classes, which all prospective parents would attend. Adults who successfully completed the course would be given a license making them eligible to take infants home from the hospital upon discharge. Children would be assigned to parents based on the list maintained by the agency.[2]

This proposal may seem preposterous. It raises questions about the capacity of state officials not only to identify what makes a good parent, but also to apply this knowledge and objectively identify who would, and would not, make suitable parents. Even more basically, this proposal presumes an authority for the state that is highly questionable. Under such an arrangement, children seemingly "belong" to the state upon their birth and the state assumes the responsibility for placing them into good homes. But the notion that children belong in the first instance to the state is repugnant to many Americans who would be left wondering how it could happen that a parent needs to petition a state agency for the privilege of raising children.

The plan could be developed in greater detail. Under one version, the state agency would endeavor to place children with their biological parents, without any guarantee. The agency might regard it as more equitable to provide the maximum number of adults who want to raise children with the opportunity to do so. Thus, the agency might decide to cap the number of children any parent or set of parents may have, at least until there was no waiting list of interested adults with fewer children in their custody.

Now the plan is plainly beginning to bother us. Well beyond our concern about the agency's talent to identify good prospective parents, the concept is beginning to take on the patina of a totalitarian undertaking. We are appalled at the thought of government intruding so actively into the realm of childrearing. It is for this reason that the United States grants asylum status to Chinese immigrants who are subject to China's harsh population control policies, including forced abortion and sterilization of its citizens.[3] For these and other reasons, we can rather quickly reject this plan.

But even an imprudent plan can produce important introductory lessons. Two are especially informative. First, every child must be associated at birth with some adult who has caretaking responsibility and will make the major life decisions for him or her so that society will know the rules regarding the allocation of their custody when they are born. This may seem unduly complicated to those who regard our current arrangement as involving no such allocation. As is well known, biological parents are responsible for their children at birth. They have the right, above all others, to raise them in their own home or to authorize another to raise them instead. (There are, as we shall see in the next chapter, important ambiguities about this rule; fathers of children born out of wedlock, for example, may be required to demonstrate an interest in their children before the law will recognize their rights as parents.) However familiar the rule, it nonetheless reflects at least some of the components of an allocation arrangement. Under our rules, parents self-identify by putting their names on a child's birth certificate. The birth certificate is a legal document maintained by a state agency. It may be altered only in limited circumstances upon court order. Moreover, a myriad of legally significant consequences follow from the formal recognition of parenthood.

To the extent we are uncomfortable characterizing this as any kind of allocation or are unable even to conceptualize it as such is itself a reflection of the deeply embedded understanding that parents "naturally" have rights to their children. Our immediate purpose in exploring this subject is to try to obtain a deeper understanding of our commitment to parents' rights. Strong intuitions are a good starting point for such an understanding, but we must delve into those intuitions to find the reasons for, and parameters of, our belief that parents "naturally" have rights to their children if we are to truly understand the substance of those rights. As we will see, articulating the reasons American law is firmly built upon the parental rights doctrine will help diffuse a murkiness that has crept into recent legal debates.

The second lesson our vain effort of imagining the state allocating children to selected adults teaches is that the subject is deeply political. The topic of parents' legal rights is far more an inquiry into the political structure of a community than may seem apparent; it is inextricably bound up with the limits of state power. It is impossible to answer the most basic questions about parents' rights without engaging in political inquiry.

Some have attempted to justify parents' rights in terms almost identical to our discussion of a natural ordering. The formal name for this theory is natural law. The theory advances that certain rights are God-given and exist beyond the institution of the state. Closely related to this reasoning is the claim that individuals exist prior to the state's formation. In coming together to form government, individuals bring with them certain rights that are beyond the control of state officials. Among these is the right to form a family and beget children.[4] Under this reasoning, family formation happened before the state came into being; it is pre-political and beyond the state's authority to control. The Supreme Court has, on occasion, relied on this reasoning.[5]

This form of reasoning closely resembles Jean-Jacques Rousseau's theory that individuals enter into an implied contract with government when they form the modern state and that certain aspects of individual freedom remain outside of the contract and are not ordinarily subject to governmental restriction.[6] Since, according to Rousseau, this form of government depends on the consent of the governed, only those rights individuals intend to submit to government authority are properly within that authority to regulate. John Locke developed similar ideas, arguing that many natural rights of men and women, including the parental power to raise children, are beyond government's power to invade.[7]

But natural law theory has the troubling quality of not being subject to proof; things are as they are because God wants it so, because it always has been so, or because it is the right way to do things. The reasoning works for those persuaded by it; but it does little to convince skeptics.[8] Even Rousseau's or Locke's theories, although helpful starting points for our discussion, only suggest that some basic human conditions begin outside the state's business.

A number of writers reject entirely this idea of a naturally ordered private sphere of family life.[9] They correctly observe that the political decision to permit families to form as they wish *is,* after all, a decision about the family's regulation. In this sense, it is inarguable that families exist within society and that society, through its laws and rules, has the power to set the conditions under which actions within families are regulable. In this conception, the state intervenes even when it chooses not to.[10]

Moreover, there is value in clarifying that the decision not to regulate behavior within a family is actually a *decision* rather than an unavoidable result. This makes is easier to uncover who benefits by the decision. Thus, for more than a century in the United States, marital rape, domestic violence, and a good deal of child abuse were protected from outside restraint. Efforts to open the family to public regulation, in other words, began with efforts to reduce male dominance over weaker and more vulnerable family members.

Among the complexities in delineating the limits of parental rights are that many who favor strict regulation of the family see themselves as engaged in a struggle similar to the one that overcame the law's reluctance to limit the authority of men to own the property of their wives and to make all decisions for and about the family and its members, including the children. Although I noted in Chapter 1 that some children's liberationists have misused the rhetoric of overcoming historical oppression, there really is a connection between modern laws that protect the decisions parents make concerning their children and the now discarded laws that protect men's authority over the family.

In addition, an added impetus for those who support greater regulation of the family to regard themselves as being on the correct side of this historical struggle is that some of their opponents would, in the name of libertarian, fundamentalist religious, or patriarchal principles deny the state even the power to insist that children receive an education, that sick children get medical care, or that bigamy may be prohibited. For these reasons, the defense of the parental rights doctrine must rest on more than history if for no other reason than that much of the history with which it is intertwined has properly been repudiated.

In particular, we need to examine the reasons parental rights, over the past two generations, have come to be regarded in American constitutional law as among the most protected and cherished of all constitutional rights. A wide range of explanations have been offered for the primacy of parental control in childrearing. Perhaps the most important is based on the relationship between citizen and state and the role of childrearing in developing and shaping future generations of an informed citizenry.

American law is built on a number of fundamental tenets. Among its first principles is that government exists to serve the will of the people. As a direct consequence, our special brand of constitutional democracy places significant limits on the power of government to regulate speech. We can regard the First Amendment's guarantee of freedom of speech as a basic right because it advances an individual's freedom to think and express him- or herself as he or she pleases.

But one can also think of freedom of speech as the outcome of a rule that constrains government from restraining speech. Here the emphasis is not on the speaker's right, but on government's limitation. Where speech is seen as the means by which the people's will is to be expressed, it is elemental that government ought to be prohibited from tinkering very much with speech. A society committed to maintaining a government that serves the will of the people will find it necessary strictly to limit the circumstances under which government may constrain speech. Any other result leaves too great a danger that government will prevent speakers from saying what those in positions of power in government do not want others to hear. Once those in power control what is allowed in public debate, the capacity to change government is greatly diminished.

The less government is permitted to suppress speech, the greater the range of ideas that can be expressed. An unregulated private marketplace of ideas fosters pluralism in its best sense: free people are permitted to consider the widest range of possibilities about how to live their lives and to shape their society.

Seen in these terms, free speech is basic to a society committed to democratic rule. It both restricts the government's capacity to silence speakers and forbids government from taking sides by preferring one idea over another. This does not mean government never tries to take sides. But the First Amendment prohibits government from engaging in content-based regulation of speech or "viewpoint discrimination."[11]

A second fundamental tenet of American law that bears directly on the rules of parental rights is the extremely limited role assigned to government in connection to religion. The First Amendment guarantees to citizens the free exercise of religion; it also prohibits government from establishing a religion. As a result, government is obliged to allow religion to flourish and also is forbidden from preferring one religion over another.

Why are these basic principles of American law pertinent to a discussion of allocating childrearing responsibility in the United States? Because childrearing involves considerably more than providing sustenance to infants and children.

It is impossible to raise children without teaching them at the same time. Moreover, it is inconceivable to teach them anything without shaping their values and outlook on life. Everything that goes on in a household is fodder for learning. Well beyond speech and communication skills, we teach our children manners, and inculcate them with lifelong values. And, of course, religion is something into which children are raised. Parents are free to attempt to inculcate their preferred religious beliefs or disbeliefs in their children. Children may not share their parents' beliefs in later life, but their views are shaped by, or at least defined in relation to, their parents' teachings as opposed to the state's.

Since children by definition need to be raised somewhere, who should decide where the children should be raised? If government played a significant role in choosing parents for children at birth, government would likely have entered the prohibited arena of participating in value inculcation in children. In a polity committed to the ideal of government serving the people's will, it is unimaginable to conceive of children as belonging to government. Quite the opposite. In such a polity, children must belong to the people for the theoretical political aspirations of self-control to have any meaningful chance to be realized. The best way to guard against government becoming too involved in shaping the ideas or religion of its citizens is to deregulate and privatize childrearing.

Even more important perhaps than the child allocation issue, government must be sharply restricted in its capacity to oversee the circumstances under which children are being raised. Precisely because childrearing means forming the values, interests, ideas, and religious beliefs of the next generation, we should expect American law to insist, as the Supreme Court has, that the state cannot enter the domain of family life. This realm is beyond the state's reach, consistent with American constitutional democracy, because children's value inculcation and religious training is something "the state can neither supply nor hinder."[12]

It is useful to explore the particular cases decided by the Supreme Court that established these rules. The context of the disputes settled by the Court provides insight into the broader questions of parental rights. The first two cases ever decided by the Court exploring the subject of parental constitutional rights arguably remain the most important. In developing the principles supporting the rights of parents to raise their children free from undue state interference, the Court stressed each of the issues upon which we have already touched.

Shortly after the end of World War I, the Nebraska legislature enacted a law that prohibited children under the age of fourteen from being instructed in a modern foreign language. At the time, a substantial number of German immigrants lived in Nebraska; the legislation was designed to speed the homogenization of American children by ensuring that all spoke a common language. In 1923, in *Meyer v. Nebraska,* a teacher of German challenged the law on behalf of himself, parents, and children.

The Court declared the law unconstitutional because, among other reasons, it violated a parent's liberty interest protected by the

Due Process Clauses of the Fifth and Fourteenth Amendments. To buttress this conclusion, the Court said that these provisions encompassed the rights "to marry, establish a home, and bring up children," even though none of them is mentioned in the Constitution itself.[13] The Court rejected the claim that the state may (over the parents' objection) play a primary role in childrearing, declaring that there is a "private realm of family life which the state cannot enter." Justice McReynolds, writing for the Court, reminded the reader that some societies were based on the understanding that the state was to play a primary childrearing role. Deliberately referencing an image anathema to many Americans, McReynolds cited Plato's vision of the Ideal Commonwealth, which included a provision that "no parent is to know his own child nor any child his parent," and proposed that all children would be raised in barracks and their training and education would be left to "official guardians." About these ideas, McReynolds wrote, "[a]lthough such measures have been deliberately approved by men of great genius, their ideas touching the relation between individual and State were wholly different from those upon which our institutions rest."[14]

Two years later in *Pierce v. Society of Sisters,* a decision with even greater repercussions, the Court struck down an Oregon statute requiring children to attend public schools. The justices found that this statute unduly interfered with the right of parents to select private or parochial schools for their children and that it lacked a reasonable relation to any purpose within the competency of the state.[15] In the Court's words, "The fundamental theory of liberty upon which all governments in this Union repose excludes any general power of the State to standardize its children." This is because "The child is not the mere creature of the State; those who nurture him and direct his destiny have the right, coupled with the high duty, to recognize and prepare him for additional obligations."[16]

Both the results and the reasoning remain important today. Our society would be quite different if the state could control the details of a mandatory curriculum for all children. It would be even more different if all children were required to attend public schools. This is not to suggest the particular questions before the Court were easy, or even correctly decided. It may be instructive for some to learn that Oliver Wendell Holmes was one of two justices who dissented in the German language case. It was, in his view, within the legitimate reach of state power to regulate the details of a child's education to this extent. Readers may also be intrigued to consider that McReynolds was an arch-reactionary who voted to strike down all progressive legislative efforts during the second and third decades of the twentieth century. His views on the power of the Court to declare unconstitutional legislation designed to improve social conditions were repudiated by the Court as soon as the Roosevelt appointees commanded a majority after 1935; McReynolds is today held in low esteem by most students of the Court.

Nonetheless, these two cases have formed the foundation for constitutionally protected parental rights. Our future as a democracy depends on nurturing diversity of minds.[17] The legal system's insistence on private ordering of familial life ultimately guards against state control of its citizens. Accordingly, government must allow parents wide latitude to raise children as the parents wish to raise them. Parents, not the state, must be the final arbiter of what subjects their children study.[18] (A minimum required curriculum of reading, arithmetic, and history is considered sufficiently content-neutral and necessary for the maintenance of an educated and capable citizenry to be imposed on children even when parents are opposed to such instruction.) Even more basically, parents must be free to choose educators for their children who are unaffiliated with the state. Although the state may maintain a public school system for those parents who wish to send their children there, parents are free to use private education as an alternative.

In addition to political theory justifying the parental rights doctrine, the Constitution has been an important protector of an American's right to procreate. Although this subject, to the extent it includes a discussion of abortion, covers more controversial constitutional theory than we have thus far considered, a robust understanding of the constitutional pillars buttressing parental rights doctrine requires its examination.

One of the fundamental freedoms protected by the Constitution is the freedom to procreate. The Supreme Court's first excursion into the subject, however, was an infamous 1927 decision, *Buck v. Bell,* allowing the compulsory sterilization of an eighteen-year-old woman with a low IQ who had already given birth to one child. A Virginia statute authorized the forced sterilization of certain institutionalized persons to prevent the transmission of "imbecility" to the next generation. Virginia sought to perform a "safe" procedure on Ms. Buck.

According to the Court, Buck's mother was "feeble-minded" as was the daughter to whom she had given birth.[19] Virginia asserted a right to prevent Buck from bearing additional children because the responsibility for raising her children would likely fall to the state and because allowing her to procreate freely would expose society to dangers it had a right to avoid. Reasoning that "three generations of imbeciles is enough," the Court upheld the law because "[i]t is better for all the world, if instead of waiting to execute degenerate offspring for crime, or to let them starve for their imbecility, society can prevent those who are manifestly unfit from continuing their kind."[20]

The decision proved to be a favorite of the Nazis in Germany, who relied upon it to support their use of government power to manipulate the gene pool for future generations. Thus it was unsurprising that the Court changed its mind the next time it had the opportunity to rule on a state law seeking to sterilize a person over his or her objection. In 1942, proclaiming that procreation is "fundamental to the very existence and survival of the race" and "one of the basic civil rights of man," the Court held in *Skinner v. Oklahoma* that an Oklahoma law that allowed the state to sterilize persons "convicted two or more times for crimes amounting to felonies involving moral turpitude" violated the Equal Protection Clause of the Fourteenth Amendment because it infringed upon the fundamental "right to have offspring."[21]

Ever since, the Court has advanced procreational rights of Americans. In a 1965 decision, *Griswold v. Connecticut,*[22] the Court declared unconstitutional a Connecticut law that, though still on the books, had not been enforced for many years. The law barred the use and distribution of contraceptives, even for married persons. Declaring that the Constitution protects various kinds of intimate privacy, including marriage, the Court recognized a zone of privacy that protected married couples from virtually all governmental regulation. "The home derives its pre-eminence as the seat of family life," wrote Justice Goldberg in a concurring opinion. It is protected by "[t]he entire fabric of the Constitution and the purposes that clearly underlie its specific guarantees demonstrate that the rights to marital privacy and to marry and raise a family are of similar order and magnitude as the fundamental rights."[23]

Griswold's reasoning has been broadly extended since, eventually leading to the Court's most controversial foray into the field of procreative rights, its 1973 decision in *Roe v. Wade*.[24] *Roe* famously ruled that part of a woman's constitutional right to privacy (including the fundamental right whether or not to beget a child) includes the choice to terminate an unwanted pregnancy (at least in the early stages of the pregnancy). In *Roe,* the Court restricted state power to forbid abortions, holding that a woman's decision whether to bear a child is within the sphere of privacy "founded in the Fourteenth Amendment's concept of personal liberty." The Court noted that even though the word "privacy" cannot be found in the Constitution, a "guarantee of certain areas or zones of privacy" has been constitutionally recognized in connection with "activities relating to marriage, procreation, contraception, family relationships, and childrearing and education."[25] The next year, the Court ruled that a mandatory leave rule for pregnant public schoolteachers impermissibly interfered with the decision to raise a family, declaring "freedom of personal choice in matters of marriage and family life is one of the liberties protected by the Due Process Clause of the Fourteenth Amendment."[26]

Though *Roe* has been attacked both within and outside the legal profession, the controversy is rarely about the decision to give greater priority to the privacy rights of women at the expense of government power, though the decision clearly does that. The decision to terminate a pregnancy directly impacts the potential father (in the next chapter we will explore in greater detail the clash of interests between the mother and the father) and, of course, the decision impacts the potential child.

To those who regard a fetus as human life, not merely potential life, the abortion decision authorizes the destruction of vulnerable beings in the name of advancing a woman's privacy. The law, however, has never recognized a nonviable fetus as more than potential life and has rejected the religious position that human life is formed at conception. Regardless of what we believe as individuals, Supreme Court cases that protect the right to control procreation clearly place that right with the individual, rather than with the government. *Griswold* and *Roe* do this in the context of affirming the right to choose not to have a child; the pregnant schoolteacher case does it in the context of affirming the right to have a child. Each is based on the principle that the state has a limited role in decisions about having children.

The Court has also developed an important line of cases that protect a parent's right to keep or regain custody of their children. In a significant case decided in 1972, the Court heard an appeal by an unmarried father of three children whose custody was taken from him when their mother died. An Illinois statute automatically deprived unmarried fathers of the custody of their natural children on the death of the mother. Illinois defended the law on the grounds that, in most cases, the fathers of children born out of wedlock fail to maintain a significant presence in the children's lives.

In *Stanley v. Illinois*,[27] the father lived with his children and the mother for almost all of the children's lives. Nonetheless, Illinois claimed the power to take his children into the state's custody and provide the father with the right to come forward to show why returning custody of his children would further their best interests. The Court declared the law unconstitutional, holding that unless a parent is unfit, he has the constitutional right to the care and custody of his children. In addition, the Court held that the state is barred from shortcutting its procedural obligations by presuming the father's unfitness. Most important of all, the Court made clear it was irrelevant that Stanley might be able to regain his children's custody by proving it would be best for his children to live with him. Illinois had a legitimate interest in the well-being of Stanley's children, the Court said, *only* if he were found by a court to be unfit. Illinois had the lawful power to charge him with unfitness. But it was unconstitutional to require Stanley to prove that his children deserved to be with him before such a showing of unfitness had been made.

There are few constitutional protections that have received such long-term support—from the Supreme Court of the 1920s, an extremely conservative Court; the Court of the 1960s, an extremely liberal one; and today's Court, also conservative. In 2000, the Court had occasion to write that "the interest of parents in the care, custody, and control of their children is perhaps the oldest of the fundamental liberty interests recognized by this Court," and that "it cannot now be doubted that the Due Process Clause of the Fourteenth Amendment protects the fundamental right of parents to make decisions concerning the care, custody, and control of their children."[28]

Closely related to the freedom to procreate is the even broader freedom of an adult to live the life one chooses free from all arbitrary governmental restraint. As we have seen, there are important instrumental values advanced by the parents' rights doctrine. But there are important freedom-advancing interests that are extremely valuable in and of themselves.

American constitutional law limits government's role in the affairs of its people for reasons other than protecting against the danger of homogeneity of political or religious ideas. Pluralism is also valued for itself. We are a society built on the principle of individual liberty and the right to live the kind of life we choose with as few restrictions placed in our paths as necessary to ensure the maintenance of civil order. (We can, of course, disagree about what these proper limits are; indeed, our most contentious social debates are about them.)

In 2003, for example, Justice Kennedy began writing his opinion for the Supreme Court in *Lawrence v. Texas,* which declared unconstitutional a Texas sodomy statute, with the ringing words "[i]n our tradition the State is not omnipresent in the home. And there are other spheres of our lives and existence, outside the home, where the State should not be a dominant presence. Freedom extends beyond spatial bounds. Liberty presumes an autonomy of self that includes freedom of thought, belief, expression, and certain intimate conduct."[29]

In a society committed to maximizing freedom for individuals to live the life they choose (subject to John Stuart Mill's limit that one's freedom ends when it harms another), it should be unsurprising that the freedom to procreate and to rear children would be deeply cherished. Wholly apart from whatever other values it may serve to society, protecting a parent's rights is a vital freedom in and of itself.

Consider the importance individuals attach to their intimate associations. Many define themselves first in terms of their relationship to the closest people in their lives. For complicated cultural reasons, we may first mention our careers when we make small talk at a cocktail party. But many parents would instantly say the most important relationship they have formed is with their children and even that their most important role has been as a parent.

The right to bear and raise children is at the core of an individual's autonomy because it permits him or her the opportunity to choose the kind of life that makes the most sense. In the words of David Richards, a law professor, "Child rearing plays a special role in the adult individual's development. It 'is one of the ways in which many people fulfill and express their deepest values about how life is to be lived. To this extent, one's children are the test of one's life and aspirations.'"[30] Parental rights help construct and support "an aspect of human self-definition and moral choice."[31] This is because, for so many of us, our understanding of ourselves is based on our intimate relationships with others.[32]

Given its importance to adults, "an attempt to imagine state interests that would justify governmental intrusions amounting to a practical prohibition on procreation and childbearing takes us out of our own experience and into an imaginary world of Malthusian nightmare."[33] The United States has already undergone such a nightmare. The institution of slavery, with all of its horrors and inhumane treatment of human beings, provides an important opportunity to comprehend the implications of the loss of parental rights. Slavery involved considerably more than the loss of control of one's labor. Slaves also lost the control over propagation. Adult slaves were denied the most basic human right to raise their children as their own.[34] Being denied the right to marry, to be parents with legally recognized rights, and to keep children in their custody, slaves, and the children of slaves, were denied the basic moral right "to integrate the experience of their ancestors into their lives, to inform their understanding of social reality with the inherited meanings of their natural forebears, or to anchor the living present in any conscious community of memory."[35]

New York University law professor Peggy Cooper Davis has shown that in the immediate aftermath of the Civil War, federal legislators focused on the loss of family that slaves experienced and enacted the Thirteenth and Fourteenth Amendments in part to guarantee all citizens the freedom to form and maintain familial relations. In Davis's words, "To think of family liberty as a guarantee offered in response to slavery's denials of natal connections is to understand it, not as an end in itself, but as a means to full personhood. People are not meant to be socialized to uniform, externally imposed values. People are to be able to form families and other intimate communities within which children might be differently socialized and from which adults would bring different values to the democratic process."[36]

Finally, and closely related to these constitutional principles, it is also important to value the labor and sacrifice associated with childbearing. Although this factor tends to emphasize a mother's right, it is Orwellian to contemplate that a woman could be expected to experience the extraordinary intrusion in her body resulting from pregnancy and childbirth and then be obliged to give birth to babies in order to permit state officials to place them as they see fit. This would mean not only that children belong to the state but, even more basically, that everyone does.

Thus far, we have considered the utility of the parental rights doctrine for advancing pluralism and an independent citizenry. We have also looked at complementary constitutional principles permitting Americans freedom to create families. But it is important for the purposes of this book to stress what we have yet to mention: children and their rights.

Despite the central place parental rights has in American culture and law, it has come under attack by some over the past generation. And the values expressed in the preceding several pages may indicate why this is so. To some, particularly those in the children's rights movement, the law focuses far too much on parents' rights and far too little on the rights of their children. It is fine to create a scheme by which adults are free to live the lives they choose; but once we appreciate that we are simultaneously licensing them to have almost complete control over the lives of children, they would argue, it is essential that we consider the degree to which parental rights advance or contravene the rights of children. Many children's rights advocates have been especially critical of the traditional parental rights doctrine.

The history of several freedom movements in the United States demonstrates that newly established freedoms for the oppressed frequently follow careful examination of venerable rules that once empowered one class of persons over another. This happened in the movement to abolish slavery and in the feminist movement. Some have applied similar reasoning to the children's rights movement, leading to the claim that the parent-child relationship contains many of the same forms of oppression found in slavery and patriarchal power.

For these children's advocates, the parental rights doctrine merely masks implicit power dominance and oppression of children by adults. They challenge the doctrine as an unfortunate descendant of outdated American property rights that men once enjoyed over their wives and children.[37] The traditional Anglo-American law of parent and children, they point out, was formed in an era of unexamined premises about the superiority and legitimate authority of white men to control the lives of others. Barbara Woodhouse, a law professor, further reminds us that the original cases upon which the parental rights doctrine are founded (including *Meyer* and *Pierce*) were "an integral part of the resistance by conservatives to a large range of programs such as mandatory free public schooling, restriction of child labor, and maternal and infant health programs supported by progressives and populists."[38] From this perspective, the only relic of illegitimate power over others remaining since the mid-twentieth century is the parent-child relationship.

For this reason, supporters of the parental rights doctrine have felt obliged to justify traditional parental authority in terms of its benefits to children, and have formulated an argument based on this claim. First, let us address the initial allocation issue.

For at least two reasons it might be said that children's interests are well served by the rule that birth parents are given first rights to rear their children above all other adults. First, the reasoning goes, parents are naturally more inclined and, thus, presumptively more motivated to do well by their children than nonparents. Thus, Locke regarded a parent's natural emotions as the principal motivating force for parents to act in the best interests of their children. In his words, "the affection and tenderness God hath planted in the breasts of parents toward their children make it evident that this is not intended to be a severe, arbitrary government, but only for the help, and preservation, of their offspring."[39]

By this reasoning, parents are predetermined to see to it that the needs of their children are met and, all things being equal, are more likely than others to do best for their children.[40] The Supreme Court similarly has reasoned that the "natural bonds of affection lead parents to act in the best interests of their children."[41] This argument differs from natural law theory (which is based on the metaphysical) because it is an empirical claim suggesting that biological parents *tend* to be better caregivers for their children. The empirical claim has never been subjected to rigorous testing, however.

A second justification may fall prey to a similar defect. There is much to suggest that children want to be raised by their biological families and that they avoid a potential cost if they are. A significant percentage of adults who have been adopted feel the need to search for and locate their birth parents at some point in their lives.[42] To the extent this reflects a natural need for children to know their biological roots, allocating children to their birth parents in the first instance avoids exposing children to the potential harm of never knowing them. In addition, many point to the stigma attached to children who are raised by someone other than their birth parents.

Despite the absence of any resolution in the continuing nature/ nurture debate, it remains a reasonable hypothesis that, all things being equal, children are well served by a rule that presumes their birth parents ought to raise them. This statement does not prove that being raised by nonbiologically related "parents" would be harmful to children, however.

Once there is agreement that children should be with their parents from birth, and that the state should play an extremely limited role in overseeing the conditions of their lives, we have established the principal structure of the parental rights doctrine. Moving past the unanswerable question of whether the rule that birth parents are entitled over others to raise their biological children serves children well, we arrive at a more relevant question: Does the rule that parents are free to raise their children as they see fit serve children well? Many children's rights advocates do not dispute the first question. They begin their disagreement with the second. But, properly understood, the second is a corollary of the first.

As a consequence of the constitutional protections accorded parents, government has assumed a modest role in monitoring what happens within the family. Government gets to set the boundaries at the outer limits of what is acceptable parenting. Thus, laws protecting children from neglect and abuse, even at the hands of their parents, have come to be regarded as a proper exercise of the state's police power (regulating the conduct of citizens that has the potential to harm others). This means only that parents are obliged to exercise a "minimum degree of care" when raising their children. Unless parents fall below this (low) standard and are found to be "unfit" in court proceedings charging them with abuse or neglect, parental childrearing decisions are virtually immune from state oversight.

The classic alternative to a "fitness" standard (which limits state authority to overrule parental childrearing choices) is the child's "best interests" standard (which permits state officials to overrule such choices whenever the official disagrees with the original choice). Are children better served by a rule that limits state officials in their authority to oversee parental childrearing or by one that expands such state power?

An important goal of any society is to develop healthy adults with a strong sense of self-esteem. Children need and greatly benefit from a sense of security. That sense of security therefore deserves prominent protection.[43] By making it difficult for state officials to intrude in the family and remove children from their parents' custody, the parental rights doctrine helps cement a child's sense of security. Children know that they always will be connected—emotionally, socially, and through physical custody—to their parents and that their relationship will not lightly be destroyed.

Seen this way, the parental rights doctrine involves far more than my right to call my children my own. It allows my children to call me their parent. When parental rights are characterized as familial rights, children reciprocally share the rights of their parents. The rights now become more than parents' rights to keep the custody of their children; it is also the children's right to remain in their families.

For this reason, some prefer to regard the parental rights doctrine as the *family's* right of autonomy, emphasizing that within the family are individual but connected members. Children and parents are interdependent. All family members benefit from rules that provide security in the belief that the family unit is significant not only to them but to the society in which they live. As a result, when laws are enacted that protect the family from needless interruption and that protect the child's relationship with his parent and siblings, the parental rights doctrine can be said to advance the rights and interests of children.

Security is also furthered because children grow up in an environment in which their parents know their decisions will not be subject to close scrutiny. Parents are encouraged to care for their children by receiving maximum discretion to carry out their responsibilities, free from the worry that their behavior will be monitored and second-guessed by a third party. Children obviously benefit from rules that are calculated to reduce stress in their home. Protecting parental choice advances the interests of children because "Children . . . react even to temporary infringement of parental autonomy with anxiety, diminishing trust, loosening of emotional ties, or an increasing tendency to be out of control."[44]

Finally, the parental rights doctrine also keeps state officials, who will never know children better than the adults who have directly nurtured them, from making childrearing decisions. Government bureaucracies ("impersonal political institutions" in the language of the Supreme Court) have been criticized for being inept at many functions; because childrearing requires exquisite attention to each child's special needs, we should expect that state officials would be particularly bad at raising children. Children benefit when the important decisions concerning them are made by people they know best.[45] Current law allows a freedom within the family for self-regulation. The degree to which children benefit from this freedom is unquantifiable; but it is reasonable to suggest that many children benefit substantially from such an arrangement.

The parental rights doctrine also frees parents to decide how much involvement in family decision making to share. In many families, children's views are solicited and taken into account when familial decisions are being made. To be sure, in some families, too little regard for the child's views may be given; and in others, too much. The point is not that one result will likely be achieved more often than another, or even that one result should be preferred over another; it is that the decision makers are those intimately connected to the children. From the child's point of view, a parent's decision will often be preferred to those of a judge, psychologist, or social worker.[46]

Any alternative to the parental rights doctrine empowers state officials to meddle in family affairs and base their decisions on their own values.[47] The parental rights doctrine protects parents from having to defend their right to their children's custody on grounds that parental custody would further the children's best interests. A best interests inquiry is not a neutral investigation that leads to an obvious result. It is an intensely value-laden inquiry. And it cannot be otherwise.

In 1966, the Iowa Supreme Court decided a case that has become standard fare for study in many law schools. The case, *Painter v. Bannister,* involved a custody dispute between a father and the maternal grandparents of his seven-year-old son.[48] The facts are relatively straightforward. Harold Painter and his wife, Jeanne, lived together with Mark, their only child, until Jeanne was killed in an automobile accident. After her death, Harold asked his parents-in-law, the Bannisters, to care for Mark while he grieved and began to put his life back in order. After a little more than a year Harold remarried. At that time, he felt ready to resume the care of Mark. However, when he asked the Bannisters to give Mark back to him, they refused and went to court to try to keep Mark.

There were no traditional grounds on which to deny Painter the custody of his son. Painter was a fit parent who obviously loved his son. To the extent it even matters, Jeanne had expressly written in her will that she wanted her husband to raise Mark in the event of her death. Finally, Iowa law clearly stated that fit parents who did not abandon their children had a superior right to their children's custody over all others.

But the Iowa Supreme Court ruled that the controlling basis upon which the child's custody would be decided was his best interests. The court relied on a recently developed theory of children's rights that unless changing custody was in their best interests, children who have "bonded" with their current caregivers should not be separated from them, even to be returned to their parents.

Once the best interests test became the standard, there were no constraints on what the court was allowed to consider as relevant. Moreover, there were no guideposts for assessing best interests. Painter, it turns out, was a hippie from Berkeley, California. His unconventional lifestyle was poorly regarded by Iowa jurists. An occasional journalist, Painter never went to college. He made a modest income as an artist selling his work to tourists in Sausalito. He was also a struggling writer who hoped to publish a book someday. Among the various facts adduced at the custody trial that the

Iowa Supreme Court saw fit to highlight was that Painter attended Jeanne's funeral wearing a "sport shirt and sweater" and that he never painted the outside of his house or cut his lawn, preferring "uncut weeds and wild oats." In contrast, the Bannisters were both college graduates. Mrs. Bannister was a librarian and Mr. Bannister was the agricultural information editor for the local university. He also served on the school board and regularly taught a Sunday school class at the local church.

The Court candidly opined that Painter would provide his son with a more intellectually interesting life. In the court's words, "We believe it would be unstable, unconventional, arty, Bohemian, and probably intellectually stimulating." But, on balance, considering that Mark was already living with the Bannisters, the Court unanimously concluded that Mark's best interests would be served by remaining with them because they offered him greater "stability and security."

This case brilliantly demonstrates what is unleashed when courts are free to decide a case based on the judge's perception of a child's best interests. The reasoning and outcome in *Painter* are presented not to establish that the case was wrongly decided. The case is described to show that one's views of a child's best interests are contingent upon the decisionmakers' beliefs and values and that it is impossible to separate their views from those beliefs and values.

The best interests standard necessarily invites the judge to rely on his or her own values and biases to decide the case in whatever way the judge thinks best. Even the most basic factors are left for the judge to figure out. Robert Mnookin asks whether best interests should "be viewed from a long-term or short-term perspective . . . Should the judge ask himself what decision will make the child happiest in the next year? Or at thirty? Or at seventy? Should the judge decide by thinking what decision the child as an adult looking back would have wanted made?" The ultimate difficulty is that "Deciding what is best for a child poses a question no less ultimate than the purposes and values of life itself."[49]

Painter demonstrates that unless judges are constrained by principles, they will always be unleashing an unfettered, uncontrollable power. When we recall that the parental rights doctrine was formed in part because our constitutional scheme prohibits state officials from becoming too involved in childrearing decisions, it is especially important that judges be authorized as infrequently as necessary to decide child custody disputes based on a child's best interests. The parental rights doctrine authorizes parents to raise their children as they deem appropriate even when others could reasonably disagree and claim the child's best interests would be served by a different approach.

In divorce-related custody contests, courts regularly use the best interests standard. But in those cases, both parents have the equal right to the custody of the child and the court has become involved in settling their private custody dispute only because one of the parties has asked the court to arbitrate it. In this chapter I refer to cases in which a court is empowered to deny a parent custody by awarding custody to a nonparent. Chapter 5 will consider in greater depth the propriety of a best interests test in divorce cases.

However alluring and child-friendly the "best interests" test appears, in truth it is a formula for unleashing state power, without any meaningful reassurance of advancing children's interests. It means substituting the state's preference about some aspect of childrearing for the parents'. But this hardly ensures the second opinion is better than the first.

Although some children's rights advocates condemn the parental rights doctrine as "anachronistically despotic licenses to control the lives of" children, the doctrine can be defended as "a rejection of state omnipotence, not children's personhood."[50] In this sense, the doctrine represents an important statement about the relationship of individuals (including children and adults) to the state.

Consider the compulsory education requirement. Parents who fail to comply with the compulsory education laws are at risk of losing their children's custody. But we vest in parents very broad discretion to exercise their rights in choosing how to comply with the law. Parents may enroll their children in public or private school or even teach them at home, so long as they teach a minimum required curriculum. By this compromise, we require that parents conform with universal rules of parenting but leave them free to comply with the requirements as they see fit.

The homeschooling movement has grown at an astonishing rate in the past generation. In 1972, a mere 12,500 children were being homeschooled. Whether or not there is a consensus that homeschooling serves children or society well, the number of parents taking advantage of that option was too small to be a significant social question. As of 2000, considerably more than one million children were being homeschooled.[51]

There may well be a consensus that children who are homeschooled are being deprived of an important socializing experience. Some would even suggest that experiences with peers in school are as important as the formal lessons in a required curriculum. Parents who feel this way send their children to school. Does this mean we should prohibit homeschooling?

A strong case can be made that our society would be better off if all children were required to go to public school. In addition, the case can be advanced that these schools should be integrated racially, religiously, ethnically, by gender, and in still other ways. Such integration might advance social relations and understandings in the United States, a country troubled by class, race, and other barriers that impede social progress. Would this be better for children, furthering their best interests and those of society? The American answer to these questions is that, unless the answers are so clear that there is no room to disagree, parents are free to decide for themselves what they believe will best serve their children.

The immutable truth of childrearing is that someone has to be in charge. This means necessarily "that someone is going to make decisions about children's lives, their education, their religious training; saying it should be parents rather than bureaucrats or activists in no way makes chattel out of children, and saying it should be the State rather than parents shows no greater respect for children's dignity and autonomy."[52] Shifting parental decision making to state officials guarantees that someone else's childrearing values will predominate. Predictably, social conformity would replace individualism as a dominant value. The problem with "allow[ing] the government to override a parent's choice about her child's [upbringing] . . . is that, in the effort to make children more free vis-à-vis their parents, the government makes children less free in their relations with the state."[53]

To ensure that state officials cannot protect children from harm by using open-ended value-laden judgments, "neglect" is strictly defined by state law. The draftsman's goal in defining neglect is to proscribe parental conduct in which no one is permitted to engage without intruding into conduct that, however unacceptable it may be to some, is above the level of impermissible. Only when *no* parent is permitted to do something are state officials authorized to prevent a particular parent from exercising his or her parental rights.

How might we express the corollary of this rule? Said provocatively but accurately, parents are free to raise their children as they see fit even when their choices would be defended by few reputable experts as good for the child so long as the decision cannot be said to be extremely bad for the child. This wide range of parental freedom is not intended to allow parents the opportunity to inflict harm on their children (so long as it happens to be above the level of *impermissible* harm). But the rule has this consequence. It is for this reason that some children's rights advocates condemn the parental rights doctrine.

The conclusion is that children have the right to be raised by parents who are minimally fit and who are likely to make significant mistakes in judgment in childrearing. We may no longer be comfortable with the parental rights doctrine when it is expressed in this way. How, we might reasonably ask, can we call this any kind of right at all?

Empowering Children Themselves

Thus far, we have only considered one part of the critique of the parental rights doctrine as developed by children's rights advocates. Even accepting that it is reasonable to allocate childrearing authority to parents rather than the state, we still must consider whether children should themselves be empowered to make important decisions about their own lives. To some, this is akin to permitting the inmates to run the asylum. To others, it is nothing less than a moral issue of autonomy. To most, the question only arises with any poignancy for older children, particularly adolescents.

The notion of a child's right to autonomy raises a completely different set of claims than those previously discussed. We have so far only examined which adult or set of adults should be empowered to make childrearing decisions. Within that inquiry, there was no suggestion that children had any power. We considered neither the possibility of requiring courts to consult children before ruling on their best interests nor whether parents should consult with their children before making important decisions about them.

Here, the challenge is to the basic premise that children are dependent and that, as a result, some adult must be authorized to decide their upbringing. This challenge to the parents' rights doctrine seeks to liberate children from all adults' care, at least for certain aspects of their upbringing.

Among the most controversial and well-known parental rights decisions is *Wisconsin v. Yoder*,[54] decided in 1972. In that case, the Court reversed the conviction of an Amish parent who removed his daughter from school in violation of Wisconsin's compulsory education law so that the child could complete her religious training at home while preparing for life in the Amish community. Though it is rare for the Court to allow parents to ignore the compulsory education laws, the Court permitted an exception for Mr. Yoder because a core element of religious upbringing was at stake.

Yoder argued successfully in the Court that if he were obliged to send his daughter to public school for the additional two years Wisconsin law required, there was too great a danger that his daughter would be inadequately prepared for her life as a member of the Amish community. In ruling for the father, the Court held that the father's right as a parent, combined with his religious liberty, exempted him from the application of the education law, reminding the reader that "The history and culture of Western civilization reflect a strong tradition of parental concern for the nurture and upbringing of their children. This primary role of the parents in the upbringing of their children is now established beyond debate as an enduring American tradition."

The case was controversial because many saw it as a clash between the rights of parents and what is best for their children. The person whose future was directly affected by the ruling in *Yoder* was a fifteen-year-old girl named Frieda Yoder. Wisconsin defended its compulsory education statute as a valid exercise of state power to provide Frieda with an opportunity for whatever life she preferred to live when she became an adult. Wisconsin argued in the Supreme Court that if her father was permitted to withdraw Frieda from school at age fifteen, Frieda would be ill-equipped to make an intelligent and informed choice about what kind of life she would want to live as an adult. Instead, withdrawing her would significantly limit her life options, making it likely she would spend her entire life on an Amish farm. Wisconsin asserted its legitimate authority as *parens patriae* (the power of the state to protect vulnerable citizens incapable of protecting themselves) to liberate Frieda from her father's control to the limited extent of keeping her in school so that she would receive the same minimal education to which all other children are entitled. The state's asserted interest was to protect children from parents who would prevent them from becoming truly autonomous adults equipped to navigate the world.[55]

Justice Douglas wrote a famous dissenting opinion arguing that if Frieda wished to continue in school her independent rights to attend were superior to her father's parental rights to make that decision for her. Douglas focused on the long-term impact of prematurely withdrawing Frieda from school. He opined that her life choices would be vastly limited when she came of age, and lamented that without state intervention, Frieda was at risk of being "harnessed to the Amish way of life" with the possibility that her entire life would "be stunted and deformed" because she might "be forever barred from entry into the new and amazing world of diversity that we have today."[56]

Douglas would have introduced a new inquiry into state challenges to parental decision making: what does the child want? He would have been satisfied with the result reached by the majority if Frieda herself was satisfied with it. No other justice was interested in pursuing that inquiry, perhaps because the original prosecution of Mr. Yoder was not brought on the theory that Frieda was unhappy with the decision to remove her from school. Moreover, Douglas's position was inconsistent with Wisconsin's. The state insisted that Frieda go to school even if she was in agreement with her father's preference because the state's views on Frieda's needs were superior to her father's and herself. It is that claim which the majority rejected.

In all events, the core of the parental rights doctrine guarantees children at least that the important decisions in their lives will be made by those who are most likely to know them best and to care the most for them. There may be no assurances that, in any given case, parents will make the best choice for their children or even make a choice based on the their understanding of what is best for their children. But the alternative of unleashing state oversight is also unable to promise any of these things. Is this a children's rights policy? One could do worse in developing such a policy.

I do not claim that children are invariably well served by the parental rights doctrine. Built into the doctrine is the premise that parents are permitted to engage in conduct toward their children that many would find disagreeable or unacceptable. No doubt some children would be better served by being removed from their parents' custody, even when it cannot be demonstrated that the parents are technically "unfit." On the other hand, the converse is also true. A scheme that preferred too much intervention, one that required removal of children whenever there was any reason to be concerned about their well-being, would surely result in some children being needlessly harmed by the removals.

When children's rights advocates condemn the parental rights doctrine after it has been shown to have harmed a particular child, they make a powerful but incomplete point. It is powerful to point out that a child has suffered a demonstrated harm that might have been prevented if our laws were different. But this hardly proves that we ought to change the law to prevent a like harm from occurring again. If the proposed change in the law were to lead to greater (albeit) different harms to children, there is no reason to be in favor of the change in the first place. Where should our errors be located? No system of enforcement will be error-free. Nor can public policy be designed with that possibility in mind. Sound policy does the opposite. It presumes errors will be made and it consciously seeks to achieve more errors of a certain kind and less of another.

Ultimately, we may be unable to resolve definitively whether or how much the parental rights doctrine advances children's interests. Though we may lack definitive proof that there is no better arrangement for children, most would agree there is much in the doctrine to reconcile with children's rights.

The more crucial point is that it may be misleading to suggest that the parental rights doctrine was developed for the purpose of serving children's interests. At the very least, it is important to acknowledge that the parental rights doctrine is unjustifiable *solely* in terms of the value it serves to children. The doctrine furthers vital interests of American society and may be defended on grounds outside of child-focused claims. In this sense, too successful a reconciliation of the parental rights doctrine and children's rights would tend to blur a more basic reality about the relationship of the laws affecting children and the circumstances under which they were formed. All such laws are made by adults in order to create the kind of society adults wish to have.

We simply are unable to untangle the relationship of child, parent, and state from the larger matters of our culture and our core political philosophy. Although there is value in articulating the ways in which parental rights are good for children, it is important to remember that parental rights also serve important, often more basic, purposes as well.

However important the subject of children's rights may be, it is only a part of a much larger subject of what rules work best for society as a whole. Even if it could be persuasively shown that the parental rights doctrine is not best for children, that should hardly condemn it. More is at stake in the parent-child relationship than what is best for children. The inquiry is obviously important, but not dispositive.

Most parents insist upon the authority to make significant child-rearing decisions without having to prove to some overseer that their choices are actually the best ones. For most parents, the point is less that their choices must be *best* for their children than that they ought not to be *bad* for them. Remarkably enough, this is precisely the constitutional rule in the United States. The unfitness rule announced in *Stanley v. Illinois* means that it is wrong to have to prove that a parent has the right to custody of his or her child before showing that the child is in danger of being harmed. Perhaps the wiser question is whether the parental rights doctrine *harms* children, rather than whether it is best for them. Some children's rights advocates may require definitive proof that the parental rights doctrine best serves children's interests. But for others, it is sufficient that there are good reasons for the parental rights doctrine apart from what is best for children and that, absent evidence that the doctrine harms children, it should be maintained.

As we end this chapter, we would do well to think about the relationship of the family to the state in terms of which institution is older. There is little doubt that families as an institution have survived because of their instrumental value in reproduction, acculturation, and assimilation of children. But to suggest they serve an instrumental value does not mean they are the instruments of the state. Law and culture are always inextricably intertwined. Our culture is based on a notion of privacy and private ordering, even though privacy is buttressed by state laws and rules. Our arrangement may not be natural or necessary. But it is ours. Consider Justice Brennan's words reflecting on this relationship: "Plato offered a vision of a unified society, where the needs of children are not met by parents but by the government, and where no intermediate forms of association stand between the individual and the State. The vision is a brilliant one, but it is not our own."[57]

One of the most deeply contentious issues in American family law is a struggle among adults over who gets to enjoy the bundle of rights parents possess. To some, the ideas expressed in this chapter will be too theoretical because they fail to address the real issues in contemporary American society. They would suggest that families have changed so significantly that the rules and principles of this chapter are outdated and ought to be irrelevant when addressing the modern family. Stepparents, foster parents, nonbiological partners of parents (either same-sex or heterosexual), and surrogate mothers are only some of the adults who have sought to be recognized by courts as having acquired parentlike rights. Today's "nontraditional" families significantly outnumber the traditional ones. Fewer children are being raised in two-parent households than ever before; a great many are being raised by people other than their biological parents. But the point of this chapter is to serve as a background for all of the arguments over children that lie ahead. Legislative and judicial responses to these disputes can be understood only within the framework of the deeply held commitment to parental rights described in this chapter.

Precisely because of the extraordinary authority over children that the law cedes to parents, it is exceedingly important to ascertain who gets to be counted as a "parent" under the law and who, as a result, obtains the bundle of rights that parents enjoy. What determines parenthood? Is it based solely on biology? Can someone be recognized as a parent based on the day-to-day caregiving that has been provided to a child? Chapter 3 considers these questions through the lens of the rights of unwed fathers. In exploring these questions, we will also be able to consider whether and to what degree a child's perspective about who is his or her parent matters.

3

Getting and Losing Parental Rights: The "Baby Jessica" Case

She went to bed on the evening of August 1, 1993 almost totally oblivious to the turmoil surrounding her in her own home and in the community around it. Three-year-olds rarely know much about the details of the conflicts the adults upon whom they depend for subsistence are experiencing. Jessica was completely unaware that she had been the subject of countless headlines in newspapers throughout the United States and featured in major magazines.[1] She knew something was not right at home; her mother and father were acting peculiarly toward her. They cried a lot, kept telling her how much they loved her, and assured her that everything would be all right. She knew something was going on around her, but not very much.

Certainly she was completely unaware when she awoke that day that her life was going to be permanently changed. Jessica was about to be taken from her parents' home—her home and the only place she had lived since she was born. She didn't know she would never see mommy and daddy again. She also did not know that for years two other people had claimed that mommy and daddy weren't really her parents, and that these other adults had succeeded in their nearly two-and-a-half-year multiple court battle to gain custody of her, The day had come when Jessica was to be taken from her home and given to her biological parents.

Jessica's life was about to be permanently altered, even though all agreed that Jessica's mommy and daddy were loving, good parents who had raised her in an exemplary manner. What is so remarkable about this story, however, is not that Jessica was being removed from her parents' home. It is that out of the nineteen judges who heard the case, sixteen concluded that the removal was the lawful and proper result.

How could this be? Didn't Jessica have the basic human right to be allowed to remain in the only home she had ever known, a home in which she had thrived? How was the parental rights doctrine described in the last chapter applied in this case? This chapter examines these and other questions by focusing on who gets to be treated as a parent under the law.

The court decision that ordered Jessica out of the home was based on a determination that her biological father was her parent, not the people who were raising her. Many regard a law that bases parenthood on biology to be insufficiently child-centered. To them, the rule that produced the forced breakup of Jessica's family is a relic derived from a now-discarded notion that children are treated as property assigned to the adult who can prove "title" to a court. In this chapter I will explain the arguments for and against the outcome in Jessica's case. Its goal is not to persuade you to prefer one outcome over the other, but to help you gain a deeper appreciation of the law as it affects children and, ultimately, to come to see how and why law sometimes appears to the public to be self-evidently wrong as it is applied in certain cases.

But it is far too early to discuss what these rules are, let alone to enter the debate of whether or not they are suitable. Let's begin, instead, by providing some of the facts in Jessica's case.

The case began when Cara Clausen, an unmarried twenty-eight-year-old woman, gave birth to a girl on February 8, 1991 in Cedar Rapids, Iowa. Throughout her pregnancy, Cara debated what to do with her baby after she was born. Ultimately, she settled on placing her for adoption. Cara let some friends know she was going to give up her baby for adoption. A cousin of a married, childless couple living in Ann Arbor, Michigan heard about Cara's plans and received permission from Cara to contact the couple, Jan and Roberta DeBoer. The DeBoers, in their mid-thirties, had been trying unsuccessfully for many years to become parents. Roberta was unable to conceive, and only three months earlier had had a hysterectomy. The state in which they lived prohibited private placement adoptions. All adoption placements in Michigan had to be made through state-licensed agencies. The DeBoers had been on wait lists to adopt for several years with nothing to show for it and no promises of success on the horizon.

Immediately after the DeBoers got in touch with Cara, they hired a lawyer in Iowa. The DeBoers waited until the lawyer had news to report. When he called to tell them that Cara had given birth to a baby girl, the DeBoers were overjoyed. It seemed that they were at last about to become parents. On February 10, forty hours after the baby was born, the DeBoers' lawyer visited Cara before she was discharged from the hospital and gave her official papers to sign, releasing custody of her child to the DeBoers and also surrendering her parental rights to the child. In these papers, she named Scott Seefeldt as the father. On February 14, Scott also signed papers relinquishing his rights to the girl.

Once both parents signed these papers, the DeBoers' lawyer phoned them and told them they should come to Iowa to take custody of their new child, whom they would call Jessica. On February 25, the DeBoers appeared in an Iowa court. At that hearing, the court gave them temporary custody of Jessica (until the adoption was finalized). Elated, the DeBoers returned to Michigan with Jessica.

Almost immediately, things began unraveling for the DeBoers. It turned out that neither one of the Surrenders of Parental Rights signed by the birth parents was lawful under Iowa law. Cara's surrender violated Iowa law because Iowa imposed a seventy-two-hour "cooling-off period" after the birth of a child during which time parents are prevented from surrendering their rights. Scott's surrender proved to be illusory because he was not the birth father. Although Cara falsely identified him as such, the actual father was a man named Daniel Schmidt, whom she had been dating at the time she became pregnant.

Things got even worse for the DeBoers when Cara told Dan the truth about his baby on February 27. Upon learning that he was the father, Dan took immediate steps to secure his parental rights under Iowa law. On March 6, nine days after the DeBoers filed their adoption petition, Cara filed a motion in the Iowa Juvenile Court to revoke her surrender. In these papers Cara stated that she falsely named the birth father and that Dan, not Scott, was the actual birth father. Later that month, Dan filed papers seeking to be declared Jessica's father and to prevent the adoption of his daughter.

The trial on all of these matters did not take place until November 4, 1991. On December 27, the court found, based on irrefutable blood matching, that Dan was the biological father of the child; that there were no grounds under Iowa law to conclude he had abandoned Jessica or that his parental rights could be terminated; and that, as a result, the adoption had to be dismissed. Because of the court's ruling, it did not need to decide whether Cara's surrender was valid. Having ruled that Dan was the legally recognized father under Iowa law, the DeBoers were ordered to give custody of Jessica to Dan.[2]

Rather than give up and return their now ten-month-old child, the DeBoers chose to appeal these rulings. To protect against the possibility of two needless disruptions of Jessica's life, the Iowa Supreme Court permitted the DeBoers to keep custody of Jessica until the appeal was decided. Unfortunately for all concerned, the appeals process took an entire year. Unfortunately for the DeBoers, they lost on all grounds on appeal.[3] Thus it was that the DeBoers were directed to appear in an Iowa court on December 3, 1992 to give custody of Jessica to Cara and Dan. By all rights, that should have ended the matter.

What About Children's Rights?

Before continuing the legal tale of what occurred next, it is useful to shift our attention to what the DeBoers and their supporters stressed was so disturbing about the outcome of their case. To many, and particularly to many in the popular media, the outcome appeared to be a travesty reflecting the status of children in American law who remain subordinated to adults' superior legal status and rights. The consistent criticism was that Jessica was being treated as a person without rights; her legal status seemed to be that of a piece of furniture that was ordered into the custody of its rightful owner. This criticism is at once powerful and inadequate. It raises the tension that always exists in custody cases between deciding cases based on the child's best interests and respecting and enforcing the rule of law.

Let's shift our focus to a simple hypothetical case. Imagine that a woman sneaks into a hospital's maternity ward, picks out the cutest baby there, and takes the baby home with her. Ten months later she is caught and charged with child-stealing. The birth parents of the child demand the child's immediate return. The "mother" who has raised the child since birth immediately files a court petition seeking to keep custody of the child. In support of her petition, she alleges that the child has psychologically bonded with her, that it is in the child's best interests for this parent-child relationship to be continued, and that, even if the childsnatcher did something wrong when the relationship was first established, the child should not be punished by destroying the only parental relationship she has ever known. If the court chose to conduct a hearing to determine whether changing custody of the child would serve her best interests, it is quite likely the evidence would favor the child remaining in the only home she has ever known.

Assuming there was no evidence to show that the child snatcher had been an inadequate parent in terms of the nurturing she had provided, most experts would agree—all other factors aside—that the child's best interests would be served by letting her stay with her "mother." Many nonexperts would also likely agree that if they were required to consider only the child's best interests, she should be allowed to remain in the snatcher's home.

There would undoubtedly be some disagreement on this issue. It is possible to try to balance the child's short-term best interests against her long-term interests by tolerating some immediate suffering to realize the long-term gain of being reunited with her birth parents. Moreover, given the possibility that the child-snatching parent would be imprisoned for her crime, even a best interests inquiry might cause some to conclude that the child should be returned to her birth parents immediately. But others would counter these points by saying that the short-term harm should be avoided, if at all possible, particularly when there is no guarantee that the child will adjust satisfactorily to the change.

Indeed, considering only what is best for the child might mean dismissing criminal charges against the child-snatching parent. Instead, the birth parents would be permitted some remedy for their loss, perhaps the right to sue for a substantial monetary judgment. Because children are not property, too much time would have elapsed to disrupt her now stable environment. Moreover, since the birth parents never even had custody of the child, their claim to her custody is based solely on biology.

Those single-mindedly focused on the child's best interest would point out that parents should never be treated as having legal title to children, especially when they have never acted as actual caregivers. Such a policy, they might claim, would prevent children from being dehumanized and considered as property. Finally, under a best interests analysis, some would say that no child should be forced to leave the care of a successful parent-child relationship simply to make whole a birth parent's legal claim to the child's possession.

Few of us, however, would be willing to put other factors aside in deciding what to do in this hypothetical case. In the real world, this case would be handled simply. There would be no hearing on the child's best interests nor any expert testimony against the child's removal. Instead, the police would summarily remove the child when they arrested the woman and would happily contact the birth parents and tell them the good news that their child was waiting for them.

The police would act in this way because the law has long operated under the principle that, whenever possible, a wrongdoer should be prohibited to benefit from her wrongdoing. This same principle, for example, is applied to deny a murderer his inheritance from the person he killed. Law, as a component of justice, is designed to advance just results. Permitting a wrongdoer to profit from illegal conduct is unjust. But there is an important, related justification for the rule. The only way to discourage illegal behavior is to have a rule that says that violators of the law will not benefit from their misconduct. Here the focus is not on justice, but on creating rules that work for society.

One of law's most important functions is to establish a code of conduct to which members of society must conform. If people knew that their failure to conform would not lead to any real consequences, the result would be anarchy. Law would be reduced to moral precepts by which people would be free to abide as they saw fit. What makes law different from mere precepts is the power to respond when the law is ignored. Take away that power and you take away the characteristic that distinguishes law from ordinary persuasion.

My hypothetical example demonstrates that there are *some* cases in which it is appropriate to order a change of custody when we have reason to believe such a change is not in a child's best interests. To be sure, we have a long way to go before knowing *which* cases. Certainly, if the child snatcher kept the child for ten or fifteen years, the case would take on a very different hue.

Many years ago, then fifteen-year-old Kimberly Mays made headlines when it was discovered that she and another child had been switched at birth as a result of a mistake at a Florida hospital. To make matters worse, the other child had died at a young age. Had the mistake been discovered after a short time, all would have insisted that the children be switched back. But by the time the mistake in Kimberly's case was discovered, many people felt strongly that it would have been wrong for a court to require that she be removed from the family that raised her for fifteen years and returned to her birth family.

The child-snatching example illustrates that, in at least some instances, it would be inappropriate even to undertake a best interests inquiry. This deserves careful consideration. This means there is a consensus that the rule of law sometimes is more important than an inquiry into what its application may mean to a particular child and that even asking what the impact of applying the law will be on a child sometimes is unnecessary.

These insights have great import in the "Baby Jessica" case. Jessica's case can be seen as having two dimensions. One is ascertaining the law and the legal principles behind it and then applying them to the circumstances of her case. The other—the one the popular media fixed upon—was concerned only with Jessica and her rights.

Why do we need a specific rule for adopting children born out of wedlock? Adoption is an important institution with deep social roots. We are a nation yielding an unprecedented number of children born out of wedlock. Particularly in a society in which abortion is deeply contentious, it makes sense to facilitate the adoption process for willing birth mothers. Society needs to develop the best rule for these situations, because when we narrow our concern only to what happens in an individual case, such as Jessica's, the focus shifts from the broader question of law and policy to the alluring but deficient focus on what should happen to her. Thus, before we are even ready to discuss the proper result in Jessica's case, we need to examine the legal principles that were established at the time of her placement.

The Rights of Unwed Fathers and the Laws Relating to Children Born Out of Wedlock

Had Jessica been placed for adoption a mere twenty years earlier, the case would have gone unnoticed as simply another of the more than 100,000 adoptions of unwed children that took place on an average basis each year in the 1970s. At that time, Jessica's birth mother would have had the sole power to decide whether to raise Jessica herself or to place her for adoption. Only she would have made that decision. She would not have been obliged to reveal who the birth father was; it would have been adequate for her to simply say "unknown" on the pertinent adoption papers. Her surrender of parental rights would have been all that was needed for the adoption to go forward. Twenty years earlier, had the DeBoers come to Iowa to adopt Jessica, they would have left completely secure in the knowledge that the adoption was final before they returned to Michigan. But by 1990, things had changed dramatically. Unwed fathers had secured legally recognized rights to their children, at least under certain circumstances.

What precipitated these changes in the law? I will next outline the evolution of the laws concerning unwed fathers and children born out of wedlock.

The term "unwed fathers," for our purposes, means men who have children by women to whom they are not married. Although the term is imprecise, since it includes both married and unmarried men, it has become the accepted term in the field. Similarly, the term "nonmarital children" is now commonly used as a substitute for what were once called "illegitimate" children. Sometimes, these children will be referred to as "children born out of wedlock." These children are the offspring of an unwed mother, an unwed father, or a wed mother who conceived the child with someone other than her husband.

For most of Anglo-American history, nonmarital children were treated very differently from marital children. The story of how, when, and why society's treatment of these children has changed in the United States is an important one, both in terms of what those changes are and in the circumstances under which they came about.

The law's treatment of children born out of wedlock initially evolved rather slowly. In the first several decades after the United States was founded, virtually every state continued to follow the extreme version of English common law doctrine that precluded a nonmarital child from ever being adopted or made legitimate.[4] Under the most severe version of English common law, children born to unmarried parents were "no one's child," a literal translation of the Latin "filius nullius." This meant such children could be taken by county officials and placed in poorhouses or apprenticed out as sailors or farmhands as state officials saw fit and not even their mothers had the right to object.

The English common law, however, proved to be far too harsh in the United States. American courts rather quickly ameliorated the most severe treatment of nonmarital children and recognized the mother as the child's legal parent. By the early 1800s, unwed mothers in the United States had the right to custody of their children. Unwed fathers, however, had no such right. Children born out of wedlock continued to be treated under American law as unrelated to the father.[5]

This differential treatment between mothers and fathers is partly explainable by reference to the laws of inheritance under the common law. The most important legal aspect of the parent-child relationship concerned the rules by which property was to be passed from generation to generation. These rules were based on legally defined kin relationships. When primogeniture was the means by which property was passed (the eldest son of a man became the primary heir of his property), it was important to establish rules that clarified who counted as a man's son and who did not. Since, for the most part, women were prohibited from owning property in the first place, it was irrelevant whether the law formally recognized the relationship between a mother and her child; the only thing that mattered was whether the law would recognize the legal relationship of a man's offspring. This assured certainty in the passage of property from one generation to the next.

A number of purposes were served by treating children born out of wedlock as nonpersons. Perhaps most important, it encouraged marriage. Men could pass on their wealth after they died only by becoming fathers through legally recognized marriages, so when an unmarried man learned that he impregnated an unmarried woman, marriage became an inevitable choice for many. Pregnant women had an even greater incentive to marry. Without marriage, they faced raising a child whom the law refused to recognize as related to the father. This scheme also provided a form of punishment to women for having sex outside of marriage.[6]

The combination of harsh economic consequences and the highly negative social stigma resulting from becoming pregnant outside of marriage were powerful disincentives from engaging in sex outside of marriage. For obvious reasons, this, too, encouraged men to marry.[7] Fixed rules of inheritance also ensured a smooth settlement of estates after a man died. There could be no contest by a person claiming to be the blood son of the deceased; the law did not care.

This is not to suggest that the law ever was a greater influence on behavior than culture and social norms. It really was and always has been the other way around. In the area of sex and human relationships, law reflects culture and social norms to a greater extent than it shapes them. For much of modern western history, the social stigma attached to women becoming pregnant out of wedlock was powerful. It pressured many women into marriage when they became pregnant. But the law helped, too.

If this book were written a hundred years ago, what would it say about unwed fathers? The category simply would not exist because the biological offspring of unwed fathers were not theirs under the law. Technically, fathers were responsible for contributing to the cost of raising their biological children. But enforcement proceedings were relatively rare, and most fathers of unwed children did not contribute anything. This meant that, at the turn of the twentieth century, men enjoyed the freedom to procreate outside of marriage with little serious risk that they would be legally or financially responsible for their behavior.[8] They were free *not* to be fathers.

This also meant that mothers had full responsibility for these children—both the privileges and responsibilities of parenting. Mothers of children born out of wedlock bore the responsibility for raising them. More precisely, the degree to which anyone other than the mother aided in providing financial support for a nonmarital child was largely a matter of choice. But these mothers also had the exclusive choice whether to raise their children themselves or place them for adoption.

With certain modifications, this remained the law in the United States until less than two generations ago. Through much of the twentieth century, legal doctrine continued to deny the connection between men and their out-of-wedlock offspring. Although men had the duty to support their nonmarital children, they were rarely compelled to do so, and thus unwed fathers had no legally recognized say about who would raise their nonmarital children.

In the story of the evolving law of unwed fathers, it took a change in the former to achieve a change in the latter. First unwed fathers were burdened by federal law with the responsibility of supporting their nonmarital children. Afterward, they gained the right to be involved in placement decisions for their children. The history of government's recognition of an unwed father's obligations for his offspring is rather convoluted. It is not really an account about children's rights; it is not even about fathers' duties. It took a cataclysmic event in the United States to get things started.

The rampant poverty and struggle for subsistence of the Great Depression set the stage for the federal government to enact legislation, for the first time, that provided public benefits for poor children. Prior to 1935, the federal government played no role in providing for needy children. It was only with the passage of the Social Security Act of 1935 that federal money was given to the states to support children whose fathers were deceased or disabled. Within a few years, the benefits were expanded to include poor children's mothers. Originally designed to assist widowed mothers, the Aid to Families with Dependent Children program gradually became the means by which government supported unwed mothers and their children.[9]

Congress's primary concern when it first held men financially responsible for their children was to reduce public funds spent on children. The requirement that unwed fathers support their children was not imposed because of a shared sense that children deserved to be supported or that fathers had a duty to support them. When caring for children was purely a private affair, the government saw little wrong with laws that failed to ensure that men financially supported children they fathered out of wedlock, even though this meant that mothers (and their impoverished children) had to fend for themselves. Only when the federal government found itself in the position of supporting children did it conclude that fathers should take over that responsibility.

Once this happened, American law and society began looking

differently at men who were fathering children outside of marriage. As society accepted the notion that children born out of wedlock, like all other children, needed to be fed, clothed, and housed, it also recognized the problems associated with laws that made these children the exclusive responsibility of government. As a result, federal laws were enacted that imposed child support responsibilities on unwed fathers for their children's care, whether or not they had custody or even were interested in custody or visitation of their children. Simultaneously, new state laws were enacted to make enforcement of child support orders more effective.

In addition to changing legal perceptions concerning an unwed father's obligations, other, profound changes in American society were taking place in the years after World War II. These societal changes fueled a remarkable transformation of the law relating to children born out of wedlock. Different social norms and economic conditions after World War II dramatically affected the marriage rates. In the past two generations, a lower percentage of adults has tied the knot than at any other time in American history. Adults who do marry have postponed marriage by a considerable number of years, and, most dramatically, a higher percentage of children have been born out of wedlock than at any time previous in the twentieth century. Consider these numbers: In 1950, a mere 4 percent of all children born in the United States had unmarried mothers; in 1970, the percentage had risen to slightly less than 11 percent; in 1980, it jumped to 18 percent; today, one in three children are born to an unwed mother.[10]

By the end of the 1970s, there were important enforcement mechanisms to ensure that unwed fathers supported their children financially if the mother chose to keep the baby. But, as we left off in our discussion of the evolution of unwed fathers' rights, they still had no say about what happened to the child during the child's lifetime.[11] At one time, this was not seen as any kind of disability. By the time of Jessica's placement for adoption, unwed fathers had achieved a constitutional right to have and maintain a legally recognized relationship with their children: the polar opposite of their rights a mere twenty years earlier.

The Supreme Court Cases

The rights of unwed fathers were first established in a groundbreaking 1972 Supreme Court case we briefly considered in the last chapter. The story of that case begins in 1950 when Peter Stanley began dating Joan in Chicago. After Joan became pregnant in 1951, Peter moved in with her and their first child was born. Over the next 17 years, Peter and Joan became the parents of two more children. Altogether Peter and Joan lived together on and off during an eighteen-year relationship, they never formalized their relationship by marrying. Even though Joan went by the name of Joan Stanley, Illinois does not have common-law marriages. Thus, according to the laws of Illinois, Peter's three children were "illegitimate."

In order to create a legally recognized paternal relationship to his children, Illinois law required that Peter marry Joan and acknowledge the children as his own or that Joan file a paternity action against Peter and secure a court order declaring Peter to be the children's father (and, thereby, financially responsible for them). For reasons unknown, Peter and Joan chose never to marry. Joan had no reason to file a paternity petition because Peter was supporting his children.

In 1969, Joan died from an illness. Shortly after her death, Peter asked a couple who were friends of the family to care for his children on an interim basis. When state officials learned that the Stanley children were without a living parent whom the state recognized, the officials took them into foster care as orphans in need of the state's protection. Peter immediately went to state court and told the court he was the children's father. But, under Illinois law, the children had "no surviving parent or guardian" recognized by the state. The court told Peter that the children had become state wards and the court now would decide where the children should reside. Peter was permitted to request that the court place the children in his custody, but the court would make whatever placement it deemed appropriate based on its assessment of what was in the children's best interests. Peter appealed the state court's ruling to the Illinois Supreme Court, which found nothing wrong with what the state court had done. Peter then appealed to the Supreme Court of the United States.

In 1972, the Court decided *Stanley v. Illinois,* one of the leading cases on parents' rights in the Court's history.[12] In the Supreme Court, Illinois defended its statutory scheme as furthering the permissible state interest of discouraging out-of-wedlock births. Illinois argued that its scheme was a rational way to place incentives on men to marry their biological children's mother if they wished to obtain legally recognized rights.

Illinois argued that Stanley should have considered the law when choosing not to marry. If he had married, there would be no court case. It was his choice not to marry and now he must suffer the consequences. This argument is a familiar example of the use of law to regulate behavior. Legislatures enact laws all the time to create incentives for people to do particular things. The Illinois law was merely an example of a universal rule in all states.

But social change frequently is recognized by the courts when legislatures are slow to react to changing social conditions. Even if the Illinois argument was highly persuasive at one time in American history, by the end of the 1960s the argument had lost a considerable amount of its power. The rising out-of-wedlock birth rate suggested that Americans' behavior was changing.

This change in real-world behavior suggests the organic relationship between law and behavior. Stanley claimed that he was being unconstitutionally discriminated against as compared with married fathers merely because he was unmarried. The Court's task really amounted to deciding whether the continued "discrimination" furthered a worthy state interest, or whether this particular law had lost its capacity to shape human behavior.

When marriage was a socially obligatory institution, states felt comfortable passing laws to "punish" those who would not bother getting married even though they became parents. The group the legislatures targeted for this punishment was fathers. But the *Stanley* Court responded (although not in so many words) by reasoning that Stanley had done virtually all of the socially responsible things society would want him to have done and, given the changing conditions of our culture, it was appropriate to reward him for his choice to rear his children. Because Peter Stanley had actually supported and cared for his children, he had acquired legally recognized parental rights despite having never married the children's mother.

Stanley began a series of cases that developed the metes and bounds of an unwed father's constitutional rights. But it took several more cases for these boundaries to take full shape. As we shall see, even today important questions remain unanswered. In all events, reasoning that Stanley's interest in retaining custody of his children was "substantial," the Court ruled that Illinois had to prove to a court that he was an inadequate parent before his children could be taken from him.

In the immediate aftermath of *Stanley,* adoption officials worried that all unwed fathers might be given all of the constitutional rights that parents enjoyed. Because Stanley was an unwed father who actually lived with, supported, and reared his children, it was unclear whether he won simply because he was the biological father of his children, because he raised them for many years and lived with them, or a combination of the two.

Six years later a case from Georgia reached the Supreme Court that provided clarification of the circumstances under which unwed fathers secured constitutional rights to prevent the adoption of their biological children. It is well established in American law that before children may be adopted, parents with legally recognized parental rights have the right to prevent the adoption absent a finding that the parent is "unfit" (a stringent finding not easily made).

Quilloin v. Walcott involved a proposed adoption of an eleven-year-old nonmarital child by her stepfather, who married the mother when the child was two years old.[13] Quilloin was the biological father of the child. Under Georgia law, before a child may be adopted both parents must have died or have given their consent to the adoption. In the case of children born out of wedlock, however, only the mother's consent was required. After the adoption was permitted to go forward over Quilloin's objection, he appealed to the Supreme Court, claiming that his rights to equal protection of the law had been violated because Georgia law only required the consent of married and divorced fathers.

It was rather easy for the Court to distinguish *Quilloin* from *Stanley*. Like Stanley, Quilloin was never married to the mother; neither did he take steps to become the legally recognized father under Georgia law (through a paternity proceeding). But that is where the similarities ended. Unlike Stanley, Quilloin never lived with his child. His only involvement with his daughter was that he occasionally visited her and offered a few insignificant child support payments. Only after the stepfather sought to adopt the child did Quilloin attempt to establish his paternity and obtain visitation rights.

The Supreme Court rejected Quilloin's argument that the law required that he be treated like Stanley, and like all other married and divorced fathers. The Court held that the mother was within her rights to decide whom the law should legally recognize as her daughter's father and ruled that there was nothing to prevent Georgia from saying that only her consent to the adoption was required.

The combination of *Stanley* and *Quilloin* did much to clarify the constitutional principles concerning unwed fathers. But it still left some important questions.

The next unwed father case to reach the Supreme Court came from New York in 1979. Like *Quilloin,* it involved the proposed adoption of nonmarital children by the birth mother's husband. New York law gave unwed fathers the right to be heard at the proposed adoption hearing, but their consent to the adoption was not required. They were only permitted an opportunity to show why the adoption would not further their children's best interests. After a New York court granted the adoption finding that the children's best interests were furthered by being raised in a home with two married parents, the unwed father appealed to the Supreme Court, claiming that his constitutional parental rights were violated. But this time, the claim was that he was denied equal protection of the law because he was being treated differently from the mother.

The facts of *Caban v. Mohammed* fit somewhere between the two previous cases.[14] Caban lived with the mother and his two children for several years, but the parents never married. After he moved out of the home, he visited with his children regularly and supported them financially. Caban's technical challenge to New York's statute was that New York gave unwed mothers but not unwed fathers the right to veto a proposed adoption of their children even when the only distinction between the parents was their gender.[15]

Caban successfully argued that he was indistinguishable from the mother in terms of the degree to which he cared for his children. The Court agreed, holding that New York's gender-based distinction was unjustified because Caban had proven himself a worthy father over a period of six years. Since he developed "a relationship with his children fully comparable to that of the mother," New York violated the Equal Protection guarantee when it gave him fewer rights than an unwed mother enjoyed.

The combination of these three cases makes clear that the Supreme Court wished to reward unwed fathers who invest in their children's lives and to discriminate among unwed fathers based on the degree to which they played a significant role in raising their children. After *Caban*, unwed fathers who played an active role in their children's lives have been rewarded even if they did not marry their child's mother. (This also makes sense from a feminist perspective. Marriage is not the crucial determinant; instead it is a commitment to be a parent and the execution of that commitment.)

It is also useful to observe that the unwed father cases did not reject the use of law to mold behavior; they reaffirmed such a purpose. Under the new rules, however, the law would confer benefits on those men who engage in the socially desirable practice of parenting. From *Caban* on, men who invested time and money in their children have been treated as parents; unmarried fathers who have not, cannot rely on the law to protect their interests to their biological offspring.

Four years after *Caban*, the Court heard the most recent case relevant to the constitutional rights of an unwed father. In *Lehr v. Robertson*, an unwed father appealed from an order than denied him even the right to receive notice that his two-year-old child was being adopted.[16] The challenged statute required that notice of adoptions be served only upon unwed fathers (1) whose name was on the birth certificate, (2) who lived with the child's mother and held themselves out to be the father, (3) who filed with the state's paternity registry, or (4) who had been legally declared to be the biological father in a paternity proceeding. Because none of these categories fit the circumstances, New York went forward with the adoption of Lehr's biological daughter without giving him even an opportunity to appear in court.

The Supreme Court upheld the adoption and ruled that Lehr never secured parental rights protected by the federal Constitution. The Court explained that unwed fathers do not acquire constitutional parental rights merely because they helped produce a child. Instead, Justice Stevens explained, unwed fathers have what he called an "inchoate" right as a parent that will ripen into a constitutionally protected right depending on what the unwed father does during the mother's pregnancy or immediately after the child's birth. The Court reasoned that an unwed father has only the right to an *opportunity* to develop a relationship with his child. In the Court's words, "[i]f he grasps that opportunity and accepts some measure of responsibility for the child's future, he may enjoy the blessings of the parent-child relationship . . . If he fails to do so, the Federal Constitution will not automatically compel a State to listen to his opinion of where the child's best interests lie."[17]

Lehr is a difficult case to analyze in part because the majority and dissenting justices disagreed on the steps Lehr had taken to develop a relationship with his daughter. All of the justices seemed to agree that the Constitution requires that unwed fathers be given some opportunity to "grasp" their parental rights. And all seemed to agree that unwed fathers who do too little do not acquire constitutionally protected parental rights. The dissent suggested that Lehr attempted to visit his daughter and to provide financial support for her, but was unsuccessful because the mother refused him a role in their lives. The majority took the position that Lehr could have listed his name with the registry. His failure to do so could be attributed only to him.

But what if the father's failure even to register was not his fault? What if, for example, the mother falsely told him she miscarried or, as in Jessica's case, the child she was carrying was not his? Despite four cases on unwed fathers in the Supreme Court over an eleven-year period, that question was unanswered at the time of Jessica's birth. It remains unanswered even today. *Lehr* could be read to suggest that unwed fathers who did everything reasonable to establish a relationship with their children but were thwarted by circumstances beyond their control did not forfeit their parental constitutional rights. But the case does not say that.

At a minimum, the Constitution requires that fathers be allowed to secure parental rights even without the cooperation and consent of the mother. For this reason, it would be unconstitutional for a state to require that an unwed father's name be on the birth certificate or that he live with the child as the only means by which he could secure parental rights, because these things cannot be accomplished over the mother's objection. In *Lehr's* wake, most states rewrote their adoption laws to establish procedures for the adoption of nonmarital children that do not depend on the mother's cooperation.

Today, many states require that unwed fathers who wish to be recognized by the state at least contribute financially toward the costs of the pregnancy and childbirth, place their name on the birth certificate, file an action to establish paternity within a relatively short period of time, or register their name with a "putative father registry" maintained by the state. Since the 1980s, a majority of states have created such registries. The minimum right an unwed father secures by filing with a registry is being assured of getting notice and an opportunity to appear at the adoption proceeding.[18]

The Iowa Decision in the "Baby Jessica" Case

By emphasizing that unwed fathers have a constitutional right to an opportunity to develop a parental relationship with their children, the Supreme Court in *Lehr* paved the way for state courts to conclude that when unwed fathers were not given such an opportunity, their constitutional rights were violated. By 1992, Iowa was among those states that saw fit to protect an unwed father's opportunity to develop a constitutionally recognized interest in his child. Once a state is committed to protecting this interest, it is reasonable to expect the state to forgive an unwed father who did not avail himself of that opportunity through no fault of his own. In such cases, the court shifts its attention from how much of a relationship had been developed by the time the child was placed for adoption to whether the unwed father should be *blamed* for the failure of such a relationship to have been formed.

The Iowa Supreme Court in Jessica's case ultimately concluded that unwed fathers may not suffer the loss of their parental rights if their conduct cannot be said to be blameworthy. Iowa and a number of other states require that an unwed father be given a fair opportunity to establish a relationship with his child. If he is not, he will be allowed to veto the proposed adoption, at least if he comes forward within a relatively short time after the child was placed.[19]

The Iowa court reasoned as follows:

> It has been urged that the court should uphold this proposed adoption on the ground that the father had abandoned his rights by failing to protect them, beginning at the time the pregnancy became known. In other words, it is suggested that this father should have acted to protect his parental rights immediately when the pregnancy became known, even though he had no indication from her that he was the father and even though she was dating another man at the time. This, of course, is totally unrealistic; it would require a potential father to become involved in the pregnancy on the mere speculation that he might be the father because he was one of the men having sexual relations with her at the time in question.[20]

Iowa applied the same rule to Jessica's unwed father that it applies to all parents who are alleged to have abandoned their child. The court must find by clear and convincing evidence that the parent *intended* to abandon. The Court concluded that because Dan Schmidt was unaware he had a child, he could not have intended to abandon the child.

A Better Rule?

It is worth repeating that this decision was not clearly required by *Lehr* or by the United States Constitution. The U.S. Supreme Court has yet to decide whether a blameless unwed father must be forgiven for failing to secure his parental rights. If the Court were to hold that such a defense is constitutionally required, all states would be bound to recognize it, as Iowa did. But if the Court were to hold that such a defense is *not* constitutionally required, states like Iowa would nonetheless be free to allow the defense.

In our American laboratory for working out complex social dilemmas, there is a mosaic of laws affecting the rights and responsibilities of unwed fathers. The only national law that applies to all cases is the constitutional requirement that fathers not lose their rights without due process of law. The U.S. Supreme Court's interpretation of a provision of the federal Constitution is binding on all courts, including state courts. But *Lehr* did not prohibit states from granting unwed fathers more rights than the federal Constitution demands. The federal Constitution creates a floor below which states may not deny fathers rights. But it is not illegal for some states to give fathers more rights than the Constitution would require.

Iowa law is more deferential to unwed fathers than many states are. Indeed, the contrast with New York's law is especially striking. Under Iowa law, Dan's consent was required before his child could be adopted. If Dan had lived in New York, the most he would have been entitled to was a right to notice of the proceeding. And it is not certain New York would have given him even that.

But the Iowa Supreme Court perceived itself as protecting and vindicating sacred parental rights by ruling for Dan. It stressed that "[c]ourts are not free to take children from parents simply by deciding another home offers more advantages" and that, unless courts scrupulously adhered to the rule of law in adoption cases, they would "be engaged in uncontrolled social engineering" by deciding for themselves who should raise children. (Considering that this is the same court that decided *Painter v. Bannister* in 1967, these words are especially significant.) One can be completely sympathetic with these principles and disagree with their application in Jessica's case.

The question the Iowa Supreme Court did not precisely consider is what steps, if any, Iowa law demands of unwed fathers *before* they acquire parental rights. It is one thing to reason that once Dan was found to have parental rights under Iowa law there was no basis to conclude that he ever intended to relinquish them. But would the best rule recognize Dan as having acquired legally recognized parental rights in the first place?

Lehr teaches us that the federal Constitution requires that unwed fathers have the opportunity to secure legally protectable parental rights. But what is the precise meaning of a right to this "opportunity"? As we have seen, it could mean, as the Iowa Supreme Court ruled in Dan's case, that he must be informed that he is (or is about to become) a father and then judged for his conduct after he has this information. When fraud or deception is involved, courts are more likely to protect the unwed father's rights. Thus, some states will forgive an unwed father for failing to register within the statutory time period when the explanation for his failure is that he did not know of the child's birth, provided that he files shortly after first learning of the child.[21]

But it could also mean that he has the constitutional right only to insist that the *state* not interfere with his opportunity to acquire legally protected parental rights. Several states explicitly bar the defense that a man's failure to secure parental rights was because he did not know he had fathered a child. These states, including New York and Texas, presume, however unrealistically, that a man is on notice that he may have fathered a child when he engages in sex with the mother.[22]

It is surely reasonable to conclude that an unwed father's rights to his child should be protected when he was unaware that he had become a father. Basic fairness might suggest that men who want to become a parent be given a meaningful opportunity to prove their intentions before losing their child permanently. In a world in which adults increasingly procreate outside of marriage, men might reasonably claim a right similar to an unwed mother's to be involved in their child's life at least until they demonstrate that they do not deserve the right. Unwed fathers who cannot be faulted for their failure to develop a relationship with their children should not be penalized.

But it is hardly unreasonable to apply a different rule. Although a different rule would surely place unwed men at a disadvantage relative to unwed women, current law already privileges women over men with respect to particular procreational rights. Women, for example, have the sole option to terminate a pregnancy. (This is true whether or not they are married.) Despite an equally powerful claim by men that their rights to procreate are violated when a pregnancy for which they are responsible is terminated over their objection, American law denies them any say in such a decision.

Women possess the obverse right as well. Under current constitutional law, men have no rights to prevent the birth of the potential offspring they contributed to producing. Women are free to decide to carry the fetus to term and give birth. On this matter, as well, women have no obligation to inform the father of their pregnancy or to consult with him about what course of action they might follow. Women have all the say; men have none.

To be sure, the choice between an abortion and an adoption is quite different. It is not only that the abortion decision exclusively affects the woman's body. Beyond this, the abortion decision involves only two choices: interrupt the pregnancy or not. Adoptions have at least three. The mother may keep her child herself. Alternatively she may seek to have the child raised by someone other than a biological parent or give the birth father the first option to keep the child.

There may be more convincing reasons to allow pregnant women alone to decide whether to terminate their pregnancy than to decide who should raise their children. Nonetheless, for a variety of reasons, many prefer to give mothers very broad choices concerning adoption. For one thing, it is quite likely that some women decide to carry their pregnancies to term based on their plan to place the child for adoption. Those women may not want the birth father involved in deciding the child's future, and might feel pressured to have an abortion as the only acceptable alternative.

The law surrounding the adoption of children born out of wedlock is a mixed set of rules by which men can far more easily forfeit their rights than their responsibilities. Moreover, these laws are about more than just giving mothers the primary decision. They also reflect policy preferences advancing the state's interests of sanctioning homes with two married parents and of meeting the demand for adoptive children.

Was the Iowa Supreme Court Right?

What, then, precisely does the Constitution require when the person responsible for the father's failure to secure his parental rights is the mother? We should be vigilant to ensure that state officials are not complicit in any arrangements by which unwed fathers are prevented from securing parental rights. But there is a huge difference between actions taken by state officials and by private individuals.

When the police search an individual's home without probable cause or a search warrant, the Constitution has been violated. But when a private citizen does the same thing, there has been no violation of the Constitution. The private citizen may have violated a duty to the individual by searching his or her home and the aggrieved person may be permitted to sue the wrongdoer for invasion of privacy. But, even though the Constitution specifically recognizes a right to privacy, the private citizen's action in no way violated the Constitution because no state action was involved.

In a similar way, when Dan was denied his opportunity to become involved in Jessica's life because of Cara's conduct, it is difficult to defend the proposition that the Constitution forbids the conduct or must provide a remedy for it. Courts should continue to use traditional justice principles when deciding these cases. If the adoptive parents contributed to any fraud or wrongdoing, it would be wrong to reward them for their misconduct. There was nothing Iowa officials did to interfere with Dan's opportunity to gain legally recognized parental rights, however. Using a closely related constitutional right as an example makes this point even clearer. As we saw in the last chapter, Americans have the constitutional right to procreate. They also have the right to marry (at least someone of the opposite sex). Nonetheless, no one would imaginably suggest that a man's constitutional right to procreate is violated when a woman refuses to have sex with him. Nor would anyone claim that his right to marry is denied when his marriage proposal is turned down. His constitutional rights only protect him against actions by state officials that interfere with his freedom to procreate or marry.

For this reason, there is probably no federal constitutional requirement that unwed fathers be given more than a theoretical opportunity to form a relationship with their children before the children may be adopted over their objection. So long as a court is satisfied that *state officials* did not interfere with the father's rights (and that the adoptive parents did not conspire with the birth mother to deny the birth father of his rights), courts may conclude that men who failed to establish a relationship with their children or to provide for their support during the pregnancy or at birth simply never acquired legally recognized status as parents in the first place.

Undeniably, these analogies are imperfect. In the case of a man being turned down when seeking to have sex with a woman or to marry her, it is not just that the state did not interfere with his constitutional rights; no one did. It is perfectly lawful for women to choose with whom to have sex or to marry. The same may not be true in the case of Cara's conduct in Jessica's case. When Cara falsely told Dan that Scott got her pregnant and when she falsely named Scott the birth father of her daughter in court papers, she did interfere with Dan's opportunity to secure legally recognized parental rights. But when a private person interferes with someone's rights, we ordinarily provide the injured person the remedy of suing for damages. Is it unreasonable to have a rule that limits Dan's remedies to an action against Cara for damages?

Limiting Dan's remedy to a damages action against Cara for her wrongful conduct may provide an important incentive for birth mothers to comply carefully with state law when placing their children for adoption. We may expect that women will take into account the duty they owe to the unwed father. Women who would otherwise be inclined to act wrongfully in connection with the birth father may be deterred from doing so in the same way people are deterred from damaging another's property because they may be held liable for their misconduct.

Indeed, such a remedy arguably provides a greater deterrence than the current Iowa rule. The rule in Jessica's case may be said to be flawed because it does not do enough to pressure birth mothers into being truthful when they place their children for adoption. Although their wrongful conduct may risk undoing the adoption, the birth mother will not directly pay for her misconduct.

On the other hand, some of these claimed benefits may prove illusory. An exclusive damages remedy may be said to give unwed mothers too much power to decide the fate of their children. Juries may be unsympathetic to unwed fathers who seek damages for the loss of their child. The birth mother may prevail in the damages action because a jury might find her failure to disclose the birth father's identity to have been reasonable.[23] Fathers may be reluctant to pursue such claims. And unwed mothers without any significant financial resources may be unafraid of having to defend such a lawsuit. If the damages remedy does not prove a useful deterrent, it may be unfair to men like Dan.

Whatever we may agree the ideal rule ought to be, it remains the case that the Iowa Supreme Court is the final arbiter of the Iowa Constitution. For better or worse, that court held in December 1992 that Dan Schmidt's constitutional rights to his daughter had been violated and that, because he had neither abandoned her nor was an unfit parent, he had the right to Jessica's custody. That should have been the end of the matter (and the end of this chapter). But it was not. The story of what happened next in Jessica's case is best told by shifting our focus to the lawyers and scholars in the legal profession who were monitoring the case and were keenly interested in its resolution.

The Importance of Jessica's Case within the Legal Profession

While Jessica's case was being litigated, various groups within the legal community kept close tabs on its progress. For a variety of reasons, the case was extremely important to them and their respective interests. Understanding the interests of these groups is essential to the larger story of this book. On the one hand were advocates keen on protecting parental rights. From what we have discussed thus far, it may seem improbable that parental rights are in need of much protection. Because parental rights are grounded in fundamental constitutional principles, it would appear unlikely there would be lawyers and scholars worried that their rights might be endangered.

The group of parents whose rights to their children are perhaps in greatest jeopardy are parents whose children are in foster care as a result of cases brought against them based on allegations of their unfitness. As of 2002, there were nearly 600,000 children in foster care, the highest in our history. As many as 40,000 children each year are the subject of court proceedings brought to permanently sever the parent-child relationship.[24]

Advocates for parents with children in foster care paid careful attention to Jessica's case. Some feared that calls to ease the way to terminate Dan's rights based on Jessica's best interests might have encouraged similar calls that would make it easier to terminate the parental rights of foster children. Ordinarily, a parent's legal relationship with a child may be extinguished over the parent's objection only if the parent seriously abused, neglected, or "abandoned" the child. Because an unwed father prevented from ever having had a relationship with his child could not plausibly be charged with abuse or neglect, courts might have an incentive to liberally construe "abandonment."

The traditional definition of abandonment, however, would preclude such a finding. Ordinarily, abandonment means conduct "which evinces a settled purpose to forgo all parental duties and relinquish all parental claims to the child."[25] Advocates for parents worried that Jessica's case would redefine abandonment in a manner that would hurt parents in other contexts.

Others in the legal community approached Jessica's case from a different direction. These lawyers and scholars are well-known children's rights advocates (although, as we shall see, the label may not have very much substantive content). Cases like Jessica's are, for them, quintessential examples of the way in which children are subordinated and harmed by exclusively adult-centered legal rules.

To these advocates, Jessica's case should have been resolved by allowing Jessica to remain with the DeBoers, and forcibly removing Jessica from the DeBoers' custody was a callous example of state power that harms the interests and rights of children.

Thus, many lawyers in the national legal community were crushed when the Iowa Supreme Court ruled as it did in Jessica's case. As luck would have it, one of the important groups of children's rights advocates, and one of the most important training grounds for children's rights lawyers, is based in Ann Arbor, Michigan, the DeBoers' hometown. Home of one of the nation's premier law schools, the University of Michigan also runs perhaps the best-known children's rights legal clinic in the country. Founded in 1978, the Child Advocacy Clinic trains law students to become children's lawyers by handling real cases in court under faculty supervision. In 1992, Suellyn Scarnecchia was teaching in the clinic. When the Iowa Supreme Court announced its ruling against the DeBoers, Scarnecchia contacted the family. Scarnecchia believed that the DeBoers had another chance.

Scarnecchia's theory had nothing to do with whether Dan should have been considered a parent with protectable rights. Even if the Iowa court was correct in ruling that Dan had such rights, Scarnecchia wanted to argue that the case was wrongly decided because both the process by which it was litigated and the result reached violated Jessica's rights.

The DeBoers were thrilled to learn that there was strong support in the legal community for their position and that they might have another chance in court. Thus it was that, instead of appearing in an Iowa court on December 3, 1992 for the purpose of returning Jessica to her birth father as they had been directed to do by the Iowa Supreme Court, the DeBoers filed a new proceeding in a Michigan court arguing that the Iowa judgment did not have to be obeyed.

The Michigan Proceedings

Needless to say, an argument that a state court need not recognize a final judgment of a different state's court poses substantial problems in a federal system with fifty sovereign states. If states were free to disregard final judgments of other states, litigants would be able to keep moving about the country, filing an action every time they lost the previous one in the hope that eventually the other side would run out of money or the new state court would see the correctness of their claim. For this reason, one of the most important procedural clauses in the Constitution, the "Full Faith and Credit Clause," obliges states, with limited exceptions, to respect and enforce another state's final judgments.[26]

Among the complicated rules of "full faith and credit" is that states are permitted to hear applications to modify another state's judgment when the other state would be allowed to modify it. In all states, child custody rulings are always modifiable based on a claim of "changed circumstances"—something that happened between the time the court decided the original matter and the modification application was filed that would make it likely the court would not have made the original decision.[27] As a result, for many years parents who lost a custody dispute in one state would move to a different state and file a new case, seeking modification of the original judgment.

This created complications between states because the two states needed to agree on which court should hear the matter. Because of this, the Uniform Child Custody Jurisdiction Act was drafted in the 1960s.[28] The explicit purpose of this law was to clarify the circumstances under which these second chances would be permitted. The law neither encouraged relitigation nor created substantive bases for second actions to be filed. Even though every state signed onto the law, conflicts between states occasionally flared and uncertainties remained over when a second state court may or should modify another state court's child custody order. Because losing parents were taking advantage of these uncertainties by taking children and fleeing to a new state to try to win a court order awarding them custody, Congress enacted the Parental Kidnapping Prevention Act in 1980.[29]

The technical claim made by the DeBoers in the Michigan action was that Michigan did not have to follow the Iowa judgment because the Iowa ruling was not based on Jessica's best interests. The DeBoers (and the Michigan Child Advocacy Clinic) sought to glean from the Parental Kidnapping Prevention Act a new *substantive* rule: that all cases involving a child's custody (including efforts to prevent an adoption) must be decided on the basis of the child's best interests.

Although the trial court ruled that it had jurisdiction to hear the case, both the intermediate appeals court and the Michigan Supreme Court disagreed and dismissed the action. The Michigan Supreme Court found it ironic that the DeBoers used the federal law as a basis for justifying relitigation of Jessica's case when Congress specifically intended by its passage to avoid such relitigation efforts.[30]

The Michigan Supreme Court ruled that Michigan did not have jurisdiction to hear the case because neither the Uniform Child Custody Jurisdiction Act nor the Parental Kidnapping Prevention Act allows the Michigan courts to take jurisdiction over the custody dispute. Indeed, the court held that both of those laws require the enforcement of the orders of the Iowa courts directing that the Schmidts have custody of the child. The Michigan Supreme Court also held that the DeBoers lacked standing to bring this custody action. Accordingly, the Court ruled that the action filed in Michigan should have been dismissed at the outset without any hearing because Michigan lacked jurisdiction in the first place.

The conclusion that Congress did not intend to change the substantive basis upon which custody cases are to be decided seems overwhelmingly correct. For one thing, Congress explicitly announced that its intention was only to create procedural rules pursuant to which relitigation would be allowable. For a second, the Supreme Court had previously held that the Kidnapping Prevention Act was enacted only to clarify procedure.[31] Finally, the entire field of child custody and private adoption has always been regarded by both Congress and the Supreme Court as each individual state's concern, with virtually no federal interest at stake. Any congressional law deigning to compel states to decide child custody disputes according to a particular substantive standard would violate a legal tradition reaching back over two hundred years.

After the appellate court ruled that Michigan lacked jurisdiction to hear the DeBoers' case, a second action was brought in the Michigan courts. This new action was brought in Jessica's name by a "next friend" (the Michigan lawyer assigned as Jessica's guardian ad litem in the just-dismissed proceeding brought by the DeBoers). This new action claimed that Jessica's constitutionally protected interest in family life was violated by the Iowa result. This claim is, of course, the precise opposite of the constitutional claim made by Dan Schmidt that prevailed in the Iowa court: that *his* constitutional rights to his daughter would be violated *unless* he secured custody of her. Now, in Michigan, lawyers purporting to represent Jessica claimed *her* constitutional rights compelled the opposite result. The two claims obviously could not stand together.

Jessica's lawyer asserted that Jessica's constitutional rights were violated by the Iowa courts in two ways. First, she claimed, Jessica had a due process liberty interest in her relationship with the DeBoers. In Jessica's case, this meant that a constitutionally protected parent-child relationship ought to be based on daily contact and not on biological relationships. Her second constitutional claim was that Jessica was denied equal protection of the laws because some children, but not her, have a right to remain with their long-term caregivers.

These two arguments are good examples of a lawyer's capacity to restate a claim in different language. The equal protection claim, it should be plain, stands or falls on whether the first claim prevails. If the first claim prevails—that Jessica has a constitutionally protected right to remain with the DeBoers so long as they are fit and it is in her best interests to stay there—it follows that Jessica has a right to be treated like other children with those rights. But if she does not have those rights, then equally surely, it does not offend the equal protection guarantee to decide her case on a different basis from other custody matters.[32]

The Michigan Supreme Court had little difficulty rejecting both claims. It reasoned that children do not have rights to their custodians that are independent of their custodians' rights to them. Indeed, it would be impossible if it were otherwise. In the court's words, Jessica's claim must fail because her interest in being protected against arbitrary state interference with her familial relationships is "not independent of [her] parents' in the absence of a showing that the parents are unfit." Michigan statutory law explicitly grants to parents the "custody, control, services and earnings of the minor." And Michigan courts have consistently required that "a parent's right to custody is not to be disturbed absent such a showing, sometimes despite the preferences of the child."[33]

Although the Michigan proceedings were not exactly frivolous (a New Jersey court took a position that was helpful to their claim in Michigan),[34] many experts predicted the outcome in advance. Seven months after the Michigan case was begun, the Supreme Court of Michigan, in a strongly worded decision, ruled 6 to 1 that Michigan was legally obligated to honor Iowa's judgment.

Before the case was really over, an appeal was taken to the U.S. Supreme Court from the Michigan Supreme Court judgment. A total of sixteen different parties with more than twenty lawyers participated in the appeal to the Michigan Supreme Court. When all was said and done, a total of twenty judges (including one justice on the Supreme Court of the United States) heard the case over a total of twenty-eight months. Finally, on July 31, 1993, Jessica was sent to live with Dan in accordance with the Iowa decision.

But What about Jessica's Best Interests?

When the Supreme Court finally rejected Jessica's and the DeBoers' final appeal, newspapers and writers throughout the country condemned the decision as a travesty of justice. Elizabeth Bartholet's complaint is representative: the "highest courts of two states found Jessica's interests irrelevant, and allowed blood rights to trump social bonds, and the Supreme Court of the United States refused to intervene."[35] What we have discussed so far suggests there are reasons to conclude that the Iowa court was wrong to rule that Dan's rights had been violated when Jessica was placed for adoption by the DeBoers. But the important point of this chapter has little to do with the correct result. Instead, our focus should be on the means by which we reach consensus on what the correct result should be. At the beginning of the chapter, we considered a number of questions about Jessica's rights. But for the vast portion of the chapter, despite engaging in a complicated discussion of the law and policy of unwed fathers' rights when their children are placed for adoption, not a single word was spent discussing Jessica or her rights.

And this is for a significant reason. The discussion about unwed fathers' rights was conducted with a focus on the principles and general applicability of law and practice: Should unwed fathers have any say into whether their children are placed for adoption? Should unmarried mothers be entitled to place their children for adoption without consulting the birth father?

We are, of course, obliged to attempt to answer these questions as best as we can. But, however odd this may sound, almost nothing is added when we try to factor in which rule is best for children. At some point reasonably early into the analysis, the inquiry becomes hopelessly circular.

One can say, with as much fervor and sincerity as possible, that the best interests of children are served by giving mothers complete control over the placement decisions of nonmarital children. But, in the end, the argument does nothing to buttress the claim except add emotional appeal. There will certainly be those with opposing views who will claim that children's best interests are served by being raised by fit birth parents whenever one of them wishes to take on the responsibility. Those inclined to believe this will stress that adoption involves risk to the child's loss of self-esteem resulting from an unavoidable sense of rejection (and the concomitant sense of worthlessness). For those with this point of view, adoption may be the lesser of various evils a rejected child may experience, but it ought never be preferred over the custody of a birth parent eager and willing to raise the child.

None of this is to say that the Iowa courts got it right in the first place when they ruled that Dan had constitutionally protected parental rights that he did not forfeit. The *only* notion being challenged is that the final result in Jessica's case was wrong because it failed to consider her best interests or because it failed to comport with them. It is this claim that most disturbed the American media and public. But the Michigan courts were surely right in rejecting it. My goal is to persuade you that this is so.

In the last chapter, we explored the source and purpose of the parental rights doctrine. Those who preferred that Jessica's case had been decided based on her best interests were making a direct challenge to the adult-centered perspective on which parental rights claims are based. To them, such claims should have been based on Jessica's life experience, not Dan's. Based on the world Jessica experienced, they argue, it is silly to suggest that Dan or Cara were her parents. She *knew* who her mommy and daddy were and the law should have recognized, and given protection to, the parent-child relationship that Jessica actually formed. To do otherwise, it is suggested, is to hold children hostage to the "rights" of adults at the expense of the emotional well-being of children. But this reasoning is extremely problematic.

There really are two separate best interests claims that the "child-centered" advocates make. The first is that law should define who is a parent with legally protected rights with reference to the child's life experience, not the adult's. The second is that, wholly apart from any conclusion about an adult's parental right, a child has an independent right not to have his or her life disrupted simply to make whole an adult's rights. If there must be a conflict between the rights of an adult and those of a child, the child's rights should prevail. These claims seem to blend together, but they really are separate. The first claim challenges the means by which parental rights are defined. The second addresses remedies that courts may or must impose after someone's rights have been identified.

Let's consider these claims in reverse order, beginning with the child-centered claim that Jessica's custody should not have been changed because, by the time the court finally decided the case, Jessica's best interests were plainly served by remaining with the DeBoers. There are a number of questions that need to be addressed as we begin to analyze this claim. The first concerns the time period we are talking about. Is there any point at which we would permit the clock to stop running, as we might, for example, when negotiating a labor contract or passing a state budget?

This is best explored by examining the time line in Jessica's case. The DeBoers first filed their adoption papers on February 25, 1991. Nine days later, on March 6, Cara filed papers in court seeking to undo the adoption on the ground the adoption violated Iowa law. Once this happened, the validity of the DeBoers' custody of Jessica was officially put on notice. Dan filed paternity papers in Iowa on March 12 and his legal papers challenging the adoption were filed on March 27. Should the clock have been stopped on one of those occasions? There are powerful justifications for doing so. For many, allowing the time it takes to litigate the contest ought not count in deciding the outcome.

But those arguing that it is Jessica and her experience which matters most would say that it is wrong to stop the clock at any of these points. Fair or not, they would say that Jessica's world continues during the litigation and she deserves not to have her life disrupted simply because the case drags on in court.

The next significant date was December 27, 1991, when the trial court in Iowa ruled that Dan was the legal parent and that the DeBoers must turn over Jessica to him. The DeBoers chose, however, to appeal to the Iowa Supreme Court. When they filed their appeal, they asked the Iowa Supreme Court to freeze the trial court order until the final appeal was heard. Wouldn't this be an obvious point to stop the clock?

Again, Jessica's supporters would argue that it is wrong even here. Another year and a half of Jessica's life would go by before the case was settled, and that time should be counted if we care about Jessica. The final order of the Iowa Supreme Court affirming the trial court order was handed down in December 1992. Now can we finally stop counting time? Again, Jessica's supporters would disagree.

It quickly becomes clear that it is pointless to continue identifying key points of the case; the child-centered advocates are always going to say the clock ought never to stop because to do otherwise would drastically undermine their basic position. If the child-centered advocates agree that there may be good reason—*any* good reason—to stop the clock for any purpose, they concede something fatal to their position: that, at least sometimes, policy or practical considerations justify deciding children's cases on factors other than what the impact will be on the children themselves.

There are, in fact, good reasons to consider stopping the clock. It is morally objectionable to give a presumptively equal claimant a disadvantage resulting from factors beyond his or her control. Delays in the legal system that cannot be blamed on the noncustodial party should not count against that party. In practical terms, the child-centered advocates are giving the custodial party an advantage. The longer it takes for a case to be decided, the greater the probability the custodial party will prevail. If a case can take nearly two-and-a-half years to litigate, as Jessica's did, we can state the point even more dramatically. The custodial party will always win.

If, as the child-centered advocates seek, Jessica's case should ultimately be decided based on her experience of who her "real" parents are, her "real" parents will be whichever party has had custody of her the longest. This is one way of resolving child custody disputes; but this position is flimsier than may be apparent.

Here is what would happen if the child-centered advocates had their way: Since everyone knows from the moment a child custody dispute is filed that the party that has the child the longest will win, the contest will immediately shift to the question of who should have temporary custody while the litigation is being waged. Cara would appear in court on Day One with an application for the immediate transfer of custody to her. And, because the court would understand that to deny her such custody would be tantamount to rejecting her claim at the end of the case, it is likely her application would be granted.

Cara's court papers plainly show that she signed the surrender of parental rights document sooner than is allowed under Iowa law. There was no reason to believe Cara was an unfit parent. Because the court would understand that to deny Cara application for temporary custody would be tantamount to rejecting her claim at the end of the case, it is virtually certain her application would have been granted. (We have, in describing Jessica's case, only focused on Dan's claims because the Iowa courts ruled on Dan's claims first. After Dan won in the Iowa courts, in March 1993 the Iowa courts ultimately reinstated Cara's parental rights.)

The same thing would happen with respect to Dan's petition. When he first filed his court papers claiming to be Jessica's father, he would apply for the immediate transfer of Jessica's custody to him. States such as Iowa that believe it is vital to protect rights of unwed fathers will grant the application.

This may seem like the perfect result. Since Dan won anyway after two and a half years of litigation, it is wonderful that we have figured out a way for Dan to have won without Jessica being harmed.

Or have we? Let's try to figure out what will happen once we implement this solution. Upon the filing of Cara's papers on March 6 (or Dan's on March 27), the court orders the immediate transfer of Jessica to her (or his) custody. The case proceeds to trial, right? Wrong! The DeBoers, knowing that they cannot win at the end of the protracted legal battle, have only two choices. They can appeal the order changing Jessica's custody pending the trial, or they can give up and go home without a fight. Since the winning party of any extended custody dispute will always be the custodial party, there will never be a protracted custody dispute.

All we accomplished was to change the party who will benefit from the child-centered rule; but, either way, we have denied one party his or her right to a day in court. Solomon's solution is beginning to look a bit more attractive.

The short of it is that the child-centered claimants make an alluring but hopeless claim. Either the fight in the case will shift from the end result to the interim one, with both sides insisting they have custody during the pendency of the dispute, or there will be no dispute at all. Other devices may end up being substituted to ensure fairness. Perhaps a neutral third-party custodian, like a foster parent, will be engaged to ensure that neither party will be advantaged during the litigation. This has real Solomonic implications. Wouldn't the "better" parent be the one who would oppose such a result?

In our system of law, it is important that we create the means by which rights can be vindicated. If a parent has the right to the care and custody of her child, our task is to develop a scheme by which those rights will be upheld. That means we must find a way to ensure that Dan has the chance of winning his claim to Jessica. (Or, for those who really want Dan to lose, we must find a way to ensure that the DeBoers have a chance of prevailing even though the court granted Dan temporary custody during the pendency of the litigation.)

It is important to recall, in this regard, that the DeBoers sought and obtained an order delaying the transfer of Jessica's custody after the trial court ruled in Dan's favor until the appeal was final. Does anybody imagine courts would grant such an application if the law required that the case be decided not on the basis of parental rights, but, instead, on the basis of Jessica's best interests?

Both parties would devote their entire efforts in these cases to securing "temporary" custody as quickly as possible and holding on for dear life. Even worse, the custodial party's litigation tactics would be crystal clear: Figure out a way to stretch the lawsuit long enough, any way will do, and it will be impossible to lose. This is why the law wisely refuses to permit the children's advocates their preferred result; these advocates simply have not thought through the implications for a system of law based exclusively on child-centered thinking.

Instead, all that we owe children is a commitment to reach the correct result within the meaning of the law; and to do so in as short a time as possible. But the law must be based on the understanding that the time it takes to decide the case will not be factored into the final outcome. Only such a rule fairly protects both sides of the dispute.

There is little question that our legal system is insufficiently child-centered when disputes like Jessica's reach them. Undoubtedly the most disturbing quality of the result in her case was the terrible pain inflicted on the DeBoers and Jessica when the court ordered the transfer of her custody. But it is important to appreciate how the legal profession unnecessarily contributed to that pain.

When Dan filed his petition seeking Jessica's custody, she had been with the DeBoers for only several weeks. The legal and factual claims Dan raised by his petition were remarkably uncomplicated. First, he needed to prove he was the birth father. A blood test can resolve that issue conclusively within a matter of days. The remaining questions are few and simple. Did Dan intentionally relinquish his parental rights? Is he fit? A truly child-centered legal system would insist that this case be heard and completed within a matter of weeks, if not days. Solomon's genius may have been in figuring out how to decide custody disputes promptly.

It is plain that the legal system has the capacity to resolve highly contested weighty matters of importance to adults in an accelerated fashion. Consider the way disputes over election issues are handled. These disputes commonly involve challenges to candidates' names appearing on the ballot, often because of a claimed irregularity in arcane election law procedures. They are hotly contested matters, involving complicated issues of fact. Nonetheless, courts routinely handle these claims in a highly efficient manner within weeks if not days in plenty of time for the election to take place on time, even leaving time to appeal to the state's highest court for final review before the election occurs.

What is unacceptable about Jessica's case is not the outcome; it is the adult-oriented framework of time that allowed a petition filed in March to come on for hearing in November and to be decided at the trial level in December. Then the first round of appeals took another entire year. March 1991 became December 1992 before the case was over in the Iowa courts. Two rounds of elections would have been held in the same time with two fully contested election trials and appeals having been completed in a fraction of the time. What can work for candidates for elected office can work for children, if we have the will. But if we do not, we should simply live with the consequences.

Children's rights advocates are correct in their goal of changing the *process* by which cases affecting children are resolved to take children's special needs into account. But it is incorrect to change the *results* when those results are reached to protect established rights.

The DeBoers should not be blamed for contesting Dan's petition when he first filed. It was not their fault that the case did not go to trial until eight months later. Nor should they be blamed for appealing to the Iowa Supreme Court (or for delaying the transfer of Jessica's custody by seeking and obtaining an order delaying the transfer).

The fault for both of those delays is the fault of the legal system and of a society that claims to be child-centered and to worry about how children are needlessly harmed by the fights adults have among themselves, but which does not take even the smallest steps to protect children from such harm. The cost of protracted proceedings is almost always greater than the benefit. This is particularly true given the relative simplicity of the issues.

We need to recognize that all of those who insisted that Jessica's case should be decided based on her best interests (as opposed to Iowa law) really wanted Jessica to remain with the DeBoers. There is always a great danger that the calls for children's best interests are stalking horses for the real arguments. When the law is on the side of adults, some people argue the law. When it isn't, those same people argue the child's best interests. This is a phenomenon akin to the well-worn adage that when the facts are against you, argue the law, and when the law is against you, argue the facts.

As a consequence, it becomes impossible to separate those making the best interests claim who are only concerned about Jessica from those using the claim as a subterfuge to help the DeBoers.

Moreover, the claim has a ratchet-like quality; it only works to keep the child with the custodial party. Thus, it ought to be unsurprising that the custodial party finds it an attractive claim and will use it as a tactic whenever it suits them.

Elián González's case well illustrates the phenomenon. After Elián's mother died in her failed attempt to enter the United States with her son, Elián's father demanded that Elián be returned to him in Cuba. There was no conceivable basis under either United States or international law to deny the father's request. But that did not stop his Miami relatives from arguing that the case should be decided on Elián's best interests. That claim was not really what they meant. They meant that Elián should stay in the United States and, because the law prohibited such a result, a different argument would have to be created other than the naked one that the law should not be enforced. Unfortunately, in so many custody disputes, it becomes impossible to tell when the best interests claim is simply a device to achieve a result prohibited by law. But, in many cases, that is really all the claim is about.

The second part of the child-centered claim in Jessica's case is a substantive one: the case was wrongly decided because it was based on something other than her best interests. This claim, like the process-focused one we just examined, also must be rejected.

The child-centered advocates asserted that the only appropriate question before the Iowa court should have been Jessica's best interests and that by focusing on Dan's rights the courts were violating Jessica's rights. But the question before the Iowa court when Dan filed his petition seeking Jessica's custody was this: Who has the right under Iowa law to raise her? As I demonstrated in Chapter 2, there are few questions of greater importance to a society committed to personal freedom. A person's right to raise his or her child deserves the greatest respect in any society committed to the rule of law.

It is vital here to separate the subject of how that question ought to be answered from what is the proper question before the court. This chapter already has, somewhat exhaustively, elaborated upon the subject of an unwed father's rights. As we have seen, there are compelling claims for and against recognizing parental rights for men in Dan's situation.

For our immediate purposes, it is irrelevant what the right answer is or ought to be. Instead, we are concerned with exploring the right question. Perhaps it *is* sound to conclude that Dan does not have any right to Jessica. But in exploring the question of whether Dan has any rights to Jessica, we cannot permit that question to be replaced by the one that the children's rights advocates in Michigan insisted it become: what is in Jessica's best interests? When this is allowed to occur, our system of law and rights is displaced.

The lesson of the hypothetical child-snatching case with which I began this chapter was that a society governed by the rule of law will sensibly insist that when a child has wrongfully been removed from a parent's custody (or when a parent was wronged by never having the opportunity to have custody of her child), the child should be given to the parent without inquiring into the child's best interests. This principle should also apply to Jessica's case.

We reached that result not merely because we were opposed to permitting a wrongdoer to benefit from her misconduct. The DeBoers were not wrongdoers in any sense when they took custody of Jessica. But we concluded in the child-snatching case that the parents should be given custody of their child because they have the right to her custody and law exists to enforce rights. We recognized that the child may suffer some short-term harm. We were even uncertain that her long-term interests would be advanced by placing her with her birth parents. But we insisted that the rule of law prevail and that parents be vindicated in their right to their child's custody when they blamelessly lost custody.

Finally, when we unhinge the issue of the extraordinary time it took to resolve Jessica's case from what the correct rule should be if the case had been resolved within a matter of weeks, even the concept of Jessica's best interests is hopelessly without content. Is it in her best interests to be raised by a loving, fit birth father who, had he known, would have been with her when she was born and would have never intentionally let her out of his custody? Or is it in her best interests to be raised by good, loving people who have demonstrated their commitment to giving Jessica the best upbringing they can provide?

Some child-centered advocates seek to remake the law so that rules are applied to children based on what the children themselves would have wanted if they were in a position as an adult to go back and help make the decision.[36] But even this attempt to reframe the question ultimately proves unhelpful. We will never be able to say with certainty how Jessica would have reacted as a teenager when she learned that her parents prevented her from being raised by her birth father. Nor can we know what she will say about this when she is an adult. Perhaps she would have preferred avoiding the pain and disruption that occurred by being sent to live with Dan. Or perhaps she would rather have gone through a difficult adjustment period in order to reap the benefits of establishing a relationship with and being raised by her birth father.

Jessica will never be able to know these things after she has grown up. When life takes us down a particular fork, we can never say with certainty that the road not taken would have worked out better. After Jessica is raised by her birth father, she may fantasize that the couple who got away would have served her better. Of course, the converse is also true. But no one will ever know.

Don't Children's Interests Matter At All?

There is, of course, an important difference when children's interests are used to develop public policy (and law) and when they are invoked to apply well-settled law. It is perfectly appropriate to reconsider the rule that fit parents who have not abandoned their children ought to have the right to their care and custody. In reconsidering this rule (and in creating such rules in the first place), there certainly is room to take into account what is best for children. The impact on children should be considered among other factors, however; it should not, by itself, be dispositive.

Most important, however, once we have established such a rule, the worst time to reconsider it is when we are about to apply it in a case involving a young child. There are two dangers. First, there is the risk that the child's perspective becomes all that we notice. The interests of children plainly are important and they deserve to be a prominent part of public discourse about the rules of society. But we make a serious mistake if we allow our concern for children to become so overwhelming that we lose sight of other, important values our society holds dear.

The second, closely related danger is that we will decide complicated public policy based on our emotions at the moment when we are least able to see the larger picture. This works well for newspaper columns. But it does not contribute to sound public policy. Such policy is best shaped when we create rules by considering what is best for all of the Jessicas (and all of the rest of the members of society) and then confidently apply those rules to particular Jessicas, rather than the other way around.

The child-centered advocates in Jessica's case would have us decide what the rights of unwed fathers should be when we are applying them in a gut-wrenching context. As emotional and humane people, we are most likely to want to change the rule to prevent a child from being harmed by its application. But if the rule protecting the rights of unwed fathers was developed with careful thought, and if the impact on children was already taken into account in its development, we serve children and society immeasurably better by eschewing reconsideration of the rule every time it is being enforced. Once we have concluded that sound public policy calls for faultless unwed fathers to have an opportunity to raise their children if they promptly step forward after their children are put up for adoption, it is deeply corrosive of the rule of law and the sound policy that stands behind it when we permit the argument that it is unfair to the child to apply the law in a particular case.

In light of all of this, we may now see that none of the claims made in Jessica's name in the Michigan courts requires further substantial discussion. Although many children's rights advocates commonly advance the claim that there are three sides to disputes like the one involving Jessica, there really are only two. Two sets of adults are fighting over Jessica's custody. Jessica's views on the outcome are irrelevant (putting aside the question how one could go about determining the views of a seventeen-day-old infant).

For this reason, there was no value served by assigning Jessica independent legal representation in the Michigan proceedings; nothing a court-appointed lawyer for her might say should matter. Nor is there anything the attorney could say that would not otherwise be said by one of the parties. It will always be in one party's interest to make child-centered claims in cases like Jessica's. Nothing is gained by pretending that those claims are being made *by* Jessica when they are being made by an adult assigned to speak for her.

The imagined virtue of adding Jessica's "voice" to the proceeding is lost completely when we realize that the position her lawyer takes is chosen by the lawyer. Jessica's lawyer might reasonably take the position that her rights (and best interests) are served by remaining with the DeBoers. But her lawyer just as reasonably might argue that she should be raised by her fit biological father who wants and loves her and never abandoned her. The problem is compounded when we begin to believe there is something special about the views her randomly assigned lawyer chose to take. Amazingly enough, courts sometimes believe the position really is the child's, when it is nothing more than the lawyer's.

The pertinent questions in Jessica's case were whether Dan had legally recognized parental rights and, if so, whether he was fit or had abandoned Jessica. The Iowa courts carefully addressed all of those issues. There were no additional issues to resolve. To some, however, the question is different when we are talking about separating children from an already formed parent-child relationship. In Jessica's case, she had never lived with Dan. Because of this difference, the child-centered advocates suggest, Dan ought not be considered her father. But that question—whether Dan should be regarded as her father with rights—is different from whether, once he is so considered, courts should enforce his legally recognized rights. To the child-centered advocates, this harsh rule—that fit parents have the right to the care and custody of their children—is bad for children. But only this rule meaningfully protects parental rights.

Justice John Paul Stevens's explanation for upholding the order transferring Jessica to Dan is surely correct:

> Applicants' claim that Jessica's best interests will be served by allowing them to retain custody of her rests, in part, on the relationship that they have been able to develop with the child after it became clear that they were not entitled to adopt her. Neither Iowa law, nor Michigan law, nor federal law authorizes unrelated persons to retain custody of a child whose natural parents have not been found to be unfit simply because they may be better able to provide for her future and her education. As the Iowa Supreme Court stated: "[C]ourts are not free to take children from parents simply by deciding another home offers more advantages."[37]

All members of society, including children, deserve a system of laws that promises to enforce legally protectable rights. In the long run, there is no better legacy to keep for the next generation.

4

Who Gets to Be the Parent? The Right to Relationships with Someone Else's Children

Penny was the mother of two daughters, aged one and three, when she met and fell in love with Walter. The couple married after a four-month relationship and the two adults and the children lived together for the next five years. During this five-year period, Walter and the children developed an extremely close relationship. Walter was a loving father who attended to the children's many needs. He nursed them when they were sick; he made them feel better when they were hurt; he attended programs in which they participated in school; he read to them at night; he loved them dearly. He also was the principal provider for the family's finances. Penny held a part-time job and was the primary caretaker in the family.

When the children were six and eight years old, Penny discovered that Walter had been cheating on her for about two years. Penny caught Walter in bed with a woman who worked with him at his office. Walter admitted to Penny that he had been having an affair for about a year and a half. Penny was furious with Walter and ordered him out of the house. Within a few weeks, Penny hired a lawyer to commence divorce proceedings. Walter initially thought, to help calm things down a bit, that he should stay away from the home and not try to see Penny or the kids. After about six weeks, during one of the several telephone conversations Walter and Penny had engaged in since the separation, Walter brought up the subject of visiting the children. By this time, Penny had been to see her divorce lawyer; she had discovered that Walter had no rights in New York to visit the children. Penny made it clear to Walter that she would prohibit him from visiting with the kids or having anything to do with her or the children ever again.

Walter had no choice but to consult a lawyer to begin a visitation proceeding. At the first meeting, Walter was stunned to learn that he had no rights to see the children under New York law. Walter could not imagine how or why this could be true. His lawyer could only tell him that New York law considered him to be a legal stranger to the children. Because the children are not his biologically, and because Walter never adopted them, Walter's lawyer explained to him that Penny, as the biological mother of the children, had the exclusive say regarding access to her children. Unless Walter could persuade Penny to allow him to visit with the children, there is no possibility he may do so.[1]

In 1993, Janis and Christine committed themselves to be partners for life in a formal commitment ceremony conducted by an ordained minister and attended by about fifty friends and relatives. Because they lived in New York, the couple could not legally marry. After they moved in together, the women decided to raise children and agreed that Christine, who was younger, would be artificially inseminated and stay home with the children, while Janis would support the family. Before the children were born, Christine executed a will and other documents that appointed Janis as the "co-parent" and "adoptive parent" of the children in the event of her incapacity or death. In 1996, Christine gave birth to a boy, and in 1998, she gave birth to a girl. Christine and Janis jointly chose the children's names, godparents, pediatrician, and school. They lived in the same household and shared holidays, birthdays, and vacations together. While the family was together, the children regarded both Janis and Christine to be their parents, as did everyone around them. In 1999, however, the couple had a falling out and separated. Initially, after the separation, Christine permitted Janis to visit with the children. After a short while, Christine decided not to permit any further visitation between Janis and the children.

Janis decided to bring a proceeding in court that would allow her to continue her relationship with the children over Christine's objection. But because Janis was not the spouse of Christine and had not adopted the children, the law regarded Janis as a legal stranger to the children. She, like Walter, was denied any relief from the courts.[2]

Stewart and Ann have been married for three years. They are the parents of one child, a daughter, Tess, who is almost two years old. For two and a half years, Stewart and Ann lived in a house located on the farm property of Stewart's father, Wilber. When Tess was almost one-and-a-half years old, the family moved off of Wilber's property and rented an apartment in town. They left Wilber's land after Wilber complained once too often that

Stewart was not was putting in enough hours on the farm. Stewart and Ann have had little to do with Wilber after they moved out. They wanted to get away from a man they considered to be overbearing and abusive. For his part, Wilber thought rather poorly of his son who, he believed, drank too much and did not work hard enough.

While they lived on Wilber's land, Stewart and Ann let Tess see her grandfather. Their relationship was not a particularly close one; but, for the most part, they saw each other most of the days the family lived on the property. Things changed once Stewart and Ann moved away. They stopped bringing Tess around to see Wilber. When Wilber tried to come to see them, they told him not to bother. One day, they received a threatening letter from an attorney whom Wilber had retained asking for visitation rights for Wilber and warning that he would sue them in court if they refused.

Shocked by the receipt of such a letter, Stewart and Ann went to see a lawyer of their own who told them that, indeed, Wilber had a right to sue them to obtain court-ordered visitation with Tess. Stewart and Ann prepared for a court battle. After a brief hearing, the court, finding that visitation between Wilber and Ann would serve her best interests, awarded Wilber the right to visit with Tess from 4 P.M. to 6 P.M. each Wednesday and Saturday.[3]

These vignettes, based on court decisions in recent years, raise an important question: Has the traditional parental rights doctrine become outdated because the norm on which it was based—a two-parent nuclear family—no longer dominates?[4] With a divorce rate hovering at 50 percent and one in three children born out of wedlock, fully 40 percent of children in the United States live in what was once a nontraditional household. Almost 30 percent live with only one parent.[5] This, in turn, means that in many households extended family members provide necessary child-rearing assistance.[6]

But the picture is even more complicated than this. In addition to the large number of single-parent households, there is also a fast-growing number of households with children in which two adults reside. One of these adults, however, is not a legally recognized parent. In some instances, these couples have chosen not to marry; in other instances, they are prohibited from marrying because state law will not recognize the marriage between people of the same sex.

Today, as many as 600,000 to one million children are being raised by gay men or lesbian women.[7] These figures include children of heterosexual relationships that ended; the figures also include children of gay and lesbian couples or individuals who are becoming parents through assisted reproductive technologies, such as artificial insemination. Estimates run as high as in the hundreds of thousands of babies who have been born in recent years as a result of artificial insemination alone.[8]

Even when couples are married, it is common today that one of the spouses is not legally related to the children the couple is raising because the stepparent has not adopted the children. Within the next generation, some predict that as many as one in four children will live with a stepparent before they reach majority.[9] Again, the failure to adopt may be the result of a personal choice; it may also be that the child still has a legal parent who has not abandoned him or her, so that the child is ineligible to be adopted by the stepparent. All of this adds up to millions of adults who may perform parent-like functions but who are denied legally recognized parental status.

There is one additional statistical fact that is highly pertinent to the subject of this chapter. Because of significant increases in life expectancy, the population of the United States is growing older. As life expectancy creeps toward eighty years, the rate of growth of the elderly population now exceeds the growth rate of the country as a whole.[10] Most pertinent of all, for the purposes of this chapter, more than 60 million Americans are grandparents.[11]

What happens to this changing family picture when it comes into conflict with the established doctrine of parental rights? And how are children's rights invoked to shift this playing field?

As we have seen in earlier chapters, the parental rights doctrine means more than that parents have the final say on how their children should be reared. It also means that parenthood has been defined based exclusively on biology. This chapter requires us to reconsider both aspects of the parental rights doctrine through an examination of the so-called "third-party visitation" movement. This movement, less than a generation old, seeks to share the parentlike privilege of obtaining court-ordered visitation with adults who lack legally recognized parental rights; it also seeks to limit the traditional power of parents to decide who may visit with their children.

There are two basic types of third-party cases and both were included in the earlier vignettes. In one, led prominently by grandparents, persons who have not necessarily served in a parentlike relationship seek to maintain or establish a significant relationship with someone else's children. In the other, the adults seeking legal recognition have performed the role of parents but have only de facto relationships with children.

The children's rights advocates who have led the charge for expanding third-party visitation rights oppose parental rights that assign children exclusively to parents based solely on biology without taking into account the needs of children. They also object to the complete control parents have over the children's upbringing, which prohibits nonparents from seeking review of parental choices. To them, "[t]he parental rights of control and custody" "confer a strange liberty that consists in the right to control not one's self or one's goods, but another human being."[12]

As we shall see, many adults are unhappy with the disproportionate power allocated to parents to make decisions about their children. And it has been these adults who have worked hardest to take away some of the traditional power of parents. The question for us to consider is whether the movement is really for and about children.

Grandparents

In common law, parents had the exclusive authority to decide whether to permit someone other than a legally recognized parent to develop or maintain a relationship with their children. Parents' choices about these third parties were seen as merely one of countless examples of the details of a child's upbringing that is within the purview of parental authority. Although visitation and custody actions have long been the business of courts in the United States, those cases were always fights between legally recognized parents. In such a dispute, the judge sits as an arbitrator between two equal rights holders who are unable to settle their differences between themselves.

Until the mid 1960s, it was almost impossible for someone other than a legally recognized parent to sue a parent for the right to custody or visitation of the parent's child. Then the law gradually began to change. New York was among the first states to enact a third-party visitation statute. Its statute, which in hindsight may seem modest, was almost revolutionary. It authorized grandparents to seek court-ordered visitation of their grandchildren over a parent's objection when one of the parents died or when the parents divorced. Before the remarkable lobbying effort of the American Association of Retired Persons was finished, every state in the country (the District of Columbia is the only exception) enacted a statute authorizing grandparents to seek court-ordered visitation. Indeed, the idea became so attractive to many legislators that what began as a grandparent movement was rapidly expanded to other designated third parties (such as aunts, uncles, siblings, nonmarital partners, stepparents, and foster parents) and, in the most ambitious of states, to "any person."

By the early 1990s, every state had a third-party visitation statute of some kind, though they vary considerably by state.[13] Some permit only grandparents to sue for visitation, excluding other extended family members who are biologically related to children (such as siblings and aunts and uncles). Others permit certain extended family members who are biologically related, including grandparents. Some statutes sharply limit the conditions under which grandparents can sue, requiring, for example, that one of the parents has died or that there be a divorce. Others permit grandparents to sue even an "intact" family, in which both the legal mother and father live together and jointly oppose the visitation. Some require the grandparent and the child to have established a substantial relationship before visitation rights may be granted. Some allow a court to grant visitation by a grandparent whenever the court concludes that visitation is in the child's best interests. A few jurisdictions permit even nonbiologically related persons to sue for visitation, along with grandparents. But no group of nonparents has fared nearly as well as grandparents, achieving a remarkable transformation of American law through legislative amendment that dramatically limits traditional parental authority.

De facto Parents

Let us now shift our attention to the efforts of those who, after having been significant parentlike figures to children as co-parents, try to maintain a relationship with the children after the adult relationship has ended. The first two vignettes at the beginning of the chapter were taken from court decisions in New York. New York allows only a limited group of people who are not legally recognized as parents to seek court-ordered visitation. Within this group are grandparents and siblings. But co-parents and stepparents lack statutory rights to seek visitation with the children they helped raise. In the two cases on which the vignettes were based, then, the question before the New York courts is very different from the question before the same court when a grandparent seeks visitation. When the grandparent seeks visitation, the judge simply looks at the language of the statute that authorizes the lawsuit. If a grandparent meets the statutory requirements (which, in New York, requires determining the largely circular and vague question of whether "circumstances exist in which equity should intervene"), the judge will rule that it has the legitimate power to decide whether to order visitation. In deciding that particular question, the judge considers what is in the child's best interests.

When the de facto parent is before the court and there is no statute upon which to rely, the judge must ask an entirely different question: Is there jurisdiction to hear the matter? A judge has no power to order visitation of someone's child to a "nonparent" (that is, a person who lacks legally recognized parental rights). In such cases, the court declares itself unable to hear the matter and dismisses the case without reaching the best interests inquiry. Thus, in New York, neither stepparents nor nonmarital domestic partners may even seek court-ordered visitation of children with whom they formed a relationship unless they are biologically related to the children or legally related through adoption.

Both stepparents and nonmarital domestic partners would fare better in other states. About one-third of the states have legislation that is broad enough to permit petitions by stepparents who seek to maintain a relationship with a child after a significant parent-child relationship was formed.[14] Some states, such as California, Oregon, and Virginia, have enacted statutes that explicitly mention stepparents as among those who may seek court-ordered visitation; in a number of other states, courts have interpreted their third-party statute to implicitly include them. An even smaller number of states allow a nonmarital domestic partner the right to visit through statute. In a few states, however, they have such a right as a result of a groundbreaking court decision granting rights to a new category of adults. The Supreme Courts of five states issued rulings in the past ten years that recognize Janis's right to maintain contact with the children she raised (Rhode Island, Massachusetts, New Jersey, Pennsylvania, and Wisconsin).[15] A few other states would also allow Janis to seek visitation. But in the vast majority of states, she would have no such right.

What's Really Going On Here?

One might begin to wonder why grandparents should be authorized to seek visitation of their grandchildren even when they have never had a relationship with them—let alone a parentlike relationship—while other adults who have had a substantial parentlike relationship with children are prohibited from doing so. To answer this requires looking both at the legislative process and the role of the courts. The legislative focus is rather straightforward.

Explaining first why grandparents might have success is rather clear. For one thing, grandparents have enormous political influence. They are numerous and popular. Nothing could demonstrate their power better than that they achieved success in every state in the country for securing visitation rights in a mere twenty-year political effort, overcoming a two-hundred-year tradition of exclusive parental authority that is almost sacrosanct in American law.

It may be that the political clout of older Americans would have been a sufficient explanation for the passage of grandparent visitation laws, but a second phenomenon should not go unremarked. As we have already seen, the percentage of families with two parents residing with children is at an all-time low in the United States. The corollary is that families headed by single women is at an all-time high. At such a moment, we may expect that the family would be most vulnerable to outside attack. The image of the family many lawmakers envision when they seek to protect parental rights is more traditional than the reality. It is one thing to develop the lofty legal principles of the sacredness of the family as a bastion of independent power when lawmakers picture the family headed by a man; it is quite another when women are at its head.[16]

It is equally unsurprising that gays and lesbians would be unsuccessful in achieving visitation rights with children they helped raise. That group is not nearly the political equal of the grandparent's lobby; even worse, their mere existence as parents is unacceptable to some lawmakers.

Law must struggle with two competing interests. The first is to conform to the changing cultural mores and protect the interests of members of nontraditional families. As Supreme Court Justice John Paul Stevens recently observed, there are an "almost infinite variety of family relationships that pervade our ever-changing society."[17] The second interest is to continue to use the law to encourage and discourage behavior, depending on whether or not it is seen as advancing the long-term health and stability of society.

Some legislators are reluctant to change laws to reflect modern life because they do not want to be seen as ratifying a lifestyle to which they are opposed. Others are concerned about the symbolic meaning of a legislative act that recognizes the legal rights of a gay or lesbian co-parent. Added to this, there is a powerful lobby against such legislation. American society today is locked in a cultural war over the family, frequently captured under the heading "family values."

On the one side are social conservatives and others unwilling to encourage the "breakdown of the family" and the "continuing moral downward spiral of American life." They view law as a statement of proper behavior and refuse to sanction behavior they deem to be wrong. After the Hawaii Supreme Court started things off in 1993 by ruling that Hawaii law requires the provision of certain benefits to some same-sex relationships, many states enacted legislation restricting marriage to opposite-sex couples. Conservatives succeeded in persuading Congress in 1996 to pass the Defense of Marriage Act,[18] which "protect[s] the institution of marriage" by permitting states to refuse to give any kind of recognition to same-sex relationships, regardless of the benefits conferred upon the relationship in a particular state.

Others, including those comfortable with supporting nontraditional lifestyles and a group we might call "realists," support changing the laws to catch up with behavior. It was only in 2002, for example, that the *New York Times* decided to announce the "weddings" and "marriages" of same-sex couples. This socially significant decision undoubtedly reflected deep social movements already long underway, but it just as surely helps speed the movement along.[19]

Massachusetts influenced the debate rather dramatically in 2003 when its highest court ruled that same-sex couples have the right to marry under Massachusetts law.[20] That decision spurred highly publicized actions in a number of other places, most famously San Francisco, in which mayors or city clerks issued marriage licenses to same-sex couples. The result has been predictable. Fearful that the Defense of Marriage Act will prove inadequate to prevent legal recognition of same-sex relationships in states that do not want to recognize them, some have proposed a constitutional amendment that would outlaw same-sex marriages everywhere in the country.

But it is important to appreciate just how rapidly the pendulum has swung. Merely a few years ago, whether or not same-sex relationships should receive the benefits of a "real" marriage was a hotly debated issue. Once the Massachusetts decision was announced, benefits are now taken as a basic, undeniable right, at least in one state. The argument is now shifting from whether it is acceptable *only* to provide the same benefits to same-sex partnerships as marriage enjoys, or whether the symbolic power of the institution of marriage must be made available to all. Being able to enjoy the benefits of being married without being permitted to marry is no longer enough for many who would have happily settled for this outcome only a few years earlier. It is extraordinary when social change of this magnitude is achieved so swiftly that it is measured by the boundaries of the previous round of debates.

The significance of the Massachusetts decision (and the ones that are sure to follow) is that among the benefits the nonbiological and nonadoptive parent will obtain are the same parental rights that his or her partner enjoys, at least with respect to children born during the marriage. Given the breakdown of support for this issue across demographic lines, it is only a matter of time until same-sex marriages or their full equivalent are recognized throughout the United States. Once the current generation of Americans over fifty lose their political influence, the next generation will more than likely eliminate a barrier to equality they simply do not recognize as sensible.[21]

It is useful, by the way, to see this example of social change as a piece of the children's rights puzzle. Children, ultimately, have the power to repudiate and eliminate the rules of their parents' lives. It is true that they cannot exercise this power until they leave childhood. But this is one of the ways "children's rights" differs from all other examples of disempowerment of minorities by majorities. In all other examples, the minority remains oppressed forever. Here, by contrast, children not only get to join the ranks of adulthood, they get to take it over completely and rearrange society in accordance with how they and their contemporaries see things.

In all events, as of 2004, depending on where you live, states may but need not confer any kind of parental rights to same-sex partners who are not biologically related to the children or have not adopted them, even if they played a major role in raising and caring for the children. However understandable the political explanation, it is important to appreciate how deeply paradoxical this result really is.

First, we learn that legislatures have willingly granted parentlike rights to persons who have never served in parentlike roles with the children. Moreover, the granting of such rights comes at the direct expense of the traditional parental rights holders. As such, the recognition of grandparent visitation rights is nothing less than an assault on the parental rights doctrine, yielding a significant modification and diminution of parental power.

By comparison, co-parents and de facto parents seek less to attack parental rights than to advance them. The millions of co-parents and de facto parents who share the daily routine of raising children but who lack legally recognized parental rights argue that third-party visitation statutes are needed to *protect* parental rights. Yet those who challenged parental rights in the legislatures were the hands-down winner. Those who sought to expand parental rights have fared considerably less well.

Thus, the third-party visitation movement has become composed of two groups with incompatible goals. The only thing these diverse challenges have in common is that both would diminish legally recognized parents' authority.

The judicial response to this movement also deserves careful discussion. Here we observe almost the opposite of what we found in Chapter 3 when we examined the judicial response to the plight of unwed fathers in the early 1970s. At that time, no legislature had modified traditional law by recognizing the rights of unwed fathers in order to account for the changing family in the United States. As a result, unwed fathers had no statutory rights to legally recognized parental status, even if they lived with and helped raise their own children. Recognizing that unless it intervened, unwed fathers would have been out of luck, the Supreme Court stepped in and ruled that unwed fathers had protectable rights. When Peter Stanley's case reached the Supreme Court in 1972, his task was to persuade the Court that he *was* a parent and that Illinois had to treat him as one. Stanley, a man without legally recognized parental rights, successfully argued that he deserved to be protected by the parental rights doctrine.

By contrast, for the most part, the judicial response in third-party visitation cases has been that whatever the legislature sees fit to do is acceptable to judges. Moreover, this is true no matter who is complaining. In most states, state supreme courts have upheld grandparent visitation statutes against challenges by parents that the statute violated their constitutionally protected parental rights. (There have been some notable exceptions in which state courts declared grandparent statutes unconstitutional. We will shortly consider one such case from Washington that reached the U.S. Supreme Court in 2000.) At the same time, when de facto parents brought third-party visitation claims alleging that the legislature's failure to grant them the right to seek visitation violated their parental rights, the overwhelming majority of state courts rejected their claims.

As the two New York cases demonstrate, many state courts have refused to recognize an adult's right to be a parent outside of what the legislature has seen fit to allow. Sometimes, courts emphasize their limited power to change the rules, leaving these decisions to legislatures to resolve. Other times, courts stress the constitutional rights of parents, suggesting that courts are powerless to expand who gets to be treated as a parent because doing so comes at the expense of persons already in possession of constitutionally protected parental rights.

What about Children's Rights?

Virtually all of the writers who support third-party visitation do so in the name of advancing children's rights. The children's rights claim is especially attractive to those adults who are reluctant to take any steps that might be construed as symbolically approving the kinds of relationships into which the adults have entered. These adults are far more comfortable focusing instead on the impact of those choices on innocent children. This is precisely where the children's rights movement meets up with the third-party visitation effort. The rhetorical device of including children's rights may be just the edge needed for those who support third-party statutes.

Litigants who bring third-party visitation claims invariably invoke children's best interests to justify their petition. They argue that children have the constitutional right to maintain an already formed, significant parent-child relationship that may not be denied them even by their own parent.[22] This claim derives from the well-known writings of Joseph Goldstein, Anna Freud, and Albert Solnit who coined the term "psychological parent" to shift the focus from the legal definition and the adult-centered notion of who is considered to be a parent to a child-centered perspective. According to these authors, a psychological parent is "one who, on a continuing, day-to-day basis, through interaction, companionship, interplay, and mutuality, fulfills the child's psychological needs for a parent, as well as the child's physical needs."[23]

This could easily lead one to conclude that third-party visitation efforts plainly pit those who support children's rights against those who support parental rights. But a principal goal of this book is to help the reader gain an appreciation that in the field of children's rights, as elsewhere, appearances can be deceiving.

This requires understanding something about the structure of the argument over visitation rights. Once a third-party visitation case gets to court, it is virtually certain that one of the parties will appear to be on the children's side and the other party will appear to be hiding behind the law's formalities simply to advance his or her own selfish interests.

Let's return to the dispute between Christine and Janis with which we began this chapter to see what happens as the case progresses. After Christine files a motion to dismiss on the ground that the court lacks jurisdiction to force her to allow visitation with a "legal stranger" to her children, we can be certain that Janis will respond that her only real interest is in the children's best interests. This is so for two strategic reasons.

First, Janis is a far less attractive party than the children. She will be able to cast them as the innocent victims of an arrangement into which two adults entered. Janis can argue on their behalf that the court has a responsibility to ensure that the children are not harmed as a result of choices made by their mother. But Janis will be unable to make an argument on her own behalf that is even remotely as compelling.

The second reason, closely related to the first, is that Janis has no rights. If she tries to pit her claims against Christine's, she begins on an extremely uneven playing field. The rights of a parent are being contrasted with the rights of someone who gets labeled by the court system as a "legal stranger." That she is a lesbian only further hinders her chances in court.

As we shall soon see, the argument that Janis is and should be recognized as a parent with rights is the more straightforward and coherent one. As a consequence, Janis should win, if at all, because courts should regard her as a parent to the same extent it would a married father after a divorce, not because of the children's best interests. Just because Janis will focus instead on the children's best interests does not make the strategic choice any less a device.

An identical set of strategies are at play in Wilber and Stewart and Ann's case. Wilber goes to court after unsuccessfully trying to persuade his son and daughter-in-law to permit him to visit with his granddaughter. After Stewart and Ann are served with court papers, they consult an attorney, who informs them that it may be unconstitutional for the court even to hear the case and that they have a sound claim that the petition should be dismissed without conducting a hearing. The lawyer further explains to Stewart and Ann the difference between "jurisdiction" (the power of the court to consider the case in the first place) and "the merits" (what the court should rule if it has jurisdiction to decide the matter). The particular statute pursuant to which Wilber sued authorizes the court to order visitation if it finds such visitation to be in Tess's best interests.

What may we expect Stewart and Ann to do in this case? The first thing their lawyer will do is file a motion to dismiss on the grounds that the statute is unconstitutional. In support of the motion the lawyer will argue that because of the parental rights doctrine, the court has no business even inquiring into whether visitation would serve the children's best interests.

And Wilber's response? He will certainly emphasize that Tess's interests are what really matter, that Tess has rights which only the court is in a position to protect, and that the parental rights doctrine must be properly balanced with the court's inherent power to protect Tess's independent right to maintain a relationship with her loving grandfather.

Most important, this lineup of arguments will not just happen some of the time. It will happen every time. Stewart and Ann may well have powerful reasons for opposing Wilber's efforts to visit with Tess. He may have said or done terrible things in the past that would lead a court easily to conclude that visitation would not be in Tess's best interests. Nonetheless, Stewart and Ann's lawyer will never mention any of this to the judge when arguing for dismissal of the case. Why is this so? Because to tell the judge the reasons the parents are opposed to visitation is to concede the very thing they deny: that the court has jurisdiction to decide whether to grant visitation in the first place. Once parents begin down the road of justifying and explaining their reasons for denying visitation, they have lost the more fundamental right not to be second-guessed or reviewed by a judge in the discharge of their parental childrearing decisions.

Grandparent Rights and the Supreme Court

By the end of the 1990s, parents in almost all states had challenged grandparent visitation laws as an unlawful invasion of their constitutionally protected authority. For the most part, state courts accepted grandparent visitation statutes as the lawful exercise of legislative discretion to enact laws that serve the well-being of children. A number of state supreme courts, however, had declared these laws unconstitutional as an impermissible infringement on parental rights. But until the U.S. Supreme Court spoke on the subject, third-party visitation statutes would remain the business of each state to work out for itself.

As we have seen, of the various significant adults in a child's life to claim an entitlement to maintain a relationship with the child over parental objection, grandparents would not obviously be first in line. The strongest such candidates would be adults who already had a significant parentlike relationship with the child. This group sometimes, but not necessarily, includes grandparents.

For better or worse, the first third-party visitation case to reach the U.S. Supreme Court was brought by grandparents from Washington who were trying to visit with two granddaughters more frequently than their mother would permit. When the Supreme Court agrees to hear a case, everyone with even the slightest interest in the legal issues raised by the case becomes keenly focused on it because whatever decision the Court renders will likely affect many thousands more. Thus it was that behind the scenes a different race was on when the Court agreed to hear *Troxel v. Granville.*[24]

Interested persons may be heard in a Supreme Court case by filing a friend-of-the-Court brief *(amicus curiae)* telling the Court what their interest in the case is and how they think the Court ought to decide the case. It is unclear just how important these briefs are in the Court's ultimate decision; occasionally an amicus curiae brief will contain a powerful new analysis that will persuade the Court to go in a particular direction which the parties had not developed. More commonly, these briefs will stake out positions that, for strategic or other reasons, the parties themselves have chosen not to take. As a result, through friends-of-the-court briefs most of a case's implications are fleshed out for the justices who have to decide it. But perhaps the most important function of these briefs is to signal to the Court the relative importance of the issue to the larger legal community.

Twenty friends-of-the-court briefs were filed in *Troxel,* a very substantial number.[25] As a consequence, no one at the Court missed the message that third-party visitation efforts were extremely important to many Americans. The same devices we have already observed were plainly evident in the strategies of these briefs. Thus, the opening sentences of the friend-of-the-court brief for Grandparents United for Children's Rights declare, "Determination of the constitutionality of visitation statutes must include consideration of the constitutional rights of children. The Washington Supreme Court erred in conducting its constitutional analysis absent recognition of the children's rights to liberty and equal protection in maintaining relationships with their grandparents." And the first paragraph in the Lambda Legal Defense and Education Fund brief reads, "That legal parents have a liberty interest in the care, custody and rearing of their children that merits both procedural protection and substantive recognition under the Due Process Clause of the Fourteenth Amendment has long been established. But the interests of others, especially children, also figure into the constitutional calculus and preclude any uniform description either of the state interest necessary to invade parental autonomy or of the procedures required to protect it."

As keen an interest as many in the national legal community had in the case, there was even greater uncertainty over how it would be decided. *Troxel* challenged the power of the state—whether through the legislature or the courts—to interfere with and overrule a parent's childrearing choices. As we have seen, ordinarily unless parents are found to be unfit, they enjoy the constitutional right to control all of the details of their child's upbringing, even when a judge disagrees with the parenting decisions.

Thus, the traditional line of family law cases that have constitutional implications suggested that third-party visitation cases would be hard to defend in the Supreme Court. These cases support a parent's right to raise children free from state interference unless the state has a *compelling* justification to interfere. It would be difficult to defend a third-party visitation statute under that high standard. On the other hand, the Supreme Court frequently looks to national trends in determining the *reasonableness* of legislation. That every state has seen fit to enact a third-party visitation statute strongly suggests the reasonableness (or the sense on the part of a majority of Americans of the reasonableness) of these laws.

The details of *Troxel* itself do not require much elaboration. The case originated in a trial court in the state of Washington. After their son died, the paternal grandparents of two girls sued the children's mother for greater visitation than the mother was allowing. For about five months after the father died, the grandparents saw the girls every weekend. Because this schedule proved too complicated for the mother, she asked the grandparents to limit the visits to one weekend each month.

Unsatisfied with this reduction in contact with their granddaughters, the grandparents filed a proceeding in a Washington state court seeking two weekends of overnight visitation per month and two weeks of visitation each summer. The statute authorizing the lawsuit provided: "Any person may petition the court for visitation rights at any time including, but not limited to, custody proceedings. The court may order visitation rights for any person when visitation may serve the best interest of the child whether or not there has been any change of circumstances."

After hearing testimony, the trial court ordered visitation of one weekend per month, one week during the summer, and four hours on both of the grandparents' birthdays. In reaching this result, the trial judge expressed the opinion that the girls would benefit from spending this time with their grandparents and that, as a result, the visitation would be in their best interests.

The Washington Supreme Court reversed, holding that the statute unconstitutionally infringed on the right of parents to rear their children. In that court's view, there were at least two problems with the nonparental visitation statute. First, according to the Washington Supreme Court, the Constitution permits a state to interfere with the right of parents to rear their children only to prevent harm or potential harm to a child. The statute failed that standard because it required no threshold showing of harm. Second, by allowing "'any person' to petition for forced visitation of a child at 'any time' with the only requirement being that the visitation serve the best interest of the child," the Washington visitation statute was too broad. The Washington Supreme Court held that "Parents have a right to limit visitation of their children with third persons," and that between parents and judges, "the parents should be the ones to choose whether to expose their children to certain people or ideas."

A sharply divided U.S. Supreme Court affirmed. Because five justices did not agree on the precise basis for declaring the Washington statute unconstitutional, no formal opinion for the Court was issued. Instead, Justice O'Connor wrote an opinion for herself and three others explaining the reasons she voted to strike the statute.

It was her view that the Washington statute was deficient because it permitted a state judge to order visitation simply because the judge regarded visitation to be in the children's best interest. O'Connor believed that, in light of the parental rights doctrine, courts must at least give special weight to the parent's reasons for opposing the visitation. This, for O'Connor, means that a court must refuse to order visitation over parental objection (without even reaching the best interests inquiry), unless the court first concludes that the parent's views are indefensible. But O'Connor and the three Justices who signed her opinion (Chief Justice Rehnquist and Justices Ginsberg and Breyer) were of the view that a properly drafted third-party visitation statute would survive constitutional challenge. Three dissenting justices were also of that view and would have upheld even the Washington statute that was before them. This means that narrowly drawn third-party visitation statutes will almost certainly survive constitutional challenge.

But it is far from clear what a statute has to include to be constitutional. This is, in part, because the grandparents in *Troxel* had a significant grandparent-grandchild relationship before they filed their petition for visitation. Would a grandparent who has never gotten to know a grandchild be allowed to bring such an action? It is also unclear what it means to give special weight to a parent's decision. Here, the difference between the U.S. Supreme Court's view and that of the Washington Supreme Court is quite telling.

The Washington Supreme Court ruled that a court must find that the parent's refusal to permit visitation would *harm* the child. A majority of the justices on the U.S. Supreme Court, however, appear prepared to uphold a visitation statute that authorizes courts to award visitation after finding the visitation would be in a child's best interests so long as some deference was first given to the parent's reasons for opposing the visitation. Two justices (Stevens and Kennedy) rejected requiring a showing of harm and they did so explicitly in the name of children's rights. In their view, children are entitled to a less severe standard in order to protect their rights to maintain significant relationships that have already been formed.

Justice Stevens went considerably further. Stressing children's rights, he would sharply limit a parent's freedom to disrupt arbitrarily already formed significant relationships. Justice Kennedy also suggested that important children's rights may be at stake in the maintenance of significant relationships that have already formed. Because of this, he was unwilling to conclude that subjecting a parent's childrearing choices to a best interests review is, in all cases, unconstitutional. Kennedy wrote that because some "relationships can be so enduring," that "arbitrarily depriving the child of the relationship could cause severe psychological harm to the child." But he went even beyond this to observe, "In the design and elaboration of their visitation laws, States may be entitled to consider that certain relationships are such that to avoid the risk of harm, a best interests standard can be employed by their domestic relations courts in some circumstances."[26]

For many in the children's rights movement, *Troxel* represented another defeat for children. Janet Dolgin, a law professor, criticized the decision in terms opposite from what the Court itself had to say. Rather than an example of the state staying out of the family, she suggested that the decision "was an [inexcusable] intrusion into [the children's] family of extended kin."[27]

Since 2000, courts in every state have had to reconsider the validity of their third-party visitation statutes in light of *Troxel*. The decision has resulted in a renewed emphasis on the constitutional importance of parental rights. Paradoxically, however, *Troxel* may prove in the long run to aid efforts to allow visitation proceedings over the objections of biological parents. This may happen by redefining who is a parent. *Troxel* pitted parents against nonparents both in the sense that the grandparents lacked legally recognized parental rights and because they had never been de facto parents to the children they sought to visit. Even in that context, there was considerable interest on the part of at least some justices to recognize the value of maintaining significant familial ties that a parent has arbitrarily severed. Surely it follows that when parents arbitrarily disrupt a significant parentlike relationship, it would be lawful for courts to review the propriety of the parent's decision.

Whose Interests: Adults' or Children's?

How might we go about deciding who the real children's rights advocates are and what rules and policies best advance children's rights or interests? To begin working through this inquiry, let us separate out two categories of cases: those in which an adult (usually a grandparent) wishes to develop a relationship with someone else's child and those in which an adult wishes to maintain an already established significant relationship with someone else's child.

NO PRE-EXISTING RELATIONSHIP

There are few adults in American society who would even attempt to advance the claim that a child's right includes developing a substantial relationship with a particular nonparent. Yet grandparents not only have made this claim over the past generation, they have succeeded in securing legislation that backs it up. But it should be plain that their success says more about the power of the grandparents' lobby than about the logic of their position.

First, consider the oddity of isolating this one discrete aspect of parenting from the multitude of ways in which parents have the authority to make decisions for their children. Among these decisions, parents get to choose where their children live; what schools they attend; the kind of clothes they wear; the food they eat; the friends with whom they associate; what they may read, watch, and listen to in books, television, film and radio; and even the religious institution to which they will belong, including the choice that they will not belong to any. Plucked out from among many of these life-altering choices comes the single claim that a parent's decision not to permit his or her child the opportunity to develop or maintain a relationship with a grandparent violates the child's right.

Why is this particular issue so important? However much one obfuscates about children's rights, the answer is, I hope, clear. It is not because a child's "right" to maintain contact with a grandparent, above all other decisions parents control, is so crucial. Most would agree that the multitude of decisions parents routinely make about their children are substantially more important to their child's best interests in the long run. The only difference is that there is an *adult* whose ox has been gored. I do not mean by this to belittle the pain of a grandparent denied access to a grandchild; rather, to acknowledge that the grandparent's pain is the motivating factor in bringing suit, not the child's. The child's best interests is the device which must be used to have any hope of the grandparent winning. But we should not let this fact fool us.[28]

Some wax nostalgic about the virtue of grandparents in the lives in grandchildren. The friend-of-the-court brief by the American Association of Retired Persons submitted to the Supreme Court in *Troxel*, for example, argued, "Research demonstrates that grandparents contribute significantly to the healthy development of their grandchildren. For instance, children who have close relationships with their grandparents were found to be more emotionally secure than other children." The same brief quotes a Connecticut state senator who spoke in support of the passage of Connecticut's grandparent visitation statute: "I have seen so many situations where the child's rights are really so disregarded by the parents who are feuding that the only people that care about the child are the grandparents . . . I think [the bill] is a step in the right direction to make certain that the child's interests are the ones that are really protected the most."

We need not dispute these generalizations to recognize that it is impossible to say one way or another whether a child's world would be advanced by knowing a particular relative. It all depends. And the thing upon which it depends most is who the person is and what kind of relationship he or she would likely form with the child. It is, in other words, no more true to say that a particular child would be well-served to develop a relationship with a particular adult, without knowing anything about the child or the adult, than it would be to assert the opposite. We simply do not know without making the effort to find out. Even when we are finished with such an effort, we may only make a prediction that carries with it an unknown risk of error.

Three important principles can be gleaned from this. First, we can't know what is best for a child without taking the time and effort to find out. Second, the time and effort can be considerable. Third, even after all of this, we can never be certain. Imbedded in these three principles is the core of the parental rights doctrine. It begins with the concept that parents are in a better position than anyone else to make the proper decisions for their children and that parents tend to have their children's best interests at heart. But it goes much deeper than this. It also recognizes the potential dangers associated with empowering state officials (judges) to make these decisions instead of parents. It is, in the end, this quality of third-party visitation statutes that matters most. Grandparent visitation laws do not so much give grandparents rights as they shift child-rearing power from parents to judges.

Not only do third-party visitation claims unleash the power of the state, judicial intervention is justified on the dubious proposition that rational inquiry through the judicial process leads to correct results. In particular, some believe that we are more likely to achieve the best outcome by requiring parents to provide a careful explanation for their parenting choices. But we have already seen in Chapter 2 that there is more myth than truth behind the idea that judges are objective, neutral investigators who have the capacity to determine in a meaningful way what course of action furthers a child's best interest. (This is why a clear majority of the *Troxel* Court refused to authorize judges to decide visitation cases merely based on a best interests test.)

There is a final problem with relying on the judicial process to resolve these kinds of disputes. Sometimes, particularly in matters of the heart and family, there is little to gain by forcing someone to explain in detail the reasons for refusing to continue a relationship with another person. When a parent-child relationship has sunk to the point that the parent decides to sue his child in a court of law in order to be permitted to visit with his grandchild, the relationship is already in deep trouble.

It is important to appreciate just how extreme a situation must become before a grandparent visitation case is filed in the first place. I have represented parents in dozens of these cases. In every one, I observed some form of pathology in the adult parent-child relationship. How could it be otherwise? These cases are commonly brought only after less extreme measures of persuasion have failed. I wonder how many readers would ever seriously contemplate suing their child to gain access to a grandchild.

The remedies most of us would use are all lawful, but private. We might send a sweet note; we might apologize; we might offer to go to counseling together; we might involve a sister or nephew or friend of the family—someone who might be able to restart the communication. We might even try to influence the parent by offering a gift of some kind. But a lawsuit is a hostile, aggressive act to which only a very few would ever resort. Although we may or may not agree that the principals would do well to consider family therapy to get past their differences and learn to become a family again, it would be deeply misguided to believe that courts are the right forum for such therapeutic intervention.

Finally, for a variety of practical reasons, there is a real likelihood that grandparents will secure judicially ordered visitation without any determination that this would be good for the child. Consider, once again, Stewart and Ann's dispute with Wilber. Let us now assume that they had excellent reasons for opposing a continued relationship with Wilber. It was important for them as young adults simply to get away from Wilber, whom they perceive to be an extremely controlling individual who is unable to separate the conflicts with his son from his relationship with his granddaughter. Stewart and Ann may fear that Wilber will use his relationship with Tess to undermine Tess's relationship with her parents.

But now let us imagine that Stewart and Ann are without much money. Wilber, on the other hand, has plenty. He can afford to hire a lawyer who will vigorously prosecute his case. Stewart and Ann seek to retain a lawyer and learn that the lawyer requires a $10,000 retainer and warns them that if the matter goes to a contested trial, the fee will almost certainly exceed $25,000. Many parents in these circumstances capitulate and accept a court order "on consent" awarding Wilber visitation.

Has this result advanced Tess's interests? It would certainly seem so on its face. The statute was enacted, after all, in the name of children's rights. Wilber's court papers stressed that he was bringing the case solely to further Tess's rights. Finally, no one even disputed the claim and Wilber obtained visitation "on consent."

Unfortunately, however, all we can say for certain is that the lawsuit advanced Wilber's interests. Indeed, on the facts we just hypothesized, Stewart and Ann's reasons opposing visitation were rather well grounded. Because of the imbalance in the adults' financial situation, however, they can ill afford to allow the case to go to trial. Under these circumstances, it is just as likely that Tess's interests were subverted.

A possible solution to this, since we are now focused on the costs associated with the litigation, would be to create a rule that would grant attorney's fees to a parent who successfully defends her reasons after trial. This might be seen to solve the problem. For one, it would create a disincentive for grandparents who do not have an obvious case on their side from even filing for visitation in the first place. In addition, this would mean that parents can afford to defend themselves, secure in the knowledge that if they prevail they won't have to pay their lawyer.

Yet much depends on how confident the parent (or her attorney) is about winning and the degree of risk the parent is willing to bear. Many rational parents, facing the choice of allowing or opposing visitation, will allow it when they realize that a full trial can cost $25,000 or more. Again, we ought not confuse the result of a parent's allowing the visitation with a good result for the child. It might, instead, be thought of as blackmail.

One possible solution, then, is to require the grandparents to pay all costs of the lawsuit regardless of who prevails. This would avoid the costs problem. But now the children's advocates (or the grandparent lobby) will be upset. They would say that the scheme is once again rigged against them. What about the grandparents who cannot afford to sue because they can ill afford to pay one lawyer, let alone two? What does this mean for children's rights when a grandparent is thwarted in bringing a case because the fee arrangement is biased so powerfully in favor of the parent? In addition, the "solution" virtually assures protracted litigation, which is itself damaging to children and their families.

In the end, it is difficult to avoid the conclusion that the real winners in grandparent visitation cases are state judges. At the heart of the grandparent claim is a question: Who should decide? Invariably, someone must decide whether or not to permit a child to form or maintain a relationship with a nonparent. American law's preference for granting parents the power to make all childrearing decisions free from state oversight may be characterized as anti-child; but it is a very difficult case to make.

It is also difficult to defend the claim that third-party statutes are pro-child. What we know for certain is that these statutes greatly enhance the power of nonparents by giving them leverage they otherwise would not have. Without such statutes, nonparents are limited to resolving their familial disputes without seeking the state's aid. They will be able to achieve only as much as they are able to persuade the parent to give them. But the force of these statutes is to place parents under the power of state officials who are vested with the authority to overrule their parenting choices.

It is true, of course, that grandparents gain something too. But grandparents may not force themselves on children even when courts agree to hear their claim. Instead, the result is that parental decisionmaking becomes ever more subject to state review. In this sense, children and families become increasingly under state control. Perhaps this is the right result because of what children gain in the long run, but we should at least recognize the degree to which aspects of childrearing have shifted from the private arena to the public.

Those concerned with the exercise of state childrearing power when the decisions at stake do not place children at risk will necessarily be wary of siding with the grandparents' efforts to secure statutory visitation rights. This doesn't make these adversaries opposed to children's rights. The ancillary costs associated with any effort to vindicate their rights are what some opponents emphasize. For them, the costs are too great to bear.

Having demonstrated that there is no way to determine whether a parent's decision to disallow visitation is good for a child or whether a court order granting visitation is preferable, let me add an additional complicating factor. For better or worse, children are assigned to their parent's custody. How confident are we that it serves children well when a court orders a parent, under contempt of court and fine or imprisonment, to permit his or her child to spend time with someone the parent genuinely believes ought not be seeing the child? What impact does this have on the child's relationship with his or her parent? On the parent's ability to be a good, loving parent? Should we expect that the anger and frustration that accompany such a loss will not impact the child in any way?

PRE-EXISTING RELATIONSHIP

It would be wrong to lump together all third-party claims. In some, especially those we have just considered, the third party is a true interloper into the affairs of an ongoing family who seeks to disrupt their privacy and autonomy. But in an ever increasing number of cases, the third party was very recently a significant member of the family unit, a full partner with the legal parent and a parentlike figure. In the case of a nonmarital partner, the parent is using the legal cloak of technical parenthood to trump the rights of someone who is truly similarly situated, except that he or she lacks legally recognized rights.

Once a parent has allowed a significant parent-child relationship to be formed, the inquiry is dramatically different. One may postulate that parents ought to be able to prevent state officials from insisting that children be permitted to form a relationship with someone outside of the nuclear family. We are not now discussing, however, whether courts should tell parents which adults should be permitted to form parentlike relationships with their children. The new inquiry is whether, after parents voluntarily allow a parentlike relationship to develop, the law is powerless to insist that the parent permit the parentlike relationship to be maintained after the adult relationship has soured.

Should the law privilege biological or adoptive parents over others who, with the full knowledge and consent of parents, have developed significant parentlike relationships with children? Domestic partners, nonbiological stepparents, and similar adults who developed a parentlike relationship with children should be allowed to continue to have access with them, even over the biological parent's objection, because biology, in our modern world, has become an arbitrary basis on which to limit the definition of parenthood.

We reach this result without any pretense of advancing children's rights. Giving a de facto parent visitation privileges is not a child's right. It is a *parent's*. Just as the requirement of marriage proved to be an unacceptable way to deny unmarried men parental rights, couples who choose to make a family together, even if unmarried or of the same sex, have taken the steps to create an arrangement that courts should be prepared to recognize. Not because it is good for children, but because families are commonly formed "entirely apart from the power of the State."[29]

We reach the conclusion that new families deserve legal recognition, paradoxically, by invoking the traditional grounds upon which the state is restricted in intervening in familial affairs. We saw in Chapter 2 that the state lacks the authority to prevent the formation of those relationships; from this it follows that it ought not be empowered to deny the adults who voluntarily formed them the associated rights or consequences that flow from their formation.

It is, of course, possible to advance this claim through a child-centered focus. This would recognize that children derive meaning from a relationship based on the "emotional attachments that derive from the intimacy of daily association," particularly because "No one would seriously dispute that a deeply loving and interdependent relationship between an adult and a child in his or her care may exist even in the absence of blood relationship."[30]

But the more straightforward claim is adult-centered. It is based on what adults expect and deserve for their investment in a child. There are many strong reasons to think that such relationships are deserving of protection. Except perhaps in rare cases, neither party intended when the relationship was formed that biology would trump the nonbiological parent's rights or that the parties joined the relationship unequally.

There is hardly anything unfair in saying to a parent who voluntarily invited someone else to share parenting and to develop a significant parent-child relationship with his or her children that the parent must allow the logical consequences of that choice to play themselves out. It is wrong both for parents and children to encourage the disruption of significant bonds for the sole reason that the biological parent prefers such a disruption.

Nonetheless, for a variety of reasons, courts are not coming to the rescue in the way they did in the case of unwed fathers. Partly this reflects the conservative shift in the courts and a greater reluctance to protect the rights of unpopular individuals than in the early 1970s. It is really more than this, however.

Also at play is a deep question about the proper role of courts in shaping society. For many judges, it is one thing to enforce a statute the legislature saw fit to enact and completely different to decide that there should be such a law in the first place. Some courts have been willing to allow visitation in these cases without waiting until the legislature acts. These courts, self-identified as "progressive," have expanded de facto parents' visitation rights when the legislature has failed to do so.

In 1995, the Wisconsin Supreme Court, for example, permitted a former partner in a lesbian relationship to seek visitation of the biological mother's child even though the former partner was neither biologically nor legally related to the child. The court ruled that individuals who can show the existence of a parentlike relationship will be permitted to seek visitation over the legal parent's objection when they lived with the child long enough to create "a bonded, dependent relationship parental in nature" by taking significant responsibility for the child's care and when the legal parent fostered the formation of the parentlike relationship.[31]

This holding is quite close to what was proposed by the American Law Institute in 2000.[32] But consider the views of one of the justices who dissented in that case. "[T]he legislature should be the body that decides what grouping of adults living together may be defined as a 'non-traditional family,'" he wrote, because "There is no justification for a court to seek to impose in the name of the law, common or equitable, its own ideas of social policy and a new found theory of family law which creates new 'rights' for those who have no legally binding relationship to the child."[33]

The arguments and reasoning needed to win in court are very different from what makes for successful arguments in the legislature. To prevail in court, a co-parent must persuade the judge either that the controlling statute authorizing visitation by nonparents is broad enough to encompass co-parents or that the Constitution *requires* that the co-parent be permitted to seek visitation. Putting aside efforts to persuade state courts that the controlling visitation statute should be interpreted to include co-parents, let us examine what arguments are available to co-parents to support the claim that the Constitution requires that courts allow such actions, using our now-familiar case involving Janis and Christine.

Plainly, Janis has a difficult burden. The party vested with constitutional rights is Christine, who is opposing the lawsuit. Indeed, as we have seen, Christine's first response to the filing of the petition will be to make a motion to dismiss it because allowing the lawsuit would violate *her* constitutional rights. It will be a challenge, to say the least, for Janis to prevail. She must overcome two significant obstacles: first, Janis must persuade a court that filing an action does not violate Christine's constitutional rights; and second, the court must allow Janis to bring her case because the Constitution protects her right to do so. The combination of these claims may not be far-fetched, but no legal expertise is needed to see just how unlikely it is that Janis will prevail.

Consider the two issues in the order they would be taken up in court. The first is Christine's claim that it would violate her constitutional rights to permit Janis to sue her. The simplest way to examine this claim is to consider whether a statute that expressly authorized a co-parent, such as Janis, to seek visitation of Christine's children is constitutional. This is hardly a hypothetical inquiry. A number of states have already enacted legislation allowing co-parents like Janis to seek visitation. In addition, a number of state courts have interpreted their third-party visitation statute broadly enough to include co-parents like Janis.

Let us consider a state law, based on the American Law Institute's Model Statute, that authorizes a de facto parent to seek visitation after the legal parent has prohibited further contact with the child. Would such a statute violate a parent's constitutional rights to control the details of her child's upbringing? Almost certainly not.

There ought to be nothing wrong with a rule that makes clear to parents the degree to which they compromise their rights when they freely permit someone to form a significant parentlike relationship with their children. Once the relationship has been formed, traditional estoppel principles would prevent the parent from changing her mind about whether it should ever have been formed in the first place.

Perhaps a preferable way to think of this is a waiver of exclusive parental rights. Even the most sacred of constitutional rights may be knowingly and intelligently waived. Inviting another adult to develop a close relationship with one's child ought to be considered a waiver of the parent's exclusive right to make all decisions for her children. Giving legal significance to this relationship should not be regarded as any kind of state intrusion into a parent's rights; the "intrusion" is by the de facto parent, who would not be permitted to sue in court if the parent had not permitted a relationship to be established. Thus, the de facto parent merely is seeking to enforce an implied contract between the parties. What else is marriage but an express contract?

Now let us consider Janis's claim that she has a constitutional right to seek visitation. Revisiting the material we considered in Chapter 3 may be useful here. Unwed fathers first secured their constitutional rights when state officials sought to remove children from Peter Stanley's home. Stanley argued successfully that he had a constitutional right to the care and custody of his children. He was not asserting a constitutional right against the mother. Because mothers were long considered to be constitutional rights holders, it would have been much more difficult for Stanley to prevail in a case against the mother.

Once *Stanley* ruled that unwed fathers had constitutional rights, unwed fathers were able to assert these rights, even against mothers. That was the precise holding in *Caban v. Mohammed*. In that case, the mother of out-of-wedlock children claimed a greater privilege to her children than the father had. Ms. Mohammed argued that the law recognized her as the sole legal parent of her children. Although it was true, she asserted, that Mr. Caban was the biological parent of her children, he had not married her or filed a paternity action as New York law required of him in order to have secured legally recognized rights. The Court rejected that argument. Although the technical grounds for the ruling was based on gender discrimination, the substantive result is that similarly situated adults who both behaved in parentlike ways should be treated similarly.

When the only difference between the parties is that one of the adults is the biological parent and the other is not and everything else about them in respect to their relationship to the children is identical, it seems plainly arbitrary to privilege one adult over another. Peter Stanley could better claim that the children he spent eighteen years raising were "his" because he sired them. Janis, who invested as much sweat and tears raising her children with Christine before their relationship ended, was unable to secure legal recognition of her parental ties because she lacked the blood connection.

In New York today, if Christine died without a will, state officials would be permitted to treat her children as state wards in the same way Illinois officials sought to do in *Stanley*. Janis might be permitted to petition a court to grant her custody, but the court would decide who should raise the children based on its assessment of the children's best interests. It is difficult to reconcile the law's continuing disparate treatment of nonmarital partners like Janis from its treatment of men like Peter Stanley.

A generation ago, men were denied the right to be recognized as a parent for the sole reason that they did not marry the children's mother. Ultimately, we came to appreciate that this requirement was arbitrary, having nothing to do with the significance of the already formed parent-child relationship. The same is true for nonmarital partners who have children by other means than making one together biologically. Janis is the loser only because she is not genetically related to her children. This is hardly a powerful or persuasive distinction in our modern world where one can be genetically related to children through artificial insemination, sperm donation, and surrogate parenting.

But let us be clear. We reach this result by reasoning about adult rights. Paradoxically, it can be persuasively advanced that recognizing de facto parents' visitation rights, despite the children's rights claims to the contrary, poorly serve children because children may end up feeling like balls in a pinball machine, getting bounced all around the place. In a modern American family, a child might have one legal mother, one legal father, one stepmother, and perhaps two other men who lived with the mother for a significant period of time.

Does this mean that children should have to spend all of their time traveling about visiting adults? One might say this should be considered at the time the court decides whether and how much visitation to order. But one might also say that it is wrong from the child's perspective even to expose a child to such problems.[34]

The Emptiness of Children's Rights

Because of the elasticity of children's rights, they can be invoked by almost anyone. The social conservatives believe they are the bulwark for protecting children by trying to maintain standards for behavior in the community. Even more interesting, many of these traditionalists support (or would like to support) grandparental visitation statutes. But, as we have seen, such statutes undermine the parental rights social conservatives hold dear.

Social conservatives would bar de facto parents even from attempting to prove to a judge that the children's best interests would be served by continued contact. Yet, they would allow grandparents who never spent a moment as parentlike figures for their grandchildren to sue for visitation. Moreover, they take these positions in the name of furthering children's interests, believing it is bad for children to grow up in a culture that encourages nonmarital relationships. They believe that, in the long term, their position better serves children's rights and, as a consequence, resent being considered anti-child. This is very much like the situation we faced in Baby Jessica's case. Those who believed she should be returned to her birth father were offended at being labeled anti-child.

Here, then, is a robust argument about children and their well-being. The child-centered advocates demand that familial relationships be given legal recognition whenever children have developed significant relationships with an adult. The social conservatives, believing that the long-term interests of children (and society) are undermined by awarding legal recognition of these relationships, refuse to recognize them.

The social conservatives have won the battle (temporarily, at least) of "protecting" the sanctity of marriage. But it is incoherent to draw the same lines when it comes to visitation rights. Even accepting the conservatives' interests and appreciating the dilemma in which they find themselves, it is indefensible to create a scheme by which unwed birth fathers have constitutionally protected rights when they have done little more than have sex with someone who became pregnant, but nonmarital partners who develop deep and meaningful relationships with children as a member of the family have none.

It is, to be sure, a losing battle for social conservatives. Though it is not fantasy to see law as an ally in advancing social policy, there is little doubt that nonmarital relationships have become quite common in American society. It simply is implausible to believe that the law can constrain the continuation of these relationships. Once one reaches that conclusion, everything changes.

The notion of children's rights is considerably more complicated than the children's rights advocates would have it. This chapter has shown how it supplies a convenient argument for adults who seek an advantage in court. It is not that the claim that children deserve the right to maintain a significant relationship is incoherent. It is that we need to appreciate who is making that claim and how limited children's rights really are. The person making such a claim usually wants something that cannot be achieved without focusing on the child's right. Even more fundamentally, it is not really the child's right we are discussing. The moment the adult no longer wants to see the child, the relationship is over. Children do not have the right to maintain a relationship with an adult. They cannot sue to insist that an adult stay in touch with them or continue to care about them. Their best interests need not be taken into account by an adult who decides to break off the relationship. Everything about the relationship hinges on the whim of the adult. The adult gets to choose the nature and extent of the relationship. So what kind of children's right is this?

5

Divorce, Custody, and Visitation

ARGUABLY, the most significant change in American family life over the past forty years involves the institution of marriage. As changing cultural values in the United States since the 1960s have increasingly tolerated familial breakup and divorce, the laws of divorce in the various states have made it ever easier for couples to end their marriages. When divorce was frowned upon culturally—as it was until well past the middle of the twentieth century in the United States—law treated marriage as a lifelong contract that could be breached only upon a few recognized grounds. Merely a generation ago, plaintiffs in most states had to prove that their spouse was at "fault" because of adultery, abandonment, or cruelty.

Although only a few states have completely eliminated fault-based grounds, between 1970 and 1985, all states either replaced fault grounds with no-fault grounds or added no-fault grounds. Today, most divorces are granted upon a showing that the parties are incompatible or that they have lived separately from each other for a prescribed period of time. One of the parties to a marriage may even go to a state that grants "quickie" divorces and obtain a divorce for no other reason than that the individual wishes it.

The divorce rate in the United States reached an all-time high within the past generation—the highest divorce rate among western nations. Between 1950 and 1997, the rate increased in the United States by 67 percent.[1] In 1970, 33 percent of marriages ended in divorce; by 1995, the percentage grew to 50.[2] Today, more than 1 million marriages end in divorce each year.[3]

This means, of course, that marriage is no longer a contract binding on both parties prohibiting dissolution unless the other party breaches a material provision. Instead, it is a unilateral contract, subject to rescission at the whim of either.[4] It is difficult to overstate the dramatic change in values this represents, leading some to label ours the "me first" generation. Our rules maximize each adult individual's freedom even when this means persons to whom we pledged ourselves have no recourse to hold us to our word.

Social conservatives, unhappy with the changes American society has experienced, like to turn their attention to what these changes have done to children. They make the claim that children fare quite poorly in this age of individualism. They argue, for example, that the divorce rate lowers academic performance, creates adjustment and behavior problems, and constitutes a significant risk factor in children for such matters as teen pregnancy, school dropouts, poverty, and delinquency.[5]

Before saying too much more about the impact on children, it is useful to recall who led the effort to change family law and what were the underlying forces behind these changes. At one time, women were subordinate to men both within and outside of marriage. Societal norms reinforced twin notions to accomplish this: within the marriage, men had the legal authority to make all decisions concerning the family; outside the marriage, an adult woman's primary function in society was to fulfill the role of a "wife." The social pressure to marry and to remain married was enormous.

For much of the twentieth century, American women struggled to achieve recognition in spheres outside of the home; many wanted to become doctors, lawyers, and corporate executives. The one role that limited their advancement, above all others, was that of "mother." Parenting in the United States traditionally had been about women committing a substantial portion of their lives to childrearing. Even worse, childrearing was little regarded and significantly undervalued.

The feminist movement played a prominent role in increasing divorce rates. Recognizing that women's choices were limited both within and outside of marriage, feminists saw the importance of easing the means by which women could leave an unhappy marriage. When divorce could be obtained based only on fault grounds, women were bound to remain married even when they wished to be single. Women wanted the simple civil right not to be bound in a relationship they grew to hate, whether or not they could persuade a judge that the husband had committed adultery. To accomplish this, feminists exploded the myth that all was well within the family. They exposed a significant amount of violence inflicted on women that was ignored by the police and the courts. To compel these women to remain in those marriages came to be seen as unconscionable.

The feminist movement alone, however, was not responsible for the changing family demographics in the United States. One of the factors that contributed to the rise in divorce rates in the 1960s through the 1980s was the availability of well-paying jobs for women. Except during World War II, there had never been many jobs available to middle-class women (although in many lower-income households women had always worked outside the home). For a variety of reasons, this began to change in the 1960s. Once women could achieve financial independence, those in unhappy marriages were able to consider leaving.

The jobs were not created to help women leave unhappy marriages. Rather, women were able to leave in unprecedented numbers because there were jobs for them. Soon women broke barriers in many fields once available only to men, and the job and salary horizon for women expanded.

At the same time, many women took paying jobs simply because of economic necessity when men's salaries failed to meet the family's needs. As a result, by 1999, 73 percent of couples had two earners; in a mere 21 percent of homes, only the husband was employed.[6] Today, not only are women more likely to be able to support themselves, many divorce schemes have created the possibility for women to share substantially in the economic gains made by the husband during the marriage.

Other conditions also have changed radically over the past century. Perhaps most important, the purpose and value of having children changed. For most of history, children were valuable to parents in economic terms, providing important labor when the children were young and ensuring support for the parents when they were old. But the value of their labor sharply diminished as the United States underwent a revolutionary change from permitting child labor to requiring education in its place and forbidding most forms of paid labor for children under age sixteen.

In addition, with the passage of Social Security guarantees in 1935, the state took over the commitment of supporting the elderly. Children became financially dispensable. As fewer adults chose to have children, one important reason for marriage was eliminated.

Some of those waging the so-called "family values" campaign are critical of the feminist movement's success in liberating women from subordinate roles in American society and the high divorce rate that has resulted from the increase in women's autonomy. So it should come as no surprise that children have been brought into the debate. Many wonder whether today's easy divorce laws harm children. Not long ago, men and women were told that remaining in a marriage, even a miserable one, was their duty if they were to put the interests of their children ahead of their own.[7] But many during the 1960s began reasoning that it was conflict, not marital status, that mattered most to children's well-being. If divorce mitigated or eliminated conflict, then divorce was good for children.[8]

Related to this notion is the common-sense idea that the mental health and happiness of the parent is an important factor for a child's well-being. If divorce leads to happier parents, the children will be the beneficiaries in the long run. Such reasoning began to influence a growing number of parents. Of course, this view coincided with the political goals of many feminists. In order to gain control over their lives, feminists argued, women needed to break the shackles restraining their freedom, shackles imposed by society's patriarchal value system. For these women, divorce was one way to achieve these ends.

In the intervening years, the controversy over the impact of divorce on children has become exceedingly complex. Today, some liberals criticize any research that shows children to be worse off from divorce (and criticize the researchers for even undertaking a fundamentally conservative effort). According to Elizabeth Scott, a law professor in Virginia, "Scientists who report harmful effects of divorce on children are branded by other researchers as conservatives whose agenda is to promote traditional marriage." Even worse, she reports that "researchers who compare outcomes for children in different family forms find themselves the targets of harsh criticism by colleagues who challenge the legitimacy of such inquiry."[9]

This happened in an interesting way to Judith Wallerstein, whose book *The Unexpected Legacy of Divorce,* published in 2000, reached the unremarkable conclusion, based on empirical research, that some children may be better off by remaining in a "good enough" marriage.[10] There are, to be sure, some flaws in her methodology. The children Wallerstein studied were all white and from middle-class backgrounds, and they were all recruited from a mental health clinic. Some have argued that her sample was not representative. In addition, she did not use a control group in her study, making it impossible to isolate the effect that divorce may have had on the children. She has also been criticized because her primary expertise is as a clinician, not as a researcher.

And yet it is difficult to suggest that her conclusions are unreasonable, or even anti-feminist. Some women make the difficult decision to divorce in part because they have been persuaded that their children will be better off if they end an unhappy marriage. To these women, Wallerstein's study may offer a new perspective.

Parents should and generally do consider the likely impact of divorce on their children before choosing to end their marriage. Most divorce despite the pain they expect their children to experience. They are not under any illusion that divorce is "good" for their children.

Nevertheless, some feminists were quick to attack Wallerstein. Katha Pollitt disputes Wallerstein's conclusions that children of divorce are harmed as a result of marital breakup. Pollitt points out that it was the very children of marriages that stayed together "for the sake of the children" (that is, this generation of adults) who did not want to subject either themselves or their children to an unhappy household. She argues that had Wallerstein studied children of marriages that remained intact in the 1950s only because law and social norms limited the possibility of divorce, Wallerstein would find countless adults who lament the conditions under which they were raised. Pollitt also wonders how to calculate the price we impose on children who must bear "the burden of knowing that one or both of your parents endured years of misery—for you."[11]

However controversial Wallerstein's work may be, most social scientists today agree that there is clear evidence that children from divorced families are worse off overall than children from two-parent families. One reason for this may be that most children after divorce live with their mothers and many single-parent homes headed by women continue to be poorer than two-parent households or households headed by men. But even if we concede that many children suffer emotionally or financially because their parents divorced, we can be certain there are children whose lives have been improved because their parents divorced.[12] Moreover, researchers will never be very good at telling parents what the impact of divorce will be on their children.

Fine-tuning this inquiry, one researcher suggests that children whose parents divorce after a very stressful relationship may suffer less than children whose parents were in a more benign relationship. Paul Amato hypothesizes that when the parents are not fighting regularly, "the separation is likely to be an unexpected and inexplicable event. Most children will not see it coming."[13] In addition, he advances the claim that unless the children have been exposed to the ugliness of the relationship, they may come to regard marriages as relationships that are dissolved for trivial or insignificant reasons.

Counterintuitively, this research suggests that it is better to expose children to conflicts in a relationship so that they come to see that the decision to end it, if such a decision is made, is at least rational. Few parents would agree with this. At a minimum, it hints that, unless children are able to see the need for the massive disruption divorce exacts, there may be trouble in their future.

One of the difficulties whenever conservatives and liberals argue over lifestyle changes is that each side sincerely believes they care more about children and that the worldview they seek to advance is better for children. Each side tends to disbelieve the other's sincerity. Feminists, for example, are concerned about conservatives' hidden agenda: conservatives focus on children's interests because it is politically safer than discussing the role of women in the home.

But feminists are also concerned that any emphasis on the negative results of divorce on children in single-parent households threatens the legitimacy of such families. It is more than easy divorce that is at stake. It is the freedom to form a nontraditional family.

Some find the conservatives' concern for the welfare of children difficult to take seriously. Conservatives are historically unwilling to use government resources to help children of single parents. Their opposition to universal health-care coverage for children or to state-subsidized child care for children from low-income families, for example, may ultimately be reconcilable with their professed interest in the best interests of children, but it is easy to appreciate why many are deeply skeptical about their invocation of children's interests in the battle over divorce. As Katha Pollitt believes, "The real aim of conservative divorce reform is to enforce a narrow and moralistic vision of marriage."

In sum, there is little hard evidence one way or the other about whether children in troubled families are better off after divorce. We might posit, as some have done, that children are better off when their parents remain married if the parents are able to live together civilly and their marriages are subjectively "good enough."[14] This may be true even if feminists complain that this observation tends to encourage women to sacrifice themselves for their children and to remain in relationships that are not personally fulfilling. But it also seems self-evident that children are not better off living in a society that compels parents to remain together even when the parents act uncivilly to each other. In between these two poles, the waters are murky.

In all events, the barriers to returning to the era of fault grounds for divorce appear insuperable. For one thing, under American laws, the lowest common denominator prevails. If any state chose to maintain a no-fault divorce statute (Nevada was the first state to have such a statute), then it would always be possible for a married person to obtain a divorce in that state by going there and remaining long enough to comply with residency requirements. Because of full faith and credit requirements of the federal Constitution, a valid divorce obtained in the easiest state must be honored in all states.

In addition, American values of limiting government interference in familial affairs also make it unlikely that our laws would become increasingly restrictive anytime soon. Here, liberals gain some support from conservatives. Though there are social conservatives who want to make divorce more difficult, there are other conservatives and libertarians disinclined to support efforts to empower government to force people to remain married.

Perhaps sound public policy would require a waiting period combined with educational sessions that would provide parents with more information about the impact of divorce on children. Although many oppose mandatory educational programs for women seeking an abortion because those programs are poorly disguised efforts to persuade women from terminating their pregnancy, efforts to educate parents about the likely impact of divorce on their children may be received rather differently.

Whatever the most sensible policy with respect to familial dissolution, it is also important to appreciate what is ignored when we consider this issue only in terms of its impact on children. We run the risk of overlooking the benefits to adults and to society that easing divorces may have wrought.

It is important to appreciate that women are not the only beneficiaries of these changes. Men benefit, too, to the extent that gendered roles constrained them from engaging in practices that a more egalitarian society regards as appropriate. For one thing, American society perceives the role of fathers vastly differently from a generation ago. American fathers today are far more likely to be more involved in the day-to-day affairs of their children (at least if they are married), even if they remain less involved than the mother. These changes contribute to a world where roles are divided less and less by gender (even though significant inequality remains). Men, women, and children benefit as members of a society in which women are contributing fully as equal participants; their talents and contributions help all members of society.

We must not forget, however, that being a child is but one stage of a long life that includes adulthood. There is nothing wrong with asking what impact liberal divorce laws have on children during their childhood. But it is also proper to consider the impact of liberal divorce laws on these same children throughout their lives, even after they grow up.

Think of how different it is to live in a society in which boys and girls are equally entitled to participate as adults. These are benefits we sometimes ignore when we focus exclusively on the impact societal changes have on children. Children will, soon enough, grow up and become the beneficiaries of these changes. If we freeze social conditions on the grounds that children are better off by keeping things as they are, we are holding adults captive to the perceived current needs of children. Moreover, we are depriving those same children of the benefits of the proposed changes once they grow out of childhood—which is to say for the majority of their lives.

Children's interests have been brought into play not only when discussing the grounds for dissolving marital relationships. They are also featured prominently once the adult relationship ends.

Who Gets to Keep the Child?

Perhaps the best-known type of legal proceeding involving children is the child custody dispute between parents after their relationship has ended. Each year hundreds of thousands of these disputes are filed in local state courts. The industry servicing these disputes is thriving, generating more than several billion dollars of income annually.

In the previous chapters, adults without parental rights were pitted against a parent for the right to some of the control over their children. In Chapter 3, the dispute was between would-be adoptive parents and biological fathers. In Chapter 4, it was between grandparents or unofficially recognized co-parents and parents. In Chapters 6 and 7 it will be between state officials and parents. This chapter considers something seemingly related but dramatically different. It considers custody and visitation disputes between legally recognized parents. These disputes most commonly arise after married parents separate or divorce. But the parents may never have married, so long as the dispute is between legally recognized biological or adoptive parents.

What distinguishes the cases in this chapter from the others is that both disputants already possess full parental rights with all of the constitutional protections described in Chapter 2. These cases get to court only because the parents are unable to resolve their differences about the upbringing of their children. The state neither requires that the dispute be brought to court in the first place nor, once in court, that it be decided by the court itself. The parties are entirely free to resolve their dispute at any time by whatever private means they should choose.

Most of the other cases we have already considered are also characterized by a preference for private resolution of familial disputes. Thus, grandparents (like other nonparents) and parents are free to set up whatever visitation arrangements they wish among themselves; indeed, this is what happens in millions of families every day. But when a grandparent and parent disagree, the grandparent's only legal remedy is to sue. The parent need not do anything to resolve the disagreement. Unless a court intervenes, the parent's choice overrules any other arrangement. For this reason, the party bringing the suit will usually be the nonparent. And when the case gets to court, the nonparent must carry the burden of proving an entitlement to sue and to win. But in the parent-parent dispute, it generally will not matter who is bringing the action and who is defending it. At least the first time the dispute is in court, both parties stand equally before the court with neither having a superior right to custody or visitation over the other parent.

I wish to demonstrate here that child custody cases are not really about children; they are about adults. What is especially interesting, however, is the extraordinary length to which adults go to deny this plain truth. Ask any professional associated with child custody disputes and the one thing he or she is sure to emphasize is that their only purpose is to resolve the dispute "in the best interests of the child." As I hope to make clear, this is not simply false, it succeeds as a coverup to hide the degree to which these disputes serve adults' interests.

But this is nothing new. The history of child custody disputes is the story of adults using the language of children and their rights to gain something for themselves. American law in the colonial days was based exclusively on English law. At the time the United States was founded, consistent with English common law, men had all of the power within the family. Everything within the family belonged to them, including wives and children. When marriages ended, women had virtually no right to their children's custody over the father's objection. In most jurisdictions, the law granted fathers a presumption that they should have the custody of their children if a dispute ever arose between a father and a mother.

For much of the nineteenth century, in many parts of the United States men continued to rule over women in virtually all aspects of familial power. For a variety of reasons, American courts in the nineteenth century began softening the rule that fathers invariably won custody after the breakup of a marriage. How were women to achieve some measure of control without rights? In an environment in which women were barred from holding public office and even from voting, it would hardly be persuasive for women to argue that they should be regarded as having equal rights to men. Women realized they could achieve a dramatic shift in the power balance nonetheless by focusing on children instead of themselves.

As a consequence, beginning in the early part of the nineteenth century, courts in a number of states shifted their focus to a new, thoroughly modern child custody standard—"the best interests of the child"—as the means by which to award custody to a mother over the father's objection.[15] This shift away from fathers' rights was, however, very gradual. As late as the 1880s, in many states men continued to enjoy a presumptive right to their children's custody. In 1883, for example, the North Carolina Supreme Court first changed the rule of fathers' rights in custody disputes. It did so by focusing on children, not women. In justifying this change of focus, the court stressed that numerous courts were moving away from notions of "strict legal rights of parents" and "look more to the interests" of children, making them "their paramount consideration."[16]

Michael Grossberg reports that this shift from parents' rights to children's interests had come so far by the end of the nineteenth century that a 1899 treatise on child custody explained "no one is entitled to the possession (of a child) as a matter of mere right or claim. The welfare and happiness of the child itself constitutes the paramount consideration in the determination of controversies affecting its custody."[17]

However much this effort to shift the focus to children might mask the real meaning of the struggle between men and women over custodial rights, the struggle was manifest. Even as early as the end of the nineteenth century, some feminists began taking off the mask of child-focused arguments, blatantly demanding "that the legislature give mothers a superior right to their children."[18] A number of early feminists comfortably argued that "women were the more fit, and more deserving, parent" because they possessed "special nurturing qualities that made them the better caregiver."[19]

Even this argument would be incoherent, however, until the question before courts in contested custody disputes had been switched from a father's to a child's right. Women needed the notion of children's rights to become prominent in order to have any hope of changing the rules to their favor. This is not meant as any criticism of their efforts. Rather, it is to help make evident the value of this shift to the adults most interested in benefiting from a change in the law.

This reasoning captured the day. By the end of the nineteenth century, courts in most states used a fairly straightforward presumption by which they awarded custody after the breakup of a marriage. Under the "tender years doctrine," mothers were presumed to be the more capable nurturer of young children and, for that reason, custody of young children (up to the age of ten) was presumptively to be given to them. Fathers would be able to obtain custody of children beyond their "tender years" in either of two ways. If the children were older than ten when the divorce occurred, courts would award fathers custody of those children. If the mothers originally obtained custody of younger children, fathers had the right to obtain custody once the children reached the appropriate older age.

In the first decades of the twentieth century, legislatures began participating in developing the rules for child custody dispute resolution. Many states enacted statutes to guide courts in how to decide these cases. Although significant variations existed, the tender years doctrine gradually came to be the principal basis upon which courts decided custody cases. But the upper age limit for including children within the category of tender years also increased. Mothers were winning custody decisions in the vast majority of cases regardless of the child's age. A wave of progressive reform during the early 1900s ended in the 1930s with most states granting mothers custody rights.[20]

By the second decade of the twentieth century, not only had the rules by which child custody cases were decided been altered, the results of custody disputes had become almost as predictable as those a hundred years before. This time, mothers were awarded custody almost routinely.

By the early 1970s, gender politics had shifted and men were able to demand equal rights at home. A father's rights movement had begun.[21] Taking full advantage of feminist rhetoric that gender roles were cultural constructs that should no longer be taken seriously, men complained that they were systematically disadvantaged in custody disputes, based on lagging gender stereotyping of women as better nurturers.

It became increasingly difficult politically for women to disagree. Indeed, the women's rights movement won a significant victory in 1971 when the Supreme Court ruled that gender-based laws would be declared unconstitutional if they were based merely on "archaic and overbroad generalizations" about the differences between men and women.[22]

As the feminist movement made greater gains, it also had to become more sophisticated. Many women recognized the cost to feminism exacted by a societal rule that presumes young children need mothers more than they need fathers. Although women obviously benefit from judicial reasoning of the sort employed in an Alabama court in the 1850s: "It is safe to presume . . . that a mother . . . would be more careful of the moral, intellectual, and physical well-being of her children than any other person in the world,"[23] the other side of that coin is Justice Bradley's famous reasoning in *Bradwell v. Illinois* in 1873 in support of the Court's decision upholding the legality of an Illinois law that barred women from becoming lawyers. According to Bradley, "the civil law, as well as nature herself, has always recognized a wide difference in the respective spheres and destinies of man and woman. Man is, or should be, woman's protector and defender. The natural and proper timidity and delicacy which belongs to the female sex evidently unfits it for many of the occupations of civil life."[24]

Arguments by women that suggested they "belonged" at home raising children, of course, provided an ideal basis for practices that preferred men over women in the work place and that generally structured society around the principle that women are "naturally" better at raising children than men. Men seeking to maintain advantages over women outside of the home were delighted to quote women as their strongest supporters.

Some feminists quickly came to appreciate that in the gender politics of the second half of the twentieth century, their own rhetoric had to become strictly gender neutral if they did not wish to end up losing more in the larger war with men than they might gain in the particular battle of child custody. What some women did not want was to risk intellectual capital in the larger arena of gender fights by continuing to rely on gender in the custody arena.

Not all feminists agreed with the strategy. Mary Becker, among a number of other writers, has argued that women had more to lose by accepting the claim that men and women were equal when it came to childrearing.[25] For most, however, gender neutrality became the mantra of the day. And, of course, men had no choice but to allow this to happen. If they argued that women are "naturally" better caregivers, they might gain something in the larger war, but they would be conceding the individual custody battle to women.

By the mid 1970s, a focus on women's superiority as caregivers would either come from women or not come at all. For the most part, women abandoned the claim.[26] This meant that the tender years presumption simply could not survive. Even though as late as 1976 in more than thirty states the mother was awarded custody of her young children, so long as she was fit,[27] the tender years doctrine was rapidly replaced by gender-neutral rules.

Feminists next asked what gender-neutral standard could act as a substitute, making it likely that women still would be awarded custody? One possibility was the "best interests of the child" standard. But best interests contained risks for women. As we have seen in several previous chapters, cases decided on a child's best interests offer judges the leeway to decide cases based on their own personal standards. Such courts could not be depended upon to award custody to women. Many feminists began to see a backlash to feminism being played out in the form of a fathers' rights counterattack.

However many gains women had made by the 1970s, they remained a distinct minority in the legal profession and, particularly, in the ranks of judges. Women's rights were therefore at great risk when predominantly male judges were authorized to decide custody cases on the virtually boundless grounds of furthering a child's best interests.

In the 1970s, in the immediate aftermath of the demise of the tender years presumption, women began losing more custody cases than at any time in the century. By this time, more women were working outside of the home than ever before. Men were remarrying early after breakups and had the upper hand in divorce fights if their new wife was willing to be the homemaker. The now-single working mother was disfavored in custody battles.

To feminists, of course, this was unacceptable. Women were poorer than men for cultural reasons. Men were paid more by employers because they were the perceived breadwinners. Men were in the paying professions longer and fared much better than women there. Now they were rewarded and women were punished simply because women needed to work.[28] Women needed an alternative that increased their odds.

But men, now active soldiers in this "gender war," also scrambled for an alternative upon which courts would decide contested custody disputes that favored them.[29] The trick for both sexes was to identify a standard that appeared to be gender neutral but that tended nonetheless to advantage one side over the other. Three new standards, in particular, were tried: joint custody, primary caretaker, and approximation.

Men initially led the movement for joint custody.[30] It was obvious what they had to gain from such a standard. But, in the beginning at least, women saw something good in it as well. Joint custody, as an ideal, might help considerably in eliminating gender roles that tended to keep women in nurturing roles and in low-income positions. Many feminists would have gladly agreed to equalize parenting roles in exchange for meaningful gender equality outside of the home. Joint custody had the potential to make it easier for women to join the workforce. Men would now be helping with childcare responsibilities, and women would be equally remunerated in the workplace. With support from both men and women, joint custody gained a foothold in the 1970s as the presumptive result in contested cases.

Joint custody suddenly became the preferred standard in a number of jurisdictions. California, in particular, advanced joint custody as the ideal means by which custody cases would be resolved and enacted the nation's first joint custody statute in 1980. California was the national leader in seeking to obtain cooperation between the separating parents and continues to advance mediation as the ideal means by which to settle differences between the parties (even requiring a couple to use divorce mediation before being allowed to obtain a judicial hearing).[31]

The idea behind joint custody is that everybody wins, including children. In practice, however, joint custody has not held up very well. Unsurprisingly, joint custody works best when the adults are equally committed to ensuring that all do well by it. But the problems that led the adults to break up their relationship in the first place commonly continue to spoil the anticipated benefits of joint custody.

It was not too long before joint custody was harshly criticized by women's advocates on several grounds. First, they objected that a presumed result of joint custody gave far too much power to fathers who were not seriously interested in having custody after divorce, but who used it as a bargaining chip in settlements.[32] When men first began fighting for custody, many did so in order to put pressure on mothers to accept smaller financial payments after the divorce. At the time, custody, child support, and financial maintenance provisions were linked, making it relatively easy for a father to place custody prominently on the bargaining table along with all monetary issues. Today, virtually all states have uncoupled custody from support and require the noncustodial parent to pay a nonnegotiable percentage of income as child support. But in the 1970s and 1980s, men gained significant bargaining leverage merely by hinting that they would seek custody.

Wholly apart from this bargaining advantage, however, many women's advocates realized that joint custody was not substantially contributing to real gains for women in the workplace. Although men were clearly benefiting from joint custody, the benefits to women were less obvious, and possibly entirely unrelated to the new custody rules.

Most of all, however, many women strongly disliked joint custody as the presumptively best outcome because it meant that men who did relatively little to help raise children during the marriage were suddenly being treated equally with mothers who had been the primary caretakers. It just did not feel fair to women that mothers would get no reward for the sacrifice of childrearing. Treating mothers equally with fathers offended many women who had played a considerably greater role in parenting than had the father.[33]

Even some child-centered advocates argued that joint custody is bad for children because it is unfair for a child to live in two different homes.[34] Other children's rights supporters suggested that joint custody only works well when parents are capable of putting their child's interests ahead of their own conflicts, something that was not happening enough.

For all of theses reasons, joint custody soon fell out of favor as the presumptive result in most states. Even California, which in 1980 made joint custody the presumptive outcome, changed its mind by 1993. Currently, California presumes joint custody is appropriate only when both parents seek it.[35] Although many states continue to allow joint custody awards, few courts now presume that it should be the preferred result.[36]

Two other new standards have been advanced since the tender years presumption was abandoned. Both were proposed by feminists. The primary caretaker standard was briefly employed in West Virginia and Minnesota in the 1980s, with the support of the leading (feminist) family law academics.[37] No state formally uses this standard today. This standard virtually assured that mothers would win custody. Women candidly criticized joint custody as unfairly rewarding fathers who were "not the primary caretakers of the children."[38] The primary caretaker presumption was offered as a gender-neutral way to achieve the same result the maternal preference yielded. Its transparency was hard to miss. It was promulgated by interested parties who knew ahead of time who would benefit most by its use.

Particularly because of its winner-take-all quality, however, the primary caretaker presumption did not have great success. As a consequence, a closely related standard continues to have support among the leaders in family law. As expressed by Elizabeth Scott, "the law's goal should be to approximate, to the extent possible, the pre-divorce role of each parent in the child's life."[39] The significant difference between the primary caretaker and the approximation standard is that the latter does not result in all or nothing. Instead, parents continue to participate in the parenting relationship after the divorce at roughly the same level as before it.

The approximation standard was adopted by the American Law Institute (ALI) in 2002. But it should be unsurprising to know that many feminists like it, too. As with the primary caretaker standard, some men criticize the approximation standard as simply a device to ensure that women win custody.

Neither should it surprise readers that the defenders of the standard protest that their only purpose is to place children's interests ahead of parents and explicitly label as "a secondary objective . . . to achieve fairness between the parents."[40] To the charge that the parental approximation standard is merely a disguised means by which to award custody to mothers, the primary draftsperson of the ALI principles, Katherine Bartlett, protests that a "parent who obtains a greater share of custodial time because of a more extensive prior role as the caretaking parent does so not because of the court's gender bias but because of the parents' own past choices about the best way to care for the child."[41]

Supporters of the approximation standard will continue to seek to change the law in each state to create a presumption that courts should award custody after a divorce based on the relative amount of time the parents devoted to caregiving during the marriage. This presumption will be difficult to apply in many cases because of the challenge of ascribing relative caregiving responsibilities to many families in which both parents work and children are cared for by paid childcare providers. But these complications need not detain us.

What matters for us is that we can predict that more women will back the approximation presumption than men. Women will appreciate how they will gain if the presumption became law; men will understand how they will lose both leverage in negotiating a divorce settlement and the prospects of securing custody themselves.

Perhaps for these reasons, the prospects for the approximation standard becoming law in a majority of states are not very bright. Also for these reasons, however, the nearly universal standard throughout the United States has long been, and remains, the best interests of the child. We now turn to examine to what extent this plainly stated child-focused rule helps adults (and, most remarkably, harms children).

The Great Compromise: The Best Interests of the Child

In between these various rules, the one standard that has endured above all others over the past thirty years in the United States is the best interests of the child. Although no two states have precisely the same list of factors that courts are supposed to consider in determining best interests, all states use the standard for deciding contested custody disputes. Most schemes use a variation on the following four factors:

1. the interaction and interrelationship of the child with his parent or parents, his siblings, and any other person who may significantly affect the child's best interest;

2. the child's adjustment to his home, school, and community; and

3. the wishes of the child as to his custody;

4. the mental and physical health of all individuals involved.

These criteria can be extremely misleading. Courts rarely are informed how much weight to give to these factors. In many states, no one factor is given greater weight than another. Other states still retain a presumption of one kind or another, but nonetheless courts may consider other factors in determining the child's best interests. A common (rebuttable) presumption, for example, is that siblings should remain together.

Moreover, no list of criteria is exclusive. Courts may take virtually anything into consideration in making a custody determination. The extremely limited considerations courts may not include actually are restrictions imposed by public policy or constitutional limitations on state officials. Thus, the Supreme Court has held that a custody court in ascertaining the child's best interests may not consider the impact others may bring to bear on a white child whose white mother chose to live with a black man. In a 1984 decision, the Court ruled that community racial prejudice may not be considered by a judge even where the judge believes in good faith that the child may be better off avoiding such prejudice by living with the other parent.[42] The Constitution also places some restrictions on courts basing judgments on religious grounds.

The "best interests of the child" standard is popular not merely because of its gender neutrality, but because it purportedly puts the children's interests above those of adults. Adults ultimately settled on this standard as the end game of a major struggle among themselves. By itself, this strongly suggests that the standard was not designed with children in mind. That hardly gets to the bottom of it. There is less connection between the best interests standard and a child-centeredness policy than even this history suggests.

The best interests standard comes into play in an extremely limited context. Parents continue to have the power to avoid a best interests inquiry by agreeing between themselves what their post-divorce family will look like. In particular, parents are free to separate from each other without getting divorced and make any custody arrangement they wish. So long as their agreement does not endanger a child, no court has any power to question the agreement. This is true even when virtually no one who would be in a position to review the agreement would conclude that it serves the child's interests.

This is so in large measure because of the principle of parental rights described in Chapter 2. Parents are free to raise their children as they see fit, so long as they do not abuse or neglect them. Upon a breakup of the family unit, parents are entitled to agree between themselves who the primary caretaker will be. When parents agree how to raise their children, the state may not intervene. Even when they disagree, parents are arguing about issues in which the state has virtually no interest.

Parents are also free to choose the mechanism by which their disagreement will be resolved. As a result, parents (when they agree) remain in charge of their case at almost every step of their divorce until the court issues its order.[43] Just as parents may avoid the court initially by making whatever agreement about their children they wish (providing, of course, the agreement does not contemplate abuse), in many states they may also settle their disagreement at any time during the litigation if they so choose.[44]

Although, technically, courts have the residual power to disapprove divorce-related agreements, private settlements are routinely approved by courts in uncontested divorces. Even in the rare instance that a court rejects a settlement and imposes a child custody arrangement that neither parent wants, parents who agree among themselves need not enforce the order once they are out of court. In this basic sense, private ordering of the family remains the rule for intact families as well as for families that separate.

But perhaps the strongest proof that custody disputes are really about parental rights is how judges view them. It is a commonplace that judges agonize over child custody cases and consider these cases among the most difficult on their docket. In 2002, for example, one state supreme court justice had occasion to write in a child custody decision, "if one were to poll the judges of this state as to what type of case is the most difficult to decide, a substantial portion, if not all of them, would respond that it is in the area of child custody."[45] The Supreme Court of Alaska expressed the identical sentiment, calling "child custody determinations . . . among the most difficult in the law." One can pick up almost any book containing court decisions and find trial judges telling the reader how they "agonized in making this most difficult decision." A senior law professor recently wrote that "every judge" he ever interviewed "said that a child custody decision is the single most difficult" one they had to make.[46]

Think for a moment what it means to be judging a difficult case.

By definition, it would be one in which the judge cannot easily choose between the competing parties. "Easy" cases are those in which it is clear that one parent is inadequate or the other outstanding. So what are judges really telling us when they describe custody cases as agonizing? In an overwhelming percentage of child custody cases, judges are unable to determine to whom custody should be awarded.

If these cases were really about children, judges would experience very few cases as difficult and even fewer as truly agonizing. If these cases were about children and their best interests, judges would hardly agonize simply because they are unable to conclude that one parent was superior to the other. This would mean (if these cases were really about children) that the judge could not make a mistake. Cases in which judges cannot go wrong hardly make the list of the year's most troubling legal decisions.

Let's consider the opposite situation. Judges would have no reason to designate as difficult those cases in which it was clear that a child's best interests would be served by awarding custody to one of the parents. Judges have little difficulty entering orders when there is abundant evidence that no real alternative exists.

The *only* conditions under which a judge could feel agonized—if these cases were really about children—is when the judge believes neither parent is an adequate resource for the child, but the law gives the court no choice but to choose between two bad options. Fortunately, those cases are few. It is plain from reading judges' speeches and decisions that these extreme situations are not the only ones that give them difficulty, however.

Rather, judges are referring to cases in which both parents are obviously good enough to deserve to win, but one of them must be designated the loser. We can certainly sympathize with judges who have to make what often amounts to an arbitrary choice, realizing the real world costs to the losing party.

In a world in which the judge's purpose is to issue an order watching out exclusively for children, the troubling quality of arbitrariness would be nonexistent. In such a world, the judge would understand from the beginning that the child will be sent to live (at least primarily) with one of the competing parties. The judge would further know that his or her job is to enter an order that does not harm (ideally that best serves) the child. If, after hearing the evidence, the judge is comfortable concluding that the child will be (reasonably) well served by living with either parent, the judge should be content that in either case the child will be well served.

It may be that some of the discomfort judges experience is based on their sense that no matter what they do, children are suffering a loss. Regardless of how well a judge decides (and regardless of the fact that often both parents would be good caretakers), the child may be hurt by the parents' separation and sometimes by the poor handling of their separation. Judges, like friends of divorcing couples, may well find it difficult to see children hurt in such ways; and judges, like friends, may often feel helpless to prevent it. Not only do custody cases tend to bring out the worst in adults, but those harmed are far more sympathetic than the victims found in other sorts of cases. It is certainly unpleasant to see how badly people can treat their former life partners and to see their inability to put their children's interests over a desire to hurt the other parent.

Having said this, much of the judges' discomfort stems not from their concern for the children; it has to do with their concern for the parents. Parents demand (one might even say *need*) the opportunity to prove they have the right to be with their child, not that their child has the right to be with them. What bothers the judges is having to accept that their order will gravely hurt the losing parent. Anyone even remotely familiar with child custody litigation appreciates the emotional baggage they carry for the contesting adults.

These adults are fighting for the most important thing in their world. In the words of Lee Teitlebaum, "If there is one thing about which virtually everyone interested in divorce and custody would agree, it is that this process involves, and perhaps creates, the most deeply antagonistic relations suffered by humans in modern society."[47] Because of this, I do not mean to mock the sentiments of the judges who find these cases so difficult. They *are* difficult. But they are difficult because they are about adults fighting over something very precious to them. As Jon Elster explains, "the knowledge that the decision will have momentous importance for the parties directly involved and the recognition that it may not be possible to have a rational preference for one parent over the other . . . conspire to create a psychological tension in decision makers that many will be unable to tolerate."[48]

It is against this backdrop that we are able to appraise the true significance of the best interests standard. We have seen how the standard represents a compromise in an ongoing fight between adults. The compromise works at many levels for adults. It provides useful cover for those uncomfortable with the possibility that their actions are harmful to their own children. It also allows judges and legislators to feel they are doing their part to advance children's well-being.

All the while, another set of adults gains by this, too. These are the professionals who service the multi-billion dollar custody and visitation industry. They are lawyers both for parents and, as we shall see, for children. They are also psychologists, psychiatrists, and other forensic experts who are hired to interview, investigate, provide written reports and recommendations, and testify in court proceedings. And they are mediators, lay counselors, and others who become involved with parents fighting over custody.

It should also be easy to see how transparent the whole business is and that these rules were not designed principally with the children in mind. The best interests standard solves various conflicts adults have with each other and allows adults to feel noble in their fight for children because they, along with the judge and other court personnel (if not their ex-spouse), are only pursuing the case in order to do what is best for their child.

Yet, a remarkable thing has happened along the way. A significant number of adults who ought to know better have taken far too seriously the importance of furthering a child's best interests through the complete investigation and resolution of custody disputes. Indeed, it is astonishing to observe how much the best interests and child-centered rhetoric is taken seriously by countless children's advocates. Thus, it is typical to read, as one highly influential family law scholar has written, that in custody and visitation cases,

"The parents' interests are to be ignored" because "all states expect courts to make the children's interests the sole focus of their attention."[49] This child-centered focus is touted both as a major change of emphasis and a wonderful new form of children's rights.

If this were all there is to it, perhaps this would be merely a problem of self-delusion. But what is most disturbing is the degree to which the best interests standard does not serve children. So much is said in praise of the standard that the pervasive problems it causes too commonly are ignored. Among these problems is that, paradoxically, by relying on such an indeterminate standard, parents are encouraged to litigate their dispute with their ex-partner. Since the best interests standard can be used to support virtually any result, parties cannot be certain who is most likely to win a contested custody dispute. As a result, in the years since the best interests standard has replaced the tender years presumption, custody cases have become exponentially more disputatious in many jurisdictions.

Unsurprisingly, child custody disputes were relatively rare when the parties knew that mothers would win custody almost every time. Fathers had little incentive to bother contesting the custody arrangement. In many jurisdictions today, by contrast, these disputes are among the ugliest and most expensive of all lawsuits. What purpose do they serve? The reasons given by mental health professionals include the notion that "The fight for a child may serve profound psychological needs in a parent, including the warding off of severe depression and other forms of pathological organization."[50] As a direct consequence of the ubiquity of the best interests standard, parents are encouraged to roll the dice and contest a custody case in court. Fathers may be said to be better off under the child's best interest standard, but it is considerably more difficult to make the case that children are.

But the child-centered rhetoric has contributed to even worse problems for children. Not only are there more contested cases, the cases are costlier and take longer to resolve. When the question before the court is what is best for children, judges tend to insist that all of the parties (including the children) be subject to a battery of tests, interviews, and evaluations by psychologists, psychiatrists, or trained court personnel. These cases cost much more than they did twenty years ago because of the proliferation of professionals.

Lawyers for Children

Perhaps the least necessary member of this new group of costly professionals is the lawyer for the child. The children's rights movement had its greatest victory in 1967 when the Supreme Court ruled that juveniles accused of being delinquent have a constitutional right to court-assigned counsel. In *In re Gault*'s wake, many writers have reasoned that the Constitution requires counsel for children in other types of legal proceedings as well. Indeed, some have even suggested that children have a constitutional right to counsel in all divorce-related custody cases.[51]

Every jurisdiction in the United States currently permits the judge to appoint a representative for the child in a custody proceeding. Moreover, lawyers are being used to represent children in divorce-related proceedings in ever-increasing numbers throughout the country. This is happening even though vast numbers of Americans are underrepresented in legal proceedings affecting their interests in other areas ranging from landlord-tenant disputes to child welfare. Today, in some jurisdictions, it is commonplace for middle-class and wealthy parents to walk into a courtroom and realize that their children are being represented by someone who is legally antagonistic to them.

Leading the call for children's lawyers in custody proceedings are children's rights advocates. Many of these stress that children have the moral right and ought to have the legal right to be heard about their own future. They commonly seek to ensure that the child's "voice" be included in the proceeding and that the child's viewpoint be advocated. Some even seek to ensure that the child's preference be a major (perhaps even dispositive) determinant in the ultimate custody decision.

Katherine Federle, for example, insists that among children's basic rights is the right to "empowerment."[52] Barbara Woodhouse also wants children's voices to be prominently considered in all custody cases and believes that the independent representation of children is essential to further children's rights. These advocates even rely on international law to support their position. Thus, the United Nations Convention on the Rights of the Child, originally promulgated in 1989, requires that "In all judicial or administrative proceedings affecting a child that is capable of forming his own views, an opportunity shall be provided for the views of the child to be heard, either directly or indirectly, through a representative, as a party to the proceedings."[53] Woodhouse condemns the United States' failure to ratify the Convention (the only country in the world to have failed to do so), in part because it has slowed efforts to ensure that children everywhere are represented in custody proceedings.[54]

Children's rights advocates greatly exaggerate the legal significance of a contested custody dispute. These advocates criticize a system that forces children to live with one of their parents even when they would prefer to live with the other (or when the other would better serve them). They ignore the obvious truth that children are forced to live with a parent whenever the parents mutually agree on which adult gets custody. After all, why make such a fuss to ensure that children's best interests are being served after a divorce? As we have seen, there is no requirement to ensure that children's best interests are being served *before* divorce. Children are forced to live with adults whose parenting skills are limited or even inadequate so long as the parenting remains above a minimum standard of fitness.

Forcing children to live with one of two fit parents without determining which parent is more fit (assuming for these purposes this is even possible to do) is not significantly different from forcing children to live with parents without making a preliminary determination of their fitness as parents. Why is it that we are so comfortable eschewing this inquiry before divorce, and yet so manifestly uncomfortable with the prospect of a court saying to divorcing parents that the court is neither capable of nor interested in determining which parent is better for the child?

We (properly) subordinate the interests of children when they are being raised by their parents before divorce (or when the adults are not contesting the terms of a divorce). Yet, some would allow the excuse of parents' disagreeing with each other to become the justification for placing the child's interests above their parents. If it *is* sensible to insist that children's interests come before their parents after a divorce one would expect a greater movement to try to put children's interests ahead of parents all of the time.

Such a goal, of course, is an unachievable fantasy. We are not at risk of this happening both because adults do not want it to happen and because we could not accomplish it even if we had the will. We can ensure that a judge's opinion about what is best for a child controls, but we cannot be confident that the judge's opinion is on the mark or superior to the parents. Recalling the real reason we ended up with the best interests standard, we need to clarify more precisely what it means.

The children's best interests is simply the method for resolving the dispute; it is a means for deciding the case, not a manifesto for children. Children have no say in whether their parents decide to terminate their relationship. Parents are free to end their relationship with each other without requiring them to take into account the impact of their decision on their children.[55] Even when the adults decide to end their relationship, only if parents cannot agree between themselves and go to court to settle their dispute do they delegate their legal decisionmaking power over their children to the state.

Yet advocates of separate counsel in custody proceedings argue that, even though the court is making the same decision that the parents could have made themselves without participation by the child and even though it is making that decision at the request of the parents, the child now has a right to be heard through counsel in the proceeding. The child's right to participate in the decision-making process and to have his or her preferences and interests consulted is triggered by whether the parents have been able to reach their own decision concerning custody.

It is far from clear that giving children a significant voice in these

disputes is a good thing. In the ordinary adult client-lawyer relationship, the client is the principal and the lawyer serves as his or
her agent. Clients set the objectives of the case and the lawyer's most
important task is to seek to secure the objective set by the client.
Lawyers, as counselors, also are expected to perform the important role of helping a client clarify the objectives that best serve the
client's interests. In performing that counseling role, however, lawyers are expected to help clients find their own answers. The central
purpose of the representation is to advance the client's autonomy.

For many reasons, we should not want children's lawyers in custody proceedings performing this role, despite the call for the child's
"empowerment" by some children's advocates. For one thing, such
a role would be inconsistent with the basis upon which the case itself is to be decided. Judges are expected to learn a child's preferences in order to factor them in when making the ultimate custody
determination. But no state wants the child's preferences to become
too significant a factor in the outcome. This is, in part, to prevent
children from becoming too entangled in the case (and suffer from
the cajoling and influencing that would surely take place if their
parents knew the child's preferences mattered too much). It is also
because we do not believe that children have the maturity or experience to make the best decision for themselves.

Custody proceedings are emotionally difficult, often involving a
mixture of feelings of rejection, guilt, pain, and anger. Placing children at the center of the dispute by informing them that their preference as to custody is the primary or even a central factor in deciding custody may make them feel the need to choose—and thereby
reject—one parent over the other.[56] Protecting children from being
forced to choose where to live may, in the long run, best serve the
interests of most children. When the child's preference will be accorded prominence by the child's lawyer, there is a danger that one
or both parents will be encouraged to attempt to influence the child.
When this occurs, children become pawns of a different order. It
rarely will serve children's best interests to have parents actively trying to persuade children to tell their lawyers that they want to live
with one parent rather than the other.[57]

Apart from giving children a "voice," children's rights advocates insist that children be represented separately because "without separate legal representation, the child's interests are left to the inadequate protection of parents and the court."[58] This reasoning stresses the potentially adverse effects of divorce on the child and the right of children, consistent with the basic meaning of the best interests standard, to focus the proceedings and its outcome exclusively on what is truly best for the child. This effort at isolating children's interests, however, ignores the complicated calculus involved in separating the interests of children from their parents. The few existing studies of children of divorce make clear the interdependency of children's interests and their parents'. Judith Wallerstein and others consistently show that unless one takes seriously the desires of the custodial parent, the child will likely lose. An unhappy parent frequently results in an unhappy child.[59]

If there are to be lawyers for children, there must be a clear definition of the lawyer's role. Remarkably, current law fails to provide any meaningful guidelines concerning the role of these lawyers. After lawyers were representing children in custody cases in Connecticut for more than twenty years, the best the Connecticut Supreme Court could muster when asked to clarify what is expected of these lawyers was "The legislature has not delineated, nor has this court yet been presented with the opportunity to delineate, the obligations and limitations of the role of counsel for a minor child. We recognize that representing a child creates practical problems for an attorney and that this important issue, at some point, needs to be addressed."[60] Connecticut is hardly alone in its unwillingness to clarify this role. Virtually no state has done so.

It would be inconceivable for the legal profession to call for lawyers for adults without having first identified the purpose and role of the lawyer. Much is revealed when a system sets loose a cadre of lawyers to represent children in the name of advancing children's rights without bothering to clarify the lawyer's role. It suggests that adults are primarily concerned with appearing to advance the interests of children (by providing them with representation). This ought not be confused with ensuring that children actually are well served in the process.

This complete lack of clarity of the role of lawyers for children means that lawyers are free to allow their child clients to set the objectives of the case to the extent the lawyers choose to do so. But it also means that lawyers for children in these proceedings are not required to seek the outcome the child would prefer. Although there are strong reasons to be wary of lawyers for children taking their marching orders from their clients in contested custody proceedings, there are even stronger reasons to oppose lawyers deciding for themselves what outcome best serves their clients' interests.

For most of my career, I have been a critic of the assumed value of providing counsel for children in custody proceedings. Time and again I have seen lawyers choosing for themselves what outcome to argue for on behalf of their child clients and gaining the advantage in the case for no other reason than that they became the recognized voice for the children's interests. Even when the judge knows full well that the position the children's lawyer is taking is really nothing more than the product of the lawyer's personal views, judges give considerable weight to that lawyer's position.[61] It seems that because the lawyer *chose* the position (as opposed to arguing for it because that is what the client wanted), the judge thinks it deserves greater consideration. A lawyer's life experiences, values, and biases surely influence the opinion he or she is advancing; regrettably, these biases are ignored by the courts.

Consider the case of a custody dispute in which the mother, a lesbian, wants to live with her lover and have custody of her two children, a six-year-old boy and a four-year-old girl. The court assigns an attorney to represent the children. The attorney meets with all parties, including his young clients, and is impressed by the children's father, who appears to be a fine, able, and concerned parent. The attorney concludes that custody should be awarded to the father and vigorously presses for this result in negotiations with the attorneys for each of the parents and in chambers with the judge; at trial, he critically cross-examines the mother while supportively cross-examining the father.

Now assume that a different attorney had been assigned to represent the same children. This attorney similarly meets with all parties, including the children. Impressed with the mother, she concludes that the children will be served best by having them remain in their mother's custody. The attorney vigorously presses for this result in negotiations with the attorneys for the individual parents, in chambers with the judge, and at trial in supportive cross-examination of the mother. Moreover, the attorney presents an expert witness of his own, allegedly "for the children," who testifies that exposing young children to homosexuality has no bearing whatsoever upon their sexual preferences.

It is highly probable that the outcome of this imagined case will depend on which position the child's attorney adopts. The judge may be impressed by the number of advocates supporting each parent's cause (two against one) or may believe that the particular outcome sought by the children's attorney is what the children themselves desire. Or the judge, viewing the attorney as the children's spokesperson, may simply defer to his or her "informed" judgment about what is best for the children.

For these reasons, the appointment of a lawyer for children in custody proceedings who is free to decide what position to advocate injects an unacceptable element of arbitrariness into the outcome. Which party wins in such cases will depend less on the factual and legal arguments made to the court than on the position taken by the child's lawyer. Furthermore, the more difficult a case is, the more probable it is that different lawyers would disagree on which result to seek. In the closest cases, the judge will be least certain of the best outcome and more likely to be tempted to rely on the children's lawyer's judgment. For every lawyer who would advocate a particular result in a close case, there will be a different lawyer who would urge the opposite outcome. In the end, it will be the child's attorney, and not the judge, who decides the case.

I have been involved in countless cases in which young children were represented by counsel. The one constant through these cases is the crucial need for the parent's attorney to win the support of the child's attorney to maximize the chances for success. This does not mean the child's lawyer's view always controls. But it is vitally important because it often can be devastating to a party's hopes for success if the child's lawyer proves to be a foe.

Children's advocates sometimes seek counsel for children in custody disputes to protect them from the travails of the litigation process itself. This is a laudable but ironic goal. It is certainly sensible to worry about the choices parents and their lawyers make when cases become deeply contentious. Anyone who has seen just how ugly contested divorces can become certainly understands that parents may lose their ability to think rationally about what is best for their children in the midst of battle.

For this reason, it is hardly irrational to favor providing children with legal representation to constrain the worst of the free-floating adversary system currently employed.[62] Lawyers performing this role should seek to speed up the proceedings and to ensure that the child is kept out of them to the greatest extent possible. This laudable purpose of protecting children in divorce cases is, however, more than a bit ironic. It is because of the best interests standard that children are being made ever more the focus of contested custody cases. Now, because of this focus, we find the need to provide children with special protective devices, such as their own lawyers, to protect them from the harm of bitterly contested cases. There is a simpler way to accomplish this. If we insisted that children be kept out of these cases in the first place, there would be no need for creating additional procedures to protect them.

It is useful to wonder why this is the only country in the world that even takes seriously the importance of providing three lawyers in a custody dispute. Perhaps it is because we have allowed adults to run wild in their efforts to win against their former partner. In a different culture—one in which there would be less need in the first place to speak in terms of children's rights—adults would never have reached the point where they would imagine they have the right to seek sole custody of a child born to two people. It would be inconceivable to atomize rights in this way and make us into individuals with rights separate from the intimate associations we have formed. In other cultures, certain commitments made would have lasting implications. Such a culture would be far less likely to have developed anything resembling the sophisticated notion of children's rights that has dominated American society over the past generation.

This hardly proves which culture honors children more. A society that truly cherishes children needs no prodding to do so. Nor is such a society likely to bother developing claims for children's rights.

Relocation

Reliance on the best interests standard has vastly increased the amount of litigation in still another way. Because the child's best interests are supposed to control parental decision-making even after the divorce is final, custodial parents in many states may not move away without the noncustodial parent's or a court's permission. This often means that parents who have primary or sole custody of children after a divorce are subject to an entire new round of costly litigation to justify their decision to move. Moreover, moves as short as fifty miles may lead to major court fights if they would "materially disrupt" the visitation schedule already established.

In some states, there is a presumption against such moves, requiring the parent who seeks to move to justify the plan. Other states presume that a custodial parent is entitled to move to another state. These states place the burden on the opposing parent to show why the move should be prohibited.[63] As recently as the mid-1990s, both New York and California were rather restrictive in allowing relocation requests. Both states tended to require the custodial parent to remain in town or forfeit custody. Each liberalized its rules in recent years.[64] Many states, however, continue to set a high standard before permitting relocations..[65]

In whose name are these relocation battles waged? The answer, for all familiar with this book, is plain: the children's best interests. As Connecticut's Supreme Court wrote in 1988, "At the heart of" all relocation disputes, "is the child, whose best interests must always be the court's paramount concern. Those interests do not necessarily coincide, however, with those of one or both parents."[66] Indiana's highest court similarly noted, "The child's welfare, not that of the parents, should be the primary concern of the trial court."[67] It is also typical to read the writings of academic family law scholars, who stress that the "focus" in all of these cases "is on the child's needs and the best way to meet the child's needs in light of the relocation."[68]

At the risk of overkill, let us count the ways in which these proceedings are anything but about children. We begin by noting the extremely limited conditions under which relocation cases may be litigated. Unless the custodial parent seeks to move away and take the child with him or her and the noncustodial parent chooses to litigate, the case does not even get to court. Custodial parents may move when the noncustodial parents do not try to bar the move.

More to the point, *noncustodial* parents may move and neither the custodial parent nor the child may complain. There is no such thing as a relocation cause of action by a custodial parent to prevent a noncustodial parent from moving out of state even though this happens innumerable times. Finally, custodial parents may move, regardless of the court order, if they choose to do so. At most, a court may order that the custodial parent must leave town without the child by transferring custody.

The subject is so confused that the only issue the court is supposed to consider—the best interests of the child—has nothing to do with the result. If it is not in the child's best interests for the custodial parent to move with the child (because the child will be unable to see the noncustodial parent regularly), then transferring custody of the child so that the current custodial parent will move without the child still leaves the child with only one parent in town. The former noncustodial parent is the obvious winner; the former custodial parent the obvious loser.

But the child? It is difficult to say anything about whether the child gained something. What we can say with certainty is that, to the extent the move was disallowed because it would reduce time the child would spend with one of his or her parents, that precise result is achieved anyway when the moving parent gives up custody.[69]

It may well be that many custodial parents give up on their plans to move when the court refuses to permit them to relocate with their child. When this is the outcome, it is clearer that the child gains something. But the law does not require the parent to choose to stay in town. When the parent leaves anyway, all of the words spoken about why the proposed move unfairly denies the child the opportunity to maintain a significant relationship with the noncustodial parent now are irrelevant.

None of this is to say that custodial parents ought to have unfettered control to move whenever they wish without any consideration for the impact on the noncustodial parent's rights. The unfortunate reality is that primary custodial parents have differing motives for relocating. Many are legitimate. But some are purely vindictive. When this is the case, the motivating purpose of moving is to punish the noncustodial parent. There is nothing wrong with allowing noncustodial parents an opportunity to challenge these vindictive moves.

But it would be a decided improvement to shed the rhetoric about children's rights and recognize that we are permitting these actions in the name of protecting a parent's rights (here, the noncustodial parent's visitation rights). We must also recognize that the noncustodial parent may be interested in thwarting the proposed move for legitimate or illegitimate reasons.

The American Law Institute has proposed creating a presumption in favor of allowing relocation without court involvement. This sensible proposal was designed to eliminate most relocation litigation. The ALI *Principles of the Law of Family Dissolution* seek to accomplish this by permitting custodial parents to relocate provided "that the relocation is for a valid purpose, pursued in good faith, and the new location is reasonable in light of the purpose."[70] Moreover, it is presumed that the move is reasonable if it is being made to pursue a significant employment or educational opportunity, to join a spouse who is moving for a similar reason, to be close to a significant family member, or even to improve significantly the family's quality of life.[71]

A Better Way?

In just one generation, we have gone from a culture that largely avoided custody fights to one that encourages them. In pursuit of ascertaining and furthering the child's best interests, custody and visitation disputes today have been allowed to become far too contentious, permitting litigants to go to unreasonable lengths to prove that awarding custody to them will further the child's best interests.

More than allowing adults to fight as hard as they want to secure custody of their child, the best interests standard ensures that parents need not apologize for appearing to be selfish when they make the fight as contentious as possible. Their perfect cover is that they are only doing it for the children.

If courts really care about children, they will begin to find ways to minimize the damage contested custody cases inflict on children. They would do well to recognize that their primary role is not to decide cases in a manner that best serves children. It borders on the impossible to isolate children's interests from their parents', particularly if a court issues an order that a custodial parent abhors. Courts are incapable of divining a child's best interests in any meaningful way that excludes the judge's own ideas about what is a good life.

Of course, divorcing parents often disagree about what is best for their children. Moreover, most parents would agree while their marriage is strong that consideration of the child's best interests should serve as one of the key principles in a custody dispute if their relationship were to end. Of course, most parents find it difficult to imagine that their child's interest will not correspond to their own. The motives typically involved in childrearing are a complex amalgam of self-serving and altruistic interests. On the whole this mix seems to be good for society. Certainly it is inescapable.

If, in the heat of custody disputes, parents are often more concerned about their self interest, a sensible societal goal is to set up rules when we are disinterested that will govern situations when we are unlikely to see things clearly. It is surely appropriate to develop rules that are designed to serve children's interests. The best interests standard, however, fails to accomplish this. Those who care about law serving children better should be concerned about continuing any standard that encourages protracted custody litigation.

If child custody disputes were really about what is best for children, society would do whatever it could to keep cases out of court. Even flipping coins has been seriously advanced as a means of resolving these disputes.[72] But proponents of the coin flip solution fail to consider its impact on bargaining.

Most child custody disputes are resolved without trial. This is undoubtedly because in many cases it is obvious to the parents which one should have primary custody after divorce. It is more than a matter of both parents agreeing on what makes the most sense for their children; it is also a shared understanding of what a neutral fact-finder would say after hearing the full story. Against the knowledge that courts will decide the dispute if parents are unable to do so, many parents choose to do the right thing in order to avoid wasteful litigation expenses.

But if the ultimate decisionmaker were a coin, many parents would see that their leverage is greatly increased. They could threaten the more worthy parent with utilizing the coin flip in order to extract concessions in the bargaining process. Adding arbitrariness to the process will almost certainly disadvantage parents whom all knowledgeable parties would agree should obtain child custody.

There are other ways to avoid trials. Those who care most about children's best interests should be advocating the abolition of the best interests standard. Substantive rules that favor one parent, such as the tender years presumption or the primary caretaker presumption, may help most children most of the time for the simple reason that most cases will be resolved without extended litigation.

Under the primary caretaker presumption, there is little incentive for the nonprimary caretaker to litigate because the rules are stacked against him or her. Unless the nonprimary caretaker can show that the primary caretaker is unfit, there would be nothing to litigate. It is, of course, true that the primary caretaker preference places too much emphasis on continuity of care when that is not the only criterion by which to determine a child's best interests. But that objection is misplaced. It is insufficient to complain that the primary caretaker rule does not guarantee serving a child's best interests. Policy makers cannot try to do the best thing for everyone. They must be more modest and try to do the least harm to the fewest. By this standard, the primary caretaker rule is quite powerful.

Another criticism of the primary caretaker rule is the potential impact it may have on the behavior of parents. One of the parents may decide not to work full-time so as to avoid the danger that, in the event of a divorce, he or she may lose custody. Moreover, the rule is not a panacea. It does not offer an obvious solution when both parents work or are away from the home an equal amount of time. It also does not avoid litigation when the substantive meaning of "primary" is enhanced by subjective factors, such as weighing the quality of interactions, as occurs in at least some jurisdictions.[73]

It may also be that this standard improperly assumes things about children's best interests. Children may, for example, do quite well if they are sent to live with the nonprimary caretaker. But for every child who would be better off if shifted from the primary to the secondary caretaker, there may be four or five children who will suffer needless harm by being subjected to a contested custody battle. The transactional costs of litigation simply are not worth the gains. Even if we knew there would be children who were better off being with the nonprimary caretaker, it is important to consider that even these children are saved from the trauma of litigation and uncertainty. In addition, litigation does not guarantee that courts will correctly identify those children who would be better off if ordered to live with the other parent. An unknown number of children who would be better off with their primary caretakers will erroneously be placed with the other parent, and vice versa.[74]

Even if it fails perfectly to state a rule for serving a child's best interests, the primary caretaker presumption at least avoids the need for contested custody cases. Those who must justify this result by focusing on children's interests need only emphasize that the costs associated with protracted litigation should be discounted from the potential benefit to be derived by awarding custody to the non-primary caretaker.

But the standard can be advanced just as forcefully without presuming anything about which outcome is best for children. It can be advanced to end the purported single-minded goal of furthering children's interests in the first place. Although there is some justification for presuming that parents who have separated and are unable to resolve disputes about their children will not act in their children's best interests, the modern solution of turning everything over to a judge and allowing the parties unlimited opportunity to present their case should not be continued. In deciding on the proper standard for resolving child custody disputes, we should assess how the various risks (including the risks of protracted litigation) would be allocated by various proposed rules. The questions raised in this chapter should be considered in such an assessment.

In the final analysis, almost *any* clearly defined rule is vastly superior to the open-ended best interests standard. Who would lose by fixed rules? Adults, not children. It is adults who are unwilling to be cut off from the possibility of trying to obtain custody of their children. Children are neither empowered nor advantaged by child custody cases. We would be far better off if we stopped deluding ourselves into thinking they are.

In the modern era, the family courts of this country operate on the unwarranted premise that judges are capable of making fine-tuned judgments about a child's best interests. While the underlying ideal and rhetoric are laudable, the unfortunate reality is that the enormous amounts of time, money, and emotional energy expended in contested custody proceedings often hurt both parents and children. For every case in which the outcome can truly be said to benefit a child, a far larger number are litigated for no good purpose. Preserving a system that produces protracted, costly custody litigation whenever parents are unwilling to resolve their custody disputes is in the best interests of a very small number of people, least of all children.

6

Child Protection, Foster Care, and Termination of Parental Rights

A man visits a small village late one evening. He notices a lot of activity on the street when he enters the town, but he is very tired from a long journey and takes a room in the only hotel. The next morning after breakfast he leaves the hotel and sees the same activity. He goes over to the scores of people working furiously near the stream that runs through the town. The townspeople are taking babies out of the stream as they pass by. They form a sort of assembly line with those at the front wading into the stream and picking up the babies as they float by and handing them to others who continue handing them off until they are wrapped and made warm and taken for more assistance. When the stranger asks someone what's happening, he is asked to join them in their efforts to save the babies. He quickly learns that the townspeople have been at this process of picking up babies at all hours of the day and night. They tell him they need his help and ask him to assist. When the stranger refuses, the townspeople become indignant.

"How can you refuse to help us in this crisis?" they ask. "Don't you have any compassion? Don't you care?"

The stranger answers quietly, but emphatically. "You can continue to pick up these babies all you like. But it strikes me that your efforts are, ultimately, inadequate. Obviously, somebody keeps putting those babies in the stream. I'm going to go upstream, find the source, and put an end to it once and for all."[1]

In Chapters 3 and 4, we considered attacks on the parental rights doctrine in several different contexts. This chapter examines its most formidable challenge: child welfare practice and policy. Child welfare policy, an enormously important subject in its own right, is particularly important within the focus of this book because it offers further insight into the influence of children's rights advocacy and rhetoric on national public policy.

"Child welfare," a technical term, sometimes also called "child protection," refers to governmental investigations of allegations of child abuse or neglect, the placement of children in foster care, and the termination of parental rights to make children eligible for adoption. Although the number of children and families affected by child welfare policy is quite large (considerably larger than most countries in the world), only a relatively small segment of American society is directly affected by the child welfare field.

For the most part, the children who are taken from parents and placed in foster care come from the poorest and least politically influential families in the country. They are also overwhelmingly minorities. For this reason, the issues discussed in the chapter are perhaps less well known than those in the previous chapters. Child welfare stories make headlines only when some tragedy occurs, such as when a foster child or a child "known to the system" dies. Fortunately, these events are rare. But their coverage greatly distorts the public's understanding of child welfare problems.

Generally, when a court declares a child neglected or abused, it may order that the child enter foster care for a specified time, usually a year at the start. When children are removed from their parent's care, the parents are expected to take steps to correct whatever problems led to the removal. If they fail to take these steps, the temporary removal may lead to permanent termination of parental rights. At the same time, except in the statistically rare circumstance of extreme or repeated abuse, foster care agencies are required by federal and state law to assist parents in overcoming the barriers to the successful and safe return of their children. This arrangement is at the heart of child welfare policy.

Agencies are also responsible for selecting the foster homes into which the children are placed and monitoring their placement to ensure the children's safety. The theoretical goal is for the child to remain in foster care for a maximum of a year or two. The foster parent–child relationship, viewed as temporary, is designed to provide children with the benefits of living in a family setting when placement outside of the child's original home is necessary.

The threat to the parental rights doctrine stemming from child welfare is obvious: child welfare law uniquely authorizes government officials to remove children from their parents' custody and even to sever permanently all legal ties between parents and children over the parents' objection. The power to remove children in order to protect them from harm is not precisely an exception to the parental rights doctrine. Instead, it is a long-accepted limit on parental rights. As we saw in Chapter 2, the Supreme Court recognized as early as 1944 that states act properly to protect children from harm, even when harm is inflicted upon them by their parents.

The power to terminate parental rights is less venerable, but it has become well-accepted that, in appropriate cases, states may sever all legal relationships between children and their birth families. In recent years, however, many have advocated a far more aggressive use of this extraordinary state power. In the 1990s, a bipartisan effort that included President Clinton and the Moral Majority supported legislation enacted by Congress in 1997 to make termination of parental rights and adoption a significantly more prominent goal of child welfare than it has ever been in our history.

What is of particular interest for the purposes of this chapter is how this change in emphasis in child welfare came to be, what the arguments for and against the policy are, and, most important, how children's rights have successfully been detached from parental rights so that the traditional parental rights doctrine as applied to poor American families is increasingly seen as anti-child.

A Supreme Court Case

Imagine being the single mother of six children—four girls and two boys. The girls are aged eight, seven, five, and four. There is a one-year-old and a newborn boy. You have always been a close-knit family. You struggled to provide a happy and healthy home for your family, and you've always been able to give them what they need, including a loving, warm family life. After the youngest was born, you experienced an unusually severe post-partum depression that left you with such low energy that you felt you were doing your children a disservice by not getting help in caring for them. However, you are quite poor and have no relatives nearby able to help you out. Through your church, you learned that the Department of Children's Services helps out families in these situations and your pastor suggested you get in touch with them.

When you met with a caseworker, you were informed that Children's Services only offers respite care in the form of foster care. To obtain foster care, you must sign a voluntary contract. The contract allows you the right to resume custody at any time you are fit to do so and spells out the agency's obligations to help you get back on your feet, requiring it to provide you with, among other things, medical assistance and counseling.

Throughout the period your children are in foster care, you visit them regularly. You love them deeply and cannot wait for the day you are all back together again. As you begin to feel like your old self, you start to press the agency for your children's return. The promises initially made by the agency fall a bit short in your estimation. Although the agency does not exactly oppose your request, it keeps stretching the time, ultimately recommending that you reunite with the children in stages.

Initially, the children were placed in three different foster homes. The two oldest, Cheryl and Patricia, were placed in one home; the younger girls, Cathy and Cindy, in a second; the boys, John and Bill, in a third. It is already in the second year of the placement when the agency finally returns the boys to you. At about the same time, the agency decides to move the younger girls into the same foster home as their other sisters.

You continue to visit with them, but you immediately detect that something is wrong. Almost from the beginning of their placement, the oldest girls started showing anger toward you. You wrote this off as a natural consequence of having placed them in foster care. In contrast, your relationship with your other four children was excellent. But after the younger girls move into the same home as their older sisters, all of the girls begin displaying a hostility and distance toward you. The agency notices this as well and starts to have its own concerns about the foster parents' influence on the children.

Two more years pass while you have custody of your sons and continue visiting with your daughters. During this time, you continue to pressure the agency to return all of the children to you. They keep putting you off. Your relationship with the girls continues to deteriorate. At some visits, none of the girls will even speak to you and only engage their brothers. Now the agency is also quite concerned and has concluded that the foster parents are undermining your relationship with your daughters.

After many futile efforts by the agency to get the foster parents to help build a better relationship between the children and you, the agency finally decides that it has no choice but to move the children out of the foster home. You are thrilled. At first, the agency plans to move the children to a new foster home. But when the case goes to court, the judge, after hearing all of the evidence, orders the agency to return the children to you immediately.

Thus far, this story, taken from a case that eventually reached the Supreme Court of the United States, could be merely one of many thousands heard every day in juvenile or family court in the United States. Currently, there are nearly 600,000 children in foster care. The overwhelming majority of these children are there temporarily and eventually will be returned to their parents. Sometimes, the children's return is accomplished in less than one year. Statistics show that when children are in foster care for longer than a year, the probability of eventual return to their families is reduced. Even for children in care for several years, however, a very large percentage still return home.

To return to our story, before the girls are reunited with you, attorneys for the New York Civil Liberties Union serve you with court papers signed by a federal district court judge enjoining the children's removal from foster care. After you meet with a lawyer, you learn that the NYCLU claims to represent both your daughters and their foster parents. You are also told that the NYCLU alleges in court that your daughters have a constitutional right to the protection of their "family"—by which they mean the foster parents with whom they have resided over the past several years. Suddenly you are in the midst of a major court battle pitting the rights of your children against your parental rights.

This case, a direct hit on the parental rights doctrine, turns some of that doctrine's most basic features onto itself. Foster parents who have raised foster children for more than one year claim a right to have *their* parent-child relationship constitutionally protected. The children, through their lawyers, claim a constitutional right to remain with their foster parents, who have become their "psychological parents." This case, filed in the 1970s, was decided by the Supreme Court in 1977. The NYCLU's strategy was simple. It sought to constitutionalize the Goldstein psychological parent theory that I have described in other chapters.

According to that theory, the *only* parent-child relationship that matters to children is the one they actually experience; it does not matter to children whether they are biologically related to the adults caring for them, because children only know their "psychological parents." Moreover, because it is vital to children's well-being to make child custody decisions within a child's sense of time, Goldstein, Freud, and Solnit's book advocates that, for very young children, their psychological parents should be given legal recognition as the adults entitled to continue raising the children after they have been in a parent-child relationship for one year. The book makes specific reference to foster families: "As the child responds to their emotional involvement and feels truly wanted, her foster parents become her psychological parents as well. Though they may be precluded from officially adopting her, they have become her parents as if by 'common law adoption'—a status that, we argue, deserves legal recognition."[2]

In this case, *Smith v. Organization of Foster Families for Equality and Reform (OFFER),* the NYCLU invoked the Constitution to attempt to protect all parentlike relationships children formed with adults that lasted for more than one year.[3] The particular remedy it sought was an order barring foster agencies from breaking up foster families that have lived together for more than one year except upon the same grounds agencies may use to disrupt birth families—to protect children from neglect or abuse. The injunction originally issued at the trial level prohibited agencies from removing children from foster homes even to return them to their birth families without conducting a hearing to determine that the removal was necessary. It doesn't take legal training to appreciate how radical this claim was or how devastating it would have been to the parental rights doctrine.

At the time the case was filed in federal court, I was an attorney with the American Civil Liberties Union, the parent organization of the New York affiliate, the NYCLU. I worked in the Juvenile Rights Project. The NYCLU case was filed by lawyers in its Children's Rights Project. But I was strongly opposed to the lawsuit and the legal propositions it sought to advance. I regarded the case as nothing less than a direct attack on what I held as among the most vital of civil liberties—the freedom of fit parents to raise their children when they were able to do so. The prosecution of the case deeply troubled me because I could not easily reconcile how the same organization (the ACLU) could have two projects, both devoted to advancing children's rights, in which one brought a case seeking to trample the core rights that the other championed.[4]

The story in this chapter, of course, is not the travails of civil liberties lawyers. Instead, it is the complicated, subtle, and too rarely considered battle within the legal profession for the right to wear the mantle of "children's rights advocate." In this particular battle, I thought I was the true children's rights advocate and the NYCLU lawyers were enemies of children's rights. For better or worse, within the legal profession, I lost that battle of monikers. For the rest of my career, I have had to accept the label "parents' rights lawyer" when I am asked to speak at conferences. The "children's rights advocates" have, at least in the field of child welfare, more often than not become spokespersons for positions antithetical to mine. This chapter is my effort to make sense of this phenomenon.

This case and the conflict surrounding it had a profound effect on my career, leading me down a path that has resulted in, among other things, this book. Ever since, I have been aware of the importance of capturing the children's rights mantle. What I realize now is that the NYCLU lawyers were like the townspeople saving the babies in the stream. But they had no interest in going upstream to find out why or how so many babies ended up in such cold water. I agree with the visiting stranger who believed it is more important to shift the focus to the conditions upstream. As we consider the issues in child welfare in this chapter, it will be useful to bear in mind the degree to which the children's rights rhetoric limits discussion by narrowing its focus to the babies in the water. Before looking at the Court's holding in *OFFER,* we should explore the broader subject of child welfare.

Child Welfare History—From Helping Families to Protecting Children

When the child welfare movement began in the United States during the late nineteenth century, it was broadly conceived; child protection was a small piece of a larger movement to rectify social ills for children. This larger movement was not to last. Instead, child welfare's purpose in the latter part of the twentieth century was dramatically narrowed to protecting children from harm inflicted upon them by their parents.

Although there has been a foster care system in place in the United States for well over 150 years, for much of that period—up to the 1970s–most children in foster care had been placed there by parents who were temporarily unable to care for them. Before then, very few foster care placements resulted from formal charges of unfitness brought against parents in civil legal proceedings. Formal coercive state intervention to protect children from harm was left largely to the criminal legal system through prosecution for such criminal acts as homicide, assault, and endangering the welfare of a minor.

Beginning in the 1830s, almshouses were built for the poor, the insane, and orphans. By the middle of the nineteenth century, children comprised approximately 40 percent of the almshouse population; at roughly the same time, public sentiment soured toward the use of almshouses. As a consequence, New York's legislature recommended the "removal of children from poorhouses and their placement in orphanages and similar institutions for special care." Throughout the 1860s and 1870s, towns and counties began contracting with private orphanages to receive and provide for children with public money. This system of placing children in state-subsidized private agencies became the standard practice within a few years.

The few entities paying attention to children's well-being in the United States were private associations, which were commonly affiliated with religious organizations. In 1877, New York was the site of the formation of the country's first Society for the Prevention of Cruelty to Children. Once such organizations were formed, states passed laws to protect children by giving the organizations the legal authority to place children on farms and away from their parents. Many thousands of children were sent from eastern states to states out West on what became known as "orphan trains," even though many of the children were not orphans. They were, instead, mostly children of Catholic recent immigrants, sent away by wealthy, Protestant "child savers."[5] Not until the twentieth century were specialized juvenile courts formed in the United States. With these courts, legal authority to remove children from homes was transferred from the private organizations to the courts.

Outside of child labor protections, the federal government's first venture into the child welfare arena was in 1935 when it enacted the Social Security Act. Through the early 1970s, federal child welfare policy was limited to providing cash benefits to needy families through programs such as Social Security and Aid to Dependent Children, including payments to families of children in foster care. Lawmakers did not perceive families as dangerous or harmful to children's well-being, so until the 1970s there were no official mechanisms to investigate allegations of child abuse. Neither child abuse nor neglect, at least as these terms have come to be understood in the United States, were regarded as serious social issues requiring public attention. Policymakers believed they had taken sufficient action to protect children by creating schemes to distribute income, food stamps, and publicly financed medicine to poor families and to families with single mothers.

Underpinning this laissez-faire policy in child welfare were two important conceptions about families in the United States. First was the parental rights doctrine: that the rights to raise children and to live within a family unit free from government oversight and regulation numbered among the core freedoms of Americans. Second was the general sense that all was well within families and that there was no need for aggressive oversight of childrearing practices.

Although today the constitutional principles supporting familial privacy remain quite vibrant in American law and culture, a dramatic change has occurred with respect to society's sense of a child's safety in his or her own home. This perception began to change in the 1960s; in that decade, medical professionals focused public attention on evidence that many physical injuries to children were apparently inflicted by parents. The medical profession labeled the pattern of unexplained physical injuries, such as multiple burns or broken bones that were inflicted on children by their caregivers, as "battered child syndrome." Doctors revealed the possibility that parents were capable both of injuring their children and falsely explaining these injuries as accidents in the home.[6] As concern for this condition increased, so did policymakers' sensitivity that children may be at risk of serious harm at the hands of family members. For the first time, child abuse became an issue of national significance.

Also during this time, the burgeoning children's rights movement encouraged policymakers to focus on the separate human rights of children to be raised in safety, even if that meant separating them from their birth families. This fueled, and was fueled by, a nascent societal consensus that children were independent persons with rights of their own, even when enforcement of those rights came at the expense of their parents.

Until this moment in time, child protection policy was a hodgepodge of various practices across the fifty states. Beginning in the 1970s and accelerating through the present day, federal law has become the dominant influence in shaping child welfare practice. By attaching conditions to the receipt of considerable federal dollars that paid for the out-of-home placement of children, Congress has been able to persuade every state to conform its child welfare laws with federal law.

It is important to understand the political forces that were at work during the 1970s—the crucial period of congressional attention to child welfare. Many Americans saw the 1960s as an opportunity to invoke the power of government to redistribute wealth and ameliorate the effects of poverty. President Lyndon Johnson, riding the wave of the civil rights movement, declared the War on Poverty as part of his Great Society crusade.

In 1967, child welfare and poverty were linked when Congress subsumed child welfare within the Aid to Families with Dependent Children (AFDC) program rather than continuing to consider it part of the Social Security Act.[7] AFDC was, by far, the largest program used to provide money for poor families.

After the election of Richard Nixon in 1968 and the prompt collapse of the War on Poverty agenda, however, poverty programs were viewed increasingly as providing tax money for poor minorities. As a result, public support for such programs eroded.[8] Conservatives were able to suggest in public debate that liberal anti-poverty legislation had exacerbated the problems of the poor.[9] Fearing that their influence in national politics was on the wane as the country seemed poised to reject poverty programs, liberals seeking to ameliorate conditions of poverty needed a new strategy to secure bipartisan support for government spending toward that end.

Chiefly through the work of Senator Walter Mondale, the new strategy found its home in the field of child abuse and protection. Mondale led the legislative effort that resulted in the passage of the Child Abuse Prevention and Treatment Act (CAPTA) in 1974. CAPTA directed a significant amount of federal money to states to fund efforts to protect children from harm. As part of a conscious plan to prevent the proposal from being viewed as a disguised poverty program, Mondale emphasized that child abuse was a "national" problem, not a "poverty problem."[10]

Stressing that child abuse affected families of all classes and that federal money would help children who were both rich and poor, Mondale won support for the proposal from politicians across party lines. Ever since, much of the public debate has ignored or understated the evidence suggesting a correlation between abuse and neglect on the one hand and poverty on the other. Indeed, a remarkable characteristic of the growth of support for child protection in the United States has been built on the claim that middle-class and upper-class children are in need of protective legislation just as much as poor children.

The consequences of this strategy have been profound. In recent years, most observers have come to see child abuse and neglect primarily as a defect in particular families, particularly those with limited or nonexistent societal roots. No longer a social problem, child welfare is conveniently defined as a matter of individual failure. Because the broader social conditions suffered by poor children who end up in foster care have been defined as outside of the proper boundaries of the subject matter, the most serious problems facing children in the United States—all related to poverty—are consistently being ignored. Any suggestion of broad systemic solutions that address poverty issues has been banned from the child welfare debate. Mondale's strategy, if you will, has resulted in frantic action on behalf of the babies in the foster care stream, with virtually no concern about why they are being put there in the first place.

The *OFFER* Decision

OFFER was decided by the Supreme Court in 1977. The Court agreed with the NYCLU that intimate relationships children form with adults are important, even when those relationships are outside of legal recognition. The Court specifically recognized that a meaningful familial relationship often "stems from the emotional attachments that derive from the intimacy of daily association." This is an important concession, because it advances the child-centered claim that legal recognition of a family should be based upon the child's experiences. The Court made clear it understood this claim well. In its words,

No one would seriously dispute that a deeply loving and interdependent relationship between an adult and a child in his or her care may exist even in the absence of blood relationship. At least where a child has been placed in foster care as an infant, has never known his natural parents, and has remained continuously for several years in the care of the same foster parents, it is natural that the foster family should hold the same place in the emotional life of the foster child, and fulfill the same socializing functions, as a natural family. For this reason, we cannot dismiss the foster family as a mere collection of unrelated individuals.

But, the Court stressed, two vitally important additional factors also need to be considered. The first concerns the circumstances under which the relationship was formed. The foster family was formed based on expectations that it would be temporary and could not, without the state's consent, be transformed into a permanent family that would gain protection against the state (or the parent). Rather than having its "origins entirely apart from the power of the State," the foster family "has its source in state law and contractual arrangements." For this reason, the Court said, it is appropriate to look to state law to ascertain "the expectations and entitlements of the parties." The Court noted, "Under New York law, the natural parent of a foster child in voluntary placement has an absolute right to the return of his child" provided the parent is fit. It also emphasized that the mother gave up her children to foster care "only on the express understanding that [they] would be returned" upon request.

The second, equally important, factor is that recognizing the foster family as a unit with legal protection would come at the direct expense of the birth family. On this point, the Court stressed that "ordinarily procedural protection may be afforded to a liberty interest of one person without derogating from the substantive liberty of another." In light of this, "It is one thing to say that individuals may acquire a liberty interest against arbitrary governmental interference in the family-like associations into which they have freely entered, even in the absence of biological connection or state-law recognition of the relationship. It is quite another to say that one may acquire such an interest in the face of another's constitution-ally recognized liberty interest that derives from blood relationship, state-law sanction, and basic human right[,] an interest the foster parent has recognized by contract from the outset."[11]

As a result, the Court ultimately rejected the claims the NYCLU brought on behalf of foster children and foster parents. It held that it is permissible for states to return foster children to their parents when their parents are able to take care of them. Many of those who call themselves children's rights advocates are harshly critical of the decision. George Russ condemns it as an example of "our courts and our social services systems routinely and mechanically remov[ing] children from long-term placements with persons they have come to believe and feel are their parents by considering only blood ties to identify their 'family' and thus return them to their 'rightful' parents." "Children," he laments, "are literally 'repossessed' by their biological parents in the same manner as though they were property, capable of ownership, without independent human rights of their own."[12] Of all areas of the law involving children, the children's rights rhetoric is voiced most strongly when it comes to protecting children from harm, particularly as a result of parental misconduct. One of the general themes of the children's rights movement, which becomes most pronounced in child welfare, is the liberation of children from the control of their parents.[13]

Child Welfare from 1980

Once the Supreme Court decided *OFFER*, the task of fixing America's foster care system remained principally in the legislative arena. In the late 1970s, Congress undertook a careful study of the foster care system and, in 1980, enacted a new law designed to change radically federal foster care policy. The study was conducted because of a widespread concern that children were spending too much time in foster care.

The hearings Congress conducted made clear that far too many children who could have safely stayed at home ended up in foster care. In addition, Congress found that in too many instances children remained in foster care for a much longer time than necessary. Even worse, Congress discovered that because of the payment methods Congress itself had authorized, federal law and policy were chiefly to blame for these problems. In particular, federal legislators became aware that although they authorized vast sums of money to states to help pay for out-of-home care for children, federal law offered virtually no money to states to help keep children safely in their own homes or to help reunify families after children were placed in foster care. The good news is that a problem Congress helped create was one it felt capable of fixing.

With this in mind, in 1980 Congress enacted the Adoption Assistance and Child Welfare Act, which changed the formula by which the federal government reimbursed states for child welfare expenditures.[14] Instead of creating financial incentives for out-of-home placements (by willingly paying for them above other services), the law stressed two new means of child welfare services. For the first time in history, Congress allocated money for services aimed at preventing the separation of children from their parents ("preventive services") and at speeding the return of children to their parents ("reunification services"). Furthermore, the Act required states to make "reasonable efforts" toward these same goals.

Unfortunately, the funds to achieve these reforms were never provided. Instead, "Under the Reagan Administration . . . [c]hild welfare services saw a virtual end to support for major demonstration programs, even though these represented a proven technology to facilitate permanency planning and reduce the number of children in foster care."[15] Out-of-home placement continued to be the principal child welfare policy in the United States through the 1980s. Between 1981 and 1983, federal foster care spending grew by more than 400 percent in real terms, while preventive and reunification spending grew by only 14 percent, and all other funds available for social services to the poor declined.[16]

As a consequence, foster care populations soared from 273,000 in 1986 to more than 429,000 in 1991.[17] Nationally, the median length of stay in foster care increased to over two years, and more children than ever experienced multiple placements. The use of crack cocaine by young mothers in the inner city led some to refer to the phenomenon as a "crack epidemic." There is little doubt that children entered foster care during the 1980s because of this problem and that some of these children would have needed to go into foster care even if preventive programs had been fully funded. But it is equally plain that the refusal of the Reagan administration to fund alternative child welfare is the predominant explanation for the growth in America's foster care population. Ironically, failing to invest in the less costly preventive services only resulted in increased government spending on foster care, which is vastly more expensive.

For more than forty years, the primary child welfare "service" the government has offered families is foster care. Numerous studies have found state efforts to keep families together to be inadequate. Three studies, in particular, document how the 1980 act was unsuccessful in reducing the number of placements. A 1987 study of foster care in New York conducted by the Child Welfare League of America found that, in 52 percent of the cases studied, the most pressing need was for daycare or babysitting, but the "service" offered most was foster care. In the same year, the National Council of Juvenile and Family Court Judges concluded that far too many judges "remain unaware of their obligation to determine if reasonable efforts to preserve families were made" and that those who are aware "routinely 'rubber stamp' assertions by social service agencies." In 1989, a third study concluded that courts made no "reasonable efforts" determination in 44 percent of cases.[18]

Thus, throughout the 1980s, researchers uniformly concluded: "treatment services for the parents of children in foster care are largely nonexistent. In fact, the child's placement usually results in a reduction in the level of services parents receive." Indeed, the 1980s can be characterized as a decade in which "the mood in society and government was turning increasingly skeptical toward social programs" and in which "expenditures for social programs were repeatedly cut."[19] These trends continued into the 1990s. The National Commission on Children came to the disturbing conclusion in 1991 that children were regularly removed from their families "prematurely or unnecessarily" because federal aid formulas give states "a strong financial incentive" to remove children rather than provide services to keep families together.[20]

It is worth stressing that Congress did not require the use of preventive and reunification services out of a sense of their duty to needy parents. These alternative services to foster care were designed to lessen government involvement. They were imposed because Congress believed that it is better for children to be with their parents, that it is less expensive to return children to their parents instead of keeping them as wards of the state, and that, if the state is to become directly involved in raising children, it ought to do so in the least intrusive manner. Many in Congress, liberal and conservative alike, preferred a minimal government role in helping to raise the children of needy parents.

This failure to implement meaningfully the "family preservation" requirements of the 1980 act is even more disturbing considering that experimental family preservation efforts initiated in the 1970s have shown real promise. For example, Alabama, California, Michigan, Minnesota, Oregon, Tennessee, Utah, and Washington, among other states, have undertaken numerous family preservation initiatives. Although the findings are mixed, these programs achieved reductions in the need for placement of children in foster care without any increase in rates of maltreatment. Despite this evidence, however, funding for these programs has ceased.[21]

The Adoption and Safe Families Act

By the mid-1990s, just about everyone familiar with the foster care system in the United States agreed: the most serious problem with the child welfare system was that too many children stayed in foster care for too long. The disagreement was over what to do about it. For many, the most pressing problems of child protection in the 1980s and 1990s were the result of children who had been trapped in the system for too long. For these reformers of child welfare, the reasons for the removals became largely irrelevant; the focus became what to do with the foster children.

A good deal of what the NYCLU tried unsuccessfully to win by constitutional rule in the 1970s was achieved twenty years later when Congress passed the Adoption and Safe Families Act of 1997 (ASFA).[22] At that time, Congress was persuaded that the solution to too much foster care was more, and speedier, adoptions. ASFA made a number of important changes in the law of foster care. Some of these have nothing to do with the issues in *OFFER*. For example, the 1997 law excuses states from directing reasonable efforts toward reunification when parents have been convicted of certain crimes against children. Nor are reasonable efforts required if a court determines that the parent has subjected a particular child to certain "aggravating circumstances" defined by state law. Together, these provisions aim to prevent reunification. The act also requires (quite appropriately) more frequent and detailed reviews of each child's placement, including more careful review of the agencies' efforts to help return children to their parents safely.

But the most significant change had to do with encouraging adoption. ASFA substantially shortens the time parents are given to regain custody of their children before states are pressured to initiate proceedings to terminate parental rights. Now promoted as a solution for foster children, the law mandates that after a child has spent fifteen consecutive months in foster care, the state must file a termination of parental rights petition unless one of three exceptions applies: the child is in the care of a relative; there is a "compelling reason" to maintain parental rights based on the interests of the child; or the state has failed to provide mandatory "reasonable efforts." In addition, under ASFA foster parents have the right to an opportunity to show that they should be permitted to keep the child permanently.

Victory for Children?

There is little doubt that child welfare policy dramatically shifted in the late 1990s. For the first time in American history, federal policy supports as a prominent aspect of foster care the permanent severance of all legal ties between foster children and their parents. This is an important shift in policy, made all the more pertinent because it was advocated in the name of children's rights. The alliance favoring ASFA included adults who support broader and easier adoption of children, sometimes for reasons having little to do with the well-being of children. These advocates nevertheless successfully invoked children's rights to make their case. The proponents of ASFA largely succeeded in labeling their opposition as "parents' rights" advocates, which in this context meant opponents of children's rights. But before concluding too quickly who are and who are not the real children's rights supporters, some additional information about child welfare is needed. In order to judge the wisdom of the current push to terminate parental rights, we need to determine how many of these children were placed in foster care to protect them from serious harm at home.

Why Too Many Children Are Placed in Foster Care

One would expect that the decision to promote the adoption of tens of thousands of America's foster children was reached only after concluding that virtually all of the children in foster care really need to be there. Nothing could be further from the truth. Studies have consistently found that the great majority of children in foster care could remain safely at home. Agencies underuse preventive and reunification services—services designed specifically to keep children out of foster care or to return them promptly to their homes after placement. Experts estimate that 40 to 70 percent of children currently in foster care have not been abused and would not need to be separated from their families if society sufficiently assisted poor families in raising their children. Duncan Lindsey, a leading child welfare researcher, evaluated placements of children in foster care and found that 48 percent of the children did not require placement.[23] Poverty is the leading reason children end up in foster care. Studies show that families earning incomes below $15,000 per year are twenty-two times more likely to be involved in the child protective system than families with incomes above $30,000.[24] Lindsey concludes not only that "inadequacy of income, more than any other factor, constitutes the reason that children are removed," but that "inadequacy of income increased the odds for placement by more than 120 times."[25]

It is also well known that countless children regularly remain in foster care simply because their parents are unable to secure adequate housing without assistance from the state. The court-appointed administrator of the District of Columbia's foster care system, for example, determined that between one-third and one-half of the children in foster care could be returned immediately to their parents if adequate housing could be found.[26]

We also know that only a very small percentage of children in foster care have suffered serious forms of maltreatment. Indeed, one respected researcher concluded in 1994 that "child abuse" is the "red herring" of child welfare.[27] Jane Waldfogel's analysis is that the current foster care population may be grouped into three categories. The most serious category, constituting about 10 percent of current caseloads, includes "serious and criminal cases." The second group encompasses serious cases that do not require criminal justice intervention. The final group of cases are those in which a child is at a relatively lower risk of serious harm, and the parents may be willing to work with an agency to secure needed services. Together, the latter two groups comprise 90 percent of the caseload.[28] Typically, these cases involve less serious physical abuse (for example, a single, minor injury such as a bruise or a scratch), charges of parental drug or alcohol abuse with no other protective issues, or less severe neglect (such as unsanitary conditions at home, lack of supervision of a school-age child, or missed school or medical appointments). Many of these lower-risk neglect cases are poverty-related, resulting from inadequate housing or inappropriate child-care arrangements while a parent needs to be away from home.

According to Lindsey, although serious child abuse receives the attention of the media, the real problems in child welfare concern poverty and the related difficulties of raising children while poor.

Although approximately 3 million child protection cases are reported each year for investigation, two-thirds are not even "substantiated" by investigating officials.

Courts and government reports alike regularly conclude that the current scheme results in a bias toward over-reporting and over-labeling child abuse and neglect. Indeed, one federal study found that investigators are more than twice as likely to "substantiate" a case erroneously than to mislabel a case "unfounded."[29] Moreover, many studies have found that as many as two-thirds of those cases labeled "substantiated" do not involve serious charges.[30] A substantiated case means merely the presence of some "credible evidence" to believe a home is unfit. As a typical example, in Illinois a report must be substantiated unless the investigator finds that there is "no credible evidence" of maltreatment.[31]

Other data on entry into foster care are also inconsistent with the notion that our child welfare system carefully monitors foster children and insists upon a compelling reason to remove a child from his or her family. Specifically, placement rates vary widely from one state to another even in the absence of any material difference between known rates of abuse or neglect. For whatever reason, twice as many children are in foster care in Minnesota than in Wisconsin and twice as many are in such care in Vermont than in New Hampshire.[32] There is also significant evidence to suggest that placements can reflect the politics of particular administrations and have little to do with child safety. States appear to use very flexible standards that depend on the policies of local child welfare officials. These policies can change dramatically from one administration to the next.

New York City's foster care population soared in the aftermath of a notorious and highly publicized case of child abuse. From 1995 to 1998, the number of new child abuse and neglect petitions filed rose 55 percent. The number of children removed from their families and placed in foster care over parental objection rose by nearly 50 percent between 1995 and 1997.[33] During this same period, however, there was no known change in the base rate of child abuse. This striking rise in prosecution suggests a change in the philosophy of the prosecutors rather than a change in the conditions of children's homes. In 2001, a federal court in New York found that it was the regular policy of child welfare officials to charge battered mothers with neglect and to remove their children from their home when the only allegation is that the children were present when the mother was the victim of domestic violence.[34] As mentioned previously, family court judges in New York have been found to approve without question agency recommendations to remove children from their parents, even in circumstances that do not constitute emergencies.[35]

The ease with which children enter foster care and the needless time they spend there should be among the highest concerns of those who care about children's well-being. Children do not thrive in foster care. The state is a poor substitute for one's family. This does not suggest, of course, that no child should ever be placed in foster care; it should be used for true emergencies, in the same way that hospitalization is used.

Not only are most children in foster care for reasons other than their immediate safety, agencies fail to do nearly enough to reunite children with their families in a timely manner. The overwhelming conclusion in the scholarly literature is that family reunification efforts have always been inadequate.[36] Although Congress concluded in 1997 when it passed ASFA that states were applying the "reasonable efforts" requirement in the 1980 act too strictly, this conclusion must be understood in context. In the 1990s, Congress reached a consensus that government had been doing too much to assist poor families and called for more modest and time-limited government assistance programs. In 1996, Congress abandoned the guarantee of basic economic support for families, which had been in place since the New Deal. Concerned about creating a "culture of dependency," vulnerable families would no longer be entitled to public assistance after they had received such benefits for a fixed period of years.

Against this backdrop, we can begin to appreciate the significance of Congress's concern that child protection officials were too assiduous in working to rehabilitate "broken" families. It is unsur-

prising that federal legislators were troubled by policy that mandated substantial expenditures in an effort to rehabilitate families
whose children had been removed from their homes because of
child abuse.[37] Nonetheless, research refutes any claim that child
welfare has been overzealous in its efforts to keep families together.

Ours is a culture struggling over how to help innocent children
but not to support their "undeserving" parents.[38] Americans have
never been very good at distinguishing between the "deserving"
and "undeserving." For some, poverty is what makes parents undeserving. The combination of race and poverty is particularly fatal
for inner-city families in our most crowded cities. ASFA makes no
distinction between parents whose children were removed because
of parental abuse and parents whose only crime is being too poor to
raise their children in a clean and safe environment without additional benefits the government refuses to supply. If we focus only on
the amount of time children remain in foster care, all cases are
treated alike.

Children's Other Needs

By failing to distinguish among cases based on the reasons children
entered foster care, ASFA continues the nearly forty-year-old tradition in child welfare of not considering the various ways children
could benefit from society's largesse by doing more than removing
children from their parents' homes. Why is ASFA so short-sighted?
A closer examination of the issues reveals that the United States is
not quite the child-loving society its politicians commonly like to
suggest it is.

Let's begin with a quick view of the larger picture of poor children in the United States. Of all industrial nations worldwide, the
United States has the highest child-poverty rate. This is not simply
an accident of fate. Many countries have developed a very different
set of priorities and policies with respect to children and families
than the United States. Britain, France, Sweden, and Canada, for
example, each spend two to three times more on children and families than does the United States.[39]

As the Children's Defense Fund regularly reminds us in its report on the state of the child in the United States, the United States ranks first in the world in many categories that reflect its status as world leader, including gross domestic product and number of millionaires. But its record with respect to children fails to reflect this fantastic wealth and power.

The United States ranks sixteenth in the world with respect to the standard of living among the poorest one-fifth of children, eleventh in the proportion of children living in poverty, and eighteenth in the income gap between rich and poor children. We are a country that has permitted the gap between rich and poor children to grow ever larger, despite our remarkable success in overcoming the worst consequences of poverty among the elderly.

Through the combination of guaranteed Social Security and Medicare for the elderly the United States ranks near the top in the world in longevity and wealth of people over the age of seventy. By contrast, children are twice as likely as adults to live in poverty. More than 12 million children in the United States live below the poverty line—nearly 17 percent of all children. Since 1969, even as the GNP has risen 50 percent, child poverty has increased by 50 percent.[40]

This larger picture is especially pertinent because of the known correlation between the poverty rate for children and the rate of out-of-home placement. A 1992 study showed that when public assistance decreased by 6 percent, the number of children entering foster care went up by 10 percent. A second study demonstrated that a 10 percent increase in benefit levels reduced out-of-home placement by 8 percent. Similarly findings have been made in Western European countries.[41]

Not only does the United States have a disproportionately high population of poor children relative to its wealth, the well-known adverse consequences of poverty for children are quite severe. For example, the United States ranks seventeenth in the world in rates of low birthweight babies, and a shocking twenty-second in the world in reducing the rate of infant morality. Life in America's inner cities holds numerous, substantial health hazards for children. Data suggest that nearly 2 million children suffer from lead poisoning, and those with lead poisoning are most often found in families in the lowest income brackets.[42]

Indigent children suffer asthma at rates twice as high as children in higher-income families, requiring hospitalization for 10,000 children between the ages of four and nine.[43] Asthma can adversely affect a child's well-being, ability to participate in sports and other activities, academic performance, and even life expectancy.

There is also a serious shortage of adequate housing for poverty-stricken children in the United States. In 1995, there were 4.4 million more low-income renters than there were affordable housing units. As a result, a vast number of families settle for substandard housing; those who seek minimally adequate conditions are often forced to pay more than half their income in rent. In a survey of thirty cities, children constituted 25 percent of the homeless population.[44] This problem grows more serious every year. The average period of time spent awaiting federal Section 8 housing assistance rose from twenty-six to twenty-eight months between 1996 and 1998; in the nation's largest housing authorities, the average waiting period increased from twenty-two to thirty-three months during this same period.

In addition, as the percentage of jobs that include health benefits decreases, the number of children without health coverage continues to grow exponentially. More than 11 million children in the United States today have no health insurance. Between 1996 and 1998, approximately 643,000 children lost Medicaid coverage.[45]

To some, these statistics will be quite troubling. To others, they will simply reflect a fact of life: the rich do well and the poor do less well. Moreover, for some, these statistics are distorting in that they fail to reflect an unfaltering improvement in the lives of all Americans, including the poor. Even if poor children suffer by comparison to well-to-do children, the poor fare reasonably well and significantly better than in many regions of the world.

The point of this snapshot of the conditions to which poor children are exposed in the United States is not to advance a call for redistribution of wealth or a reordering of society's values. That set of arguments is for another book and another time. There are complicated reasons for our failure to do more to ameliorate the negative conditions to which children are exposed and which are within our reach to improve. I have described the plight of America's poor children to see more clearly the larger child welfare picture.

The Value of "Child Welfare" to Adults

Think for a moment what you understand to be the most serious danger facing children in the United States. It would be rare if most readers did not place at the top of their list child abuse or sex abuse. This is because the news media and politicians have focused so much of their attention on these two subjects above all others affecting children. As a consequence, it is relatively difficult for the educated reader even to be aware of the significant health problems faced by millions of poor children. Yet among poor children, health problems are far more dangerous and common than child abuse. Americans have become convinced (wrongly) by the media that child abuse is a prevalent social ill.

The conditions most threatening to children, however, are far more dangerous and adverse to their well-being than child abuse. It has been estimated, for example, that of the 22,000 children who die each year in the United States from accidents, "inexpensive injury prevention programs and emergency medical systems for children" could save an estimated 6,000 to 10,000 of these children's lives.[46] An additional 4,205 children were killed by guns in 1997.[47] By contrast, child abuse fatalities appear to be a rarer event (estimated to be between 1,000 and 1,200 annually).[48]

One more point needs to be made here. The statistics in the last paragraph concern only those dangers that are relatively *preventable*. Public health officials know it is well within our capacity drastically to reduce the number of children killed or injured by firearm accidents or to improve emergency medical treatment for children. According to the Centers for Disease Control and Prevention, children in the United States under age fifteen are: twelve times more likely to die from gunfire, sixteen times more likely to be murdered by a gun, eleven times more likely to commit suicide with a gun, and nine times more likely to die in a firearm accident than children in twenty-five other industrialized countries combined.

I leave for the reader to ponder which battles adults are fighting among themselves that place these fixable problems outside of mainstream political debate. What matters for the purposes of this book is the degree to which politicians prize the topic of child abuse because it allows them to proclaim their deep concern for children by demonstrating how much money is in the "child welfare" budget, how many child abuse investigations they are conducting, how many children are in foster care, and how many children are being adopted. It also makes the rest of us feel pretty good about ourselves because this data would seem to prove that we really do care about our children's needs.

Let's suppose you were the governor of a state in which a child is killed by gunfire every three days and which ranks forty-sixth among states in the percentage of children without any health insurance, thirty-fifth among states with low birthweight babies, thirty-fifth in the percentage of children who are poor, thirty-fourth in per pupil expenditures for education, twenty-seventh among states in infant mortality rate, twenty-fifth among states in the percentage of babies born whose mothers received any prenatal care, and thirtieth among states in childhood immunizations for two-year-olds. You could take on these challenges, and the controversy and expense that would entail. Or you could try to find an easier way to demonstrate that you are committed to helping innocent children. Suppose, in other words, you were the governor of Florida, Jeb Bush. What strategies might you employ?

Whenever the subject of children comes up on the political trail, you would include as part of every soundbite an abiding concern for the safety and well-being of children who are harmed by their parents. You might talk about the new commissioner of child welfare you intend to bring into your cabinet. You could hold a press conference each April in celebration of Child Abuse and Neglect Prevention Month and issue a statement warning that "child abuse and neglect results in significant trauma to the child, family and so-

ciety as it causes children to suffer serious illness and injury resulting in impairment of physical, intellectual and emotional functioning and well-being or even death." While you're at it, you could
increase the size of the public relations budget for the Department
of Children and Families by more than 20 percent, to more than
half a million dollars. Meanwhile, you would not increase money
spent on education or raise taxes to provide affordable health care
for children.[49]

So What Should Happen to Foster Children?

What should be the policy concerning children placed in foster care
for years on end? The NYCLU children's rights advocates insisted
that a child's right includes the right not to be returned to his or her
parents once they have lived in substitute care for more than one
year, a battle they lost in court. The question remains whether children's rights rhetoric as expressed by the NYCLU deepens our understanding of the complexities of the issues or obscures our capacity to consider other factors than the impact of foster care on a
particular child.

Just as with the children's rhetoric used in the "Baby Jessica"
case, which we considered in Chapter 3, the NYCLU position focuses only on the impact of the individual child affected in a particular case. What is lost by such a focus is the far more complicated
question of the greater good that can be achieved for children. Even
worse, the very purpose of the underlying foster care policy is disregarded. As we saw in Chapter 3, an emphasis on children's rights
when we are considering a custody dispute between a current caregiver and someone else (usually a parent) is skewed in favor of a
particular result (keeping the child with the current caregiver). Such
an emphasis also stresses emotional arguments over sound public
policy, thereby discouraging the development of a policy that works
best for society.

For these reasons, let us consider the larger picture. Once we do
that, it ought to matter a great deal how a parent-child relationship
was established and what were the original understandings of the

adults who formed it or allowed it to be formed. Consider, for example, a three-year-old boy whose mother requires hospitalization for a serious heart disorder. After major surgery, she suffers a severe setback and enters into a coma for approximately six months. After coming out of the coma, she needs substantial rehabilitative services. Between the time she first entered the hospital until she is fully ready to go home and resume a normal life, twenty months have elapsed. Would even a children's advocate claim that the boy should not be returned to his birth mother because he had formed a bond with a psychological parent? Most of us would agree in this case that the parent deserves to regain the custody of her child when she is able to take care of him and that the child deserves to be reunited with his parent.

Much of our opinion about the outcome of this case, however, would depend on several parameters: who was taking care of the child during the parent's incapacity, what was the caregiver's relationship to the parent (and the child), what was the caregiver's (and the child's) expectations about long-term plans, and what was being said to the child (and the caregiver) about long-term plans.

There are countless possibilities. If the parent has an extended family, there is every possibility that the substitute caregiving would be provided by the child's grandparent or aunt or cousin. Under such circumstances, few would propose that the parent should be banished from the child's life permanently. Most of us would be disturbed if they were not reunited.

If the extended family caregiver has a good relationship with the parent, we would expect that the caregiver would regularly talk about the mother to the child, stressing how much her mother loves him, and looking forward to that wonderful day when they could be together again. Expectations are powerful for these purposes. The more the caregiver steers the child toward an eventual reunion, the more we would insist that the child should be reunited with the mother. We would also expect that the child would stay in regular contact with his mother as appropriate under the circumstances. Depending on those circumstances, this might mean visiting only occasionally when the mother is in a coma (unless doctors and other experts consider the child's visiting during this period too difficult for the child), to weekly or daily visits with her when she is stronger.

The key to a successful reunion is nurturing the relationship between parent and child during the period they are apart. Kindling the warmth and bond between them not only is feasible, it is imperative for those who really want parent and child to be reunited again.

How pertinent is this example to the subject of foster care? Admittedly, foster care is far more complex. When the foster parent is not a relative, the caregiver often will not know the parent, making it more difficult to nurture the parent-child relationship. This distinction, by itself, is hardly decisive. But there is an even greater complication: the reasonableness of kindling the relationship in light of the deep uncertainty about what the future holds for the child.

When a foster parent does not know the mother and cannot be sure that the mother will regain the custody of her child, what should the caregiver say to the child? How appropriate is it to pray for the day when the two can be reunited when there is reason to be concerned that day will never come? Is it fair or wise to hold the child's emotions hostage to a fantasy that he or she will live with the mother again when there are real reasons to doubt that will happen? How should we prepare foster children and the people helping to raise them for an outcome that is unknown?

On the one hand, we cannot afford to promise foster children that they will certainly be reunited with their parents. But does this mean the wiser course is to tell them, as AFSA proponents would have it, that unless their mother is ready within a year to take them back, they will never be permitted to live with her again? These questions deserve far more attention than they receive. They are almost never addressed in the literature and are completely absent from court cases—further proof of the ways in which children's needs are inadequately taken into consideration when they are being raised by the state.[50]

It is helpful to expand our focus to still other separations between parents and children in order to explore these issues outside of the foster care world itself, a world that has become rife with race, class, and wealth issues, and a baneful view of the value of the parents themselves. If we can isolate that last factor, perhaps we can discuss this field with more clarity and honesty than sometimes occurs.

Is it a sign of a properly child-centered society that children of soldiers who go to war for three years should be allowed, over the soldier's objection, to remain within the custody of their caregivers after the soldier comes home? Would the truly child-centered society mandate that children hidden from enemies seeking to kill them, as Jewish children were in Europe in the 1940s, be kept by their safekeepers when the enemies are defeated?

I would like to think there is a clear consensus that the children in these examples ought to be returned to their parents when the parents are able to have them. This is not to say that we would *insist* that each of these parents resume their caregiving function regardless of the length of the separation. Some may decide, for any number of personal reasons, that their children should remain where they have been raised.

Surely almost everyone would agree there would be something terribly wrong if the law *prohibited* returning children to their birth parents when the parents are again able to take care of them. It is vital that we make clear why this is so. To be sure, some examples, such as protecting children during wartime, raise broader issues of social justice and restoring life to the way it was before catastrophic events changed things. Even this example suggests that more is at stake in foster care cases than protecting children's right to maintain a relationship with their psychological parent. It is not just that the child's right is outweighed by the right of the innocent parent; more directly, we do not believe that the child has an antagonistic right in the first place.

When there is an understanding that a caregiver will care for children temporarily until the parent is able to become the custodian, it is appropriate to celebrate when the parent and child are reunited. That is why the Supreme Court reasoned in *OFFER* that New York should be held to its promise to parents that it would return their children to them when they were ready to have them.

It is crucial to recognize the degree to which the child-centered rhetoric in the United States over the past twenty years has made it difficult to see this point clearly. It is misguided to believe that we measure our love for children by the degree to which we will insist that they be allowed to remain with parentlike figures who have filled in for their parents.

What, then, is the difference between the soldier and the parent whose child is in foster care? Unfortunately, it appears that in the United States today, the difference is an unstated belief that the parent of the foster child is unworthy. I believe it is not coincidental that the call for the permanent banishment of birth parents reached its zenith when the foster care population reached an unprecedented high of being nonwhite. As a result of this major policy change, an official goal of U.S. policy today is to socially engineer the makeup of the families raising poor, nonwhite children.

Consider the astonishing statistics on the racial makeup of foster care in America's largest urban cities. In Chicago, more than 95 percent of the children in foster care are African-American.[51] In New York City, of the 42,000 children in foster care in December 1997, only 3.1 percent were categorized as "non-Hispanic white" by New York City officials.[52] How do we explain these staggeringly disproportionate numbers? To the extent that most children who end up in foster care are there because of conditions related to abject poverty, these numbers should not be too surprising. The nexus between poverty and race in the United States is well documented.[53]

And yet these numbers deserve a closer look. They also mean that, somehow or other, New York City has found a way to maintain a child welfare system for its white population that treats placement in foster care as an extremely rare event. Even with a significant white immigrant population of poor families, New York City places non-Hispanic white children in foster care at a rate of less than three per thousand. For the rest of the population, the rate soars to three in every one hundred.[54]

I have represented hundreds of parents—mostly mothers—over

the past twenty years. Most had not abused their children. They were simply overwhelmed by conditions at home exacerbated by poverty. Some did nothing to warrant the removal of their children, who were removed only because of poor judgment exercised by a social worker given a great deal of discretion. Others did terrible things to their children. And more than a few did awful things to themselves. These have included women who were addicted to drugs or alcohol; women who made money in whatever way was possible during their bleakest times, including selling their bodies for drugs or money. Many of these parents came to realize their conduct toward their children was wrong and were genuinely remorseful.

Despite all of these variations, two basic patterns emerge in the vast majority of my cases. First, I am struck by how difficult it is for the parents to regain their children's custody, regardless of the reason for the removal. Once children are in foster care, cases drag on at "agency time" or "court time," and children remain in care for as long as two years when there is nothing to justify even a day's additional separation. These delays occur despite everyone's claimed desire to speed up cases so that children do not suffer needlessly.

Two thoughtful attorneys who have wide experience representing parents in foster care–related proceedings have reached almost identical conclusions. Nanette Schorr, a tireless and compassionate lawyer for poor parents in New York City, describes how in her experience foster care commonly is extended for months on end with no real concern for the children's well-being or that of their parents. "As overwhelmed and undertrained caseworkers make arbitrary or impossible demands on them," she writes, "parents lose hope of being reunited with their children. They complete a drug treatment program only to be told they must find a job. They receive a certificate from a parental skills class, only to be told that they can get their children back only when a therapist determines that they are ready . . . Months, sometimes years, pass as cases are repeatedly adjourned and professionals who sit behind closed doors determine the fate of their families."[55]

Annette Appell, who represented parents in Chicago and in

South Carolina, reports similar experiences. Writing about three cases in which she represented parents in the child welfare system, Appell concludes that the "state's intervention was arguably unnecessary in all of the cases." But far more significantly, she believes the intervention was "certainly not helpful in any of them."[56]

In one case she describes the mother of two children who discovered that a man with whom she was having a sexual relationship had molested one of her daughters. After she confronted him and reported him to authorities, he set fire to her apartment while she and her two children were inside. When the mother turned to the child welfare system for help, it removed her two children after the mother admitted to having unmarried sexual relations with the molester. The mother was then forced to prove her entitlement to regain custody over a fourteen-month period of strict, closely supervised, one-hour visits per week. All she ever needed from the agency was an apartment to replace the one that was destroyed by the fire or transportation to another city where she could start over again with the help of her extended family.

In all three cases she discusses, Appell finds that the children were removed without the state addressing the presenting problems for the separations. The agencies chose to change the long-term behavior of the mothers. In the process, none of the families was provided with meaningful services. Instead, they were required to attend workshops, therapy sessions, skills courses, and a variety of other task-oriented programs that they did not need. The only hope of ever getting their children returned depended on satisfying the caseworkers that they "really" loved their children enough to do what was asked of them. In this way, the parents who are most compliant are the most likely to prevail and regain their children. Those who fail to "exhibit sufficient contrition or obedience" are the least likely to regain custody.

The second lesson I have been taught through experience is how difficult it is for my clients to be seen for who they really are. In case after case, I am struck by how my knowledge of my client differs from how they are described and talked about in court. There, the discussion always relies on labels: "drug user," "alcoholic," "depressed personality," as if these words adequately describe a person. In far too many cases, I have come to conclude that person who cares most about the children who are the subjects of the case is my client—the one regarded by everyone else as the child's greatest enemy. In Appell's experience, even though in the cases she wrote about "all of the mothers loved and nurtured their children," the state failed to strengthen the "relationships by assisting the mothers to strengthen ties to existing support systems," and, "instead of exhibiting sophistication, flexibility, and attentiveness regarding the mothers' needs, the state provided services according to administrative convenience."[57]

Most disturbing of all, this unstated judgment of the parents' unsuitability has been disguised and translated into a children's rights claim. AFSA was widely heralded as a children's rights victory. One columnist, with no irony intended, treated the new law as a civil rights victory for children that would be "to the abused and neglected children in our nation's foster-care system what the Voting Rights Act was to black Americans in 1965."[58] Federal legislators remarked in support of the law, "we have to start worrying about the children's rights and less about the rights of the natural parents" because "[o]ur child welfare system too often protects parents' rights rather than children's rights."[59]

There is one last way to test the depth of the children's rights advocates' insistence that the child has a right to remain with his or her long-term caregiver. Many of us can imagine substitute caregivers who would regard it as immoral or otherwise unacceptable to keep someone else's child after the parent objects. For them, it is one thing to take care of a child because the parent asks or is grateful for it, and completely another to do so over the parent's opposition. Are these caregivers acting wrongly when they are prepared to return the child after a two- or three-year separation from the parent? Even those who want foster parents to be able to keep a child over the parent's objection surely do not mean that the law should insist that a foster parent do so.

As we continue this focus, it immediately becomes clear just how important are the daily interactions between the foster parent and the foster child. These interactions depend, in turn, on the foster parent's own conception of her role and her relationship to the child and to the child's birth family. A foster parent who keeps reminding the child of the child's relationship to the birth parents helps the child maintain his or her own identity as someone else's child. This is, of course, the precise role that nannies play when helping raise children of the wealthy (some of whom spend very little time with their parents). Unfortunately, AFSA discourages foster parents from supporting the child's relationship with his or her birth family.

The contentious issues in this chapter do not resolve themselves as easily as the solution we identified in the "Baby Jessica" case. There, speedy proceedings would take care of most of the problems. The unwed father gets his chance in court to prove his right to the custody of his child. The would-be adoptive couple gets to present their claims to the child. The court is free to decide the case in accordance with the rule of law without the additional fear that the ultimate decision reached will imperil the child.

In foster care, however, things cannot be sped up in the same way. We can do a much better job of ensuring that the only children who enter foster care really need to be separated from their families. We can also work harder to speed up returning children to their birth families when the delays in return are the result of agency or court failings. Yet many children will have to spend a reasonably long period in foster care if we are to give parents the time they need to regain their own lives so they can be reunited with their children.

When we revisit the facts in *OFFER*, we can now see that the real problems developed in the case only when the foster mother undermined the foster children's relationship with their birth mother. As the tension between the foster children and their mother became more and more pronounced, the foster agency decided it had to remove the children from the foster home. When the agency attempted to do that, the NYCLU went to federal court to prevent the separation.

Who was really more faithful to the children's long-term rights, the foster care agency or the NYCLU? The agency wanted the children to be reunited with their birth mother when she was able to take them back and insisted that the substitute caregiver honor and respect the children's relationship with their mother. The NYCLU sought a constitutional rule that protects the foster relationship even when foster parents undermine state policy to preserve the birth family relationship.

When we try to identify children's rights, we need to recall how difficult it is to know what truly serves them. But we also should be ever mindful that other interests in our society may properly be regarded as even more important. Just as the justice rule we examined in Chapter 2 would preclude us from seriously entertaining the possibility that a child snatcher should keep a child, even if we believed that it would serve the child's best interests, we may believe that a parent who has been released from a concentration camp should also be given his child for the simple reason that we want a society that is committed to such results.

How do we best characterize the values behind such a preference? We might say that our society exists in part to help out others who, for whatever reason, are unable to raise their children for a particular period of time, and that we honor the parent-child relationship so much that we rejoice when we are able to participate in its restoration. To be sure, the child-centered advocates would mock the notion of privileging the biological parent-child relationship and condemn us for looking at the world exclusively through the lens of adults. They would condemn our willingness to destroy a crucial relationship the child has formed merely to restore a property right of an adult—a right simply secured through the biological process of reproduction. But we need to ask, *all* things considered—not just the interests of one child, but the interest of the greatest number of children, and the interests of adults—whether this is the society in which we want to live.

The ease with which children enter foster care and the time they are forced to endure in foster care should be among the highest concerns of those who care about children's well-being. It disserves poor children and their families to continue to ignore the true reasons so many children enter the foster care system: the lack of political will to do more to improve the lives of poor children.

The harsh conditions of poverty and despair into which millions of poor children are born are not immutable facts of life. It is helpful to determine the extent to which these conditions are caused by factors for which we may hold the larger society accountable and, therefore, could improve or eliminate. My point is not to condemn American society for failing to take the steps to ameliorate the harsh conditions in which so many children continue to live. It is that we should not be overly proud of what we do in compensation for this inaction.

Perhaps America is unable to do better for children of vulnerable families for the simple reason that it is unwilling to do better. Nina Bernstein, a *New York Times* reporter and author, helps remind us of the impossibility of isolating what we are willing to do for poor children from the larger politics of taxes and economics. "There has long been an iron rule in American social welfare policy: conditions must be worse for the dependent poor than for anyone who works. The seldom-acknowledged corollary is that the subsidized care of other people's children must be undesirable enough, or scarce enough, to play a role in this system of deterrence."[60]

Child welfare practice, however, cannot be intelligently discussed without expanding the traditional boundaries of the field. To do otherwise is to behave like the townspeople striving to save the babies in the stream. They work tirelessly to protect children. They believe in the good nature of their deeds. But they consider the subject of how the babies got into the stream to be someone else's concern. If we could start over and conceive of child welfare as a public health or shared social problem, rather than an issue focused solely on child abuse, we could develop policies that address directly and proactively those conditions that adversely affect the health and welfare of poor children in the United States.

The unfortunate turn federal legislation took in child protection in the early 1970s was to make it into an arm of the police with primary investigative and removal powers. A great opportunity was lost to transform child welfare into a program that served the needs of vulnerable families. From the investigative function, it was a short step to becoming a removal and prosecutorial agency. Although many in the field lament this shift and work in child welfare to provide services to bolster vulnerable families, child protection today, more than at any time in the past hundred years, stresses the virtue of breaking up families and freeing children for adoption.

The point of this chapter is less to persuade the reader that this direction is misguided. It is to show that adults who approve the change have been permitted to speak in the name of children and, even worse, have been successful in labeling those with contrary views as speaking for their parents (with the connotation that "pro-parent" is "anti-child"). This is the pernicious shift in the public debate.

If there is any solace in the recent trend to speed terminations of parental rights for all children in foster care longer than fifteen months, it is that these changes have been made by the legislature instead of the Supreme Court through constitutional adjudication. Had the NYCLU been successful in the 1970s in advancing its version of children's rights, there would have been little opportunity for further debate. In the 1990s, ASFA was enacted with the support of many children's rights advocates. Those who believe Congress went too far now must press their case. The debate about who is right would be far easier to conduct if the flawed rhetoric of those claiming to protect children was removed.

7

Children's Rights that Serve Adults' Needs: The Case of Adolescents' Right to Abortion

MANY of the earlier chapters in this book involved a dispute among adults over the custody of children in which "children's rights" were invoked by one party to gain the upper hand. As the last chapter demonstrates, this phenomenon extends to conflicts between parents and state officials. This chapter explores a subject that may appear to fit oddly within this book. But the story of how and why children's rights were invoked to declare unconstitutional laws that required pregnant minors to obtain parental permission to terminate their pregnancies is only a variation on this larger theme.

In this chapter I review two Supreme Court decisions in the 1970s that first declared that adolescent girls possess adultlike constitutional rights to terminate an unwanted pregnancy, purporting to identify and enforce an adolescent's constitutional right to obtain an abortion. Though I describe the law regulating adolescent abortions, the subject is explored as a case study to demonstrate how the language of children's rights helps adults reach the result they want.

In total, the Supreme Court has addressed the subject of a pregnant minor's rights a total of ten times since 1973 (when the Court first held that a woman's constitutional right of privacy encompasses a right to terminate a pregnancy).[1] There have also been a number of state court decisions, including those from California and New Jersey, that have declared laws regulating abortions for minors unconstitutional under state constitutional provisions, though they are beyond the focus of this chapter.[2]

Adolescent Pregnancy

For many years, the United States has had a significant teenage pregnancy problem. At least from the 1960s through the 1990s, teen pregnancy rates in the United States have been higher than in most developed nations—twice as high as in England, France, and Canada and nine times higher than in Japan and the Netherlands.[3] For most of these years, more than 400,000 girls under the age of eighteen become pregnant each year.[4] A fraction of these pregnancies was planned and the overwhelming percentage of these pregnant minors were unmarried.

Many would prefer that the United States address this problem by attempting to reduce the amount of sexual activity in which teens engage. They would propose that adults preach abstinence to minors and warn them of the moral, legal, health, and life-altering consequences of engaging in sex outside of marriage or when underage. As a result, there has been a mighty effort by many to talk about sex to teens in the same way many propose that adults talk to teens about drugs: "just say no" is the best they have to offer.[5]

There is an obvious problem with this. Sex is everywhere in America's popular culture, including television, film, and music. Ours is also a culture in which sexual imagery is sold to everyone beginning at a young age. We advertise goods and services with sexual innuendo and, whether we want young children to be thinking about sex or not, Madison Avenue advertising executives have ensured that they will be. For better or worse, millions of teens in the United States are sexually active.

Remarkably, however, in the last decade of the twentieth century the teen birth rate declined rather dramatically. The most recent government statistics indicate a decline in the teen birth rate by 30 percent between 1990 and 2000.[6] This appears to be the result of a combination of greater use of contraceptives and a lowering of the incidence of sexual activity among teens. Abortion is also a popular method used by many teens to avoid having unwanted births. Even with this recent impressive reduction in the teen birth rate, there remain countless teens who regularly engage in sexual intercourse. Of these, nearly 20 percent are likely to become pregnant within one year of engaging in sex. Among teens who engage in sex, about 8 percent of fourteen-year-olds and 18 percent of fifteen- to seventeen-year-olds become pregnant each year.

Until 1973, there were few lawful options available to pregnant minors. They could decide to raise their child themselves or with the help of their families or they could give up their child for adoption. Many chose the unlawful option of securing an abortion.

The 1973 Supreme Court decision in *Roe v. Wade* potentially paved the way to make this third option lawful when it ruled that adult women have the constitutional right to terminate an unwanted pregnancy (provided the procedure is performed within the first two trimesters and under a physician's care). At the time *Roe* was decided, of course, there were no special rules concerning a minor's access to abortion because abortion was illegal in almost every state in the United States. In the immediate aftermath of *Roe*, the question naturally became, what should the rule be with respect to pregnant minors?

Everyone familiar with the issue recognized the negative consequences of a society composed of, in part, a large number of unwed teenage mothers. Many indicators reveal the negative impact of a high teenage, unmarried birth rate. These births adversely affect the health, mental health, wealth, and education of both the teenage mothers and their children. The combination of growing up in a single-parent home, having parents with little education, and living in poverty with inadequate or no health insurance places the children of unwed adolescent mothers in the highest risk category.

Whichever side one takes on the abortion debate, all can agree the subject is of great importance. Wholly outside of the moral issues it raises, all societies must care about their birth rate and the demographics of new mothers. A society producing too large a number of unwanted births must confront the behavior of its citizens. Policymakers have long been aware that, for whatever reason, adoption is a relatively rarely used option for teenage pregnant girls. Fewer than 10 percent of babies born to unmarried teenagers are placed in adoptive homes.[7] For most pregnant teens, the choice has been between keeping the baby or having an abortion.

But *Roe* did not hold that pregnant minors may terminate their unwanted pregnancies. It was silent on the subject. All *Roe* held was that an adult woman has the constitutional right to terminate an unwanted pregnancy. What about minors? Did they, too, have this constitutional right?

Who Decides: The Legislature or the Courts?

Ordinarily, most public health matters are left to the judgment of legislatures to resolve. There are few instances in which courts are asked, or expected, to make basic public health decisions in the United States. The law of abortion and the rules regulating teenage access to abortion are a major departure from this ordinary arrangement.

Today, the law affecting a minor's right to obtain an abortion depends on the minor's state of residence. In eighteen states and the District of Columbia, there are no restrictions whatsoever, and pregnant minors may, in those states, terminate an unwanted pregnancy under the same rules and conditions as adult women.[8] But in thirty-two states, there are restrictions imposed on a minor's opportunity to obtain an abortion. These restrictions vary by state. In some states, the minor must first notify at least one parent (in some cases, both parents) before being allowed to have an abortion. In other states, the minor must first obtain the written consent of at least one parent (in two states, both parents) before she may get an abortion.

But in all of the states that require parental notice or consent, there is an important means by which the minor may avoid whatever restriction the state has imposed. Called a "judicial bypass," the minor may go to the local court and file a petition seeking a judge's authorization for the abortion. Once in court, the judge must provide such authorization under either of two conditions: the judge must authorize the abortion if the judge determines that the minor is "mature." If the judge is unable to conclude the minor is mature, the judge nonetheless must authorize the abortion provided the judge determines that the abortion is in the minor's "best interest." If the judge concludes both that the minor is immature and the abortion would not be in her best interests, the judge may not authorize the abortion.

What is most remarkable about these rules, however, is that they were designed by the Supreme Court of the United States. The story of how these peculiar rules came into being is an important one, all the more so because of what it reveals about the malleability of children's rights.

Roe had an unusual impact on the role ordinarily performed by legislatures, distorting the abortion conversation within the democratic process. *Roe* was decided at a relatively early stage of the women's rights movement. That movement achieved great success over relatively few years by changing the focus of the abortion conversation and allowing many to see laws compelling women to carry a pregnancy to term as taking away from women an important measure of control over their own bodies. Indeed, New York and Washington had only recently legalized abortions through the legislative process before *Roe* was decided. But before the full impact of the movement could be felt in the legislatures, lawyers in the Supreme Court succeeded in having abortions declared a woman's constitutional right.

Once the federal constitutional rule was established for adult women, everything changed at the local political level. The power positions were radically switched. Women who supported the right to abortion suddenly had the more powerful position in the American legal landscape. Once abortion became a constitutional right, there was little legislatures could do to prevent women from having abortions. (As we shall see, this does not mean that legislators opposed to abortions did nothing. They sought to place as many obstacles in the path as possible. In the process, they forced the Supreme Court to clarify the limits of the constitutional right to an abortion.)

For better or worse, *Roe* changed the debate dramatically. In some important measure, the decision impeded, rather than advanced, the resolution of the abortion debate by ordinary political process. Once *Roe* was decided, the conversation over abortion shifted from policy to law; it became less what the rules for American society ought to be and more rearrangement of laws in light of the newly announced constitutional rule. It had still another impact on the democratic process. It removed from each legislator the full responsibility of having to decide how he or she should vote when an abortion bill was presented. Secure in the knowledge that the Supreme Court stood at the ready to strike down laws that infringed on the Constitution, some legislators became willing to vote for restrictive abortion statutes.

One of *Roe*'s immediate impacts was a rush by opponents of abortion to the legislatures to enact laws placing as many roadblocks to abortions as possible. In the words of one writer, "Almost from the moment the Supreme Court legalized abortion in *Roe v. Wade* in 1973, lobbyists and activists have kept up a steady presence in every legislative chamber, including Congress."[9] As a result, beginning in 1973 a number of legislatures enacted laws testing the limits of *Roe*.

The Role of Parents

At common law, and still today throughout the United States, in the absence of specific legislation to the contrary, it is illegal for any healthcare professional to treat a minor for nonemergency purposes without parental permission. As we saw in Chapter 2, the general American rule is that parents have the constitutional authority to make all decisions concerning their child's upbringing. Though we stressed in that chapter that this rule is primarily a matter of choosing between empowering parents or empowering the state to make childrearing decisions, parents also have the authority to make most decisions about their children even when their children object.

The clash between parents' authority to make decisions about their children with which the children disagree, however, is very different from the clash between parents and state officials. State officials should not be in the business of raising children, I observed in Chapter 2, because American principles of freedom and democracy depend on limiting the state's power to shape the values of children. Since, for a significant portion of childhood at least, children are inherently dependent and some adult must be vested with the authority to make decisions about them, parents may be regarded as gaining this authority by default as the only remaining serious candidate for the job after state officials are excluded.

These fundamental rules have always mattered most with respect to young children. Although it remains true that state officials may not substitute their views about childrearing for parents, even with respect to older children, courts have granted legislatures significant leeway to liberate children to make decisions for themselves in a variety of contexts. When this happens, the general principles from Chapter 2 are abrogated to the limited extent that older children are authorized to make specific decisions about their own lives regardless of what their parents would want.

Legislatures have much greater leeway to free children from their parents' authority for specific purposes than the discussion in Chapter 2 may have implied. For the most part, legislatures are free to do what they think is best and any choice will be consistent with the Constitution. They may, if they see fit, apply the default rule that parents must be consulted about all decisions concerning their children's upbringing. Or they may allocate to children a limited emancipation for particular purposes. When legislatures do this, courts will uphold the legislative choice as within constitutional boundaries.

Legislators have proven to be extremely practical in fashioning rules about children's access to medical procedures that legislators want to encourage children to use. Consider, for example, treatment for sexually transmitted disease, sexual abuse, drug or alcohol use, or counseling for psychological problems. Every state has passed special laws that permit minors (of any age) to obtain treatment for most of these conditions without obtaining parental consent. These laws go so far as to prohibit professionals who treat these minors from notifying the parents that their children have been treated.

Many children's rights advocates emphasize the importance of liberating older children from the shackles of their parents' authority in order to advance the personal autonomy and rights of the children themselves. But when legislatures enact these kinds of laws, they are not focused on the rights of children. Instead, they are concerned with the public costs associated with a rule that authorizes only parents to permit children to receive treatment for certain conditions. These laws reflect decisions by the legislature that it advances the public interest to remove barriers to children choosing to receive the services involved. They are, in other words, tacit support by the legislature for minors to avail themselves of the services the laws address.

A well-known truth about adolescents is that when laws require them to obtain parental consent before they secure various medical treatments, these requirements serve as a powerful barrier. The same is true even for laws merely requiring professionals to notify parents when they are treating teens. Many teens, facing the choice between receiving or avoiding medical treatment for a condition they prefer not telling their parents about, will forgo the treatment rather than tell their parents. At best, they will delay the treatment, putting off telling their parents for as long as possible (which often means too long).

At the same time, the general rule remains that, in the absence of special legislation to the contrary, children may not receive any professional services without parental consent. Often, this common-law rule means two things. First, professionals who treat children without parental consent realize that, unless the children pay for their services in cash, there is a real possibility they will never be paid. It also means that professionals are at risk of being sued by parents for treating their children without consent.

In the absence of special legislation, when a healthcare professional treats a minor without parental permission, technically the professional has committed the common law tort of battery. Derived from ancient notions of children as the property of their parents, this law has survived today. It is similar to entering one's property without permission (a trespass). A dentist who treats a child without parental permission may be charged with battery by the parents.

The harshness of the common law has been ameliorated in virtually every state today. An "emergency exception" allows professionals to justify their decision to treat a minor when taking the time to seek parental consent would be placing the child at unnecessary risk. A closely related exception, based on the notion of the parent's implied consent, allows treatment of minors without parental consent when it would be unreasonable to contemplate that the consent would be withheld. In effect, a jury may relieve a professional of the decision to treat a minor without parental consent when, under all of the circumstances, the professional's decision is considered reasonable. Parents are also not legally responsible for the debt incurred as a result of the nonconsensual treatment of their minor child, unless it was an emergency treatment, or the professional could reasonably have concluded there was implied consent. Because minors are not legally responsible for debts they incur in these situations, many professionals are unwilling to treat minors without parental consent, even when a lawsuit seems unlikely, simply because they may not paid for their services. If the parents refuse to pay, the professional has no recourse since the minor cannot be sued for the debt.

The law also recognizes a very limited "mature minor" exception to the common-law rule that only parents may consent to a minor's nonemergency health care. For the most part, this exception serves as a device to indemnify a physician sued by a parent for "providing non-negligent care that is both low risk and within the mainstream of medical opinion to a minor who is capable of giving informed consent."[10] A small number of states, including Alaska, Arkansas, Idaho, and Nevada, have enacted special legislation allowing unemancipated minors to consent to medical treatment when, in the opinion of the treating physician, they are sufficiently mature and intelligent to understand and appreciate the consequences of their decision.[11] In these few states, adolescents have adultlike rights to seek medical care.

Sometimes, however, the professionals providing the service are willing to treat children without parental consent. Common examples include tattoo artists or body piercing stores. In these cases, the "professionals" require that minors pay for the services in cash and are willing to take the chance that they will not be sued by the parents. When legislatures become aware that children are getting services to which their parents object, sometimes the remedy is to enact special legislation making it a crime for adults to provide services to children without parental consent. It is for this reason that many states have enacted laws prohibiting tattoo parlors giving tattoos to persons under the age of eighteen without parental consent. It is also the reason specially enacted laws prohibit minors in many states from getting their ears or other parts of their bodies pierced without parental consent. These special laws are passed not to change the law regarding who gets to decide whether children are entitled to certain services. Instead, they are enacted to reinforce the common-law rule that parents have this authority.

Parental Consent in Missouri and Massachusetts

Among the many legislatures in the 1970s seeking to limit *Roe* as much as possible were Missouri and Massachusetts. Both of these states' legislatures were dominated by anti-abortion legislators. Other states, such as New York, made no effort to amend their legislation. Seeking to permit citizens the broadest right under the Constitution to secure a desired abortion, those state legislatures that were compatible with the result in *Roe* stayed out of the fray.[12] But those states unhappy with *Roe* did otherwise.

The question in the immediate aftermath of *Roe* was whether minors, like adults, could obtain an abortion when they wanted one, or whether, consistent with the general rules of the parental rights doctrine, parental consent was required. In the absence of any special legislation, there was every reason to believe that physicians could no more perform an abortion on a minor without parental consent than they could perform any other nonemergency medical procedure. If any special legislation were needed, therefore, it would have been to clarify that minors would be allowed to decide for themselves whether to have an abortion.

At the same time, doctors affiliated with Planned Parenthood in many states were more than willing to treat pregnant minors who came to them seeking an abortion. Missouri and Massachusetts, two states strongly opposed to the holding in *Roe*, wanted to make clear to the medical profession that abortions were no different from any other kind of nonemergency medical treatment. For this reason, both enacted laws that reemphasized the common-law rule requiring parental consent.

The two state legislatures were not only clarifying a rule, however. By making explicit that parental consent was required before minors may obtain an abortion, Missouri's and Massachusetts's goal was to discourage them. The legislators who supported the laws and their opponents understood that parental consent laws would make it less likely that pregnant minors would choose to terminate a pregnancy. The differing rulings by the legislatures on abortion and sexually transmitted disease make their stance obvious. Although there is only one correct response in public health terms to someone with a sexually transmitted disease (treatment), there is more than one response to an unwanted pregnancy. And the Missouri and Massachusetts legislatures preferred childbirth to abortion.

Thus, Massachusetts and Missouri could rely on the traditional parental rights doctrine as cover for their actions, but there was no mistaking that the laws were enacted to make it less likely a minor would choose to abort an unwanted pregnancy. Indeed, one study subsequently found that as many as 9 percent of pregnant minors would carry their fetus to term rather than inform their parents of their decision to abort their pregnancy.[13] The defenders of the laws understood this; their opponents understood this. Most important, for purposes of this chapter, this was certainly the understanding of the justices of the Supreme Court.

The Supreme Court Comes to the Rescue

Shortly after *Roe* was announced, the Missouri legislature enacted a new law whose purpose was to limit the reach of *Roe* to as small a range of cases as constitutionally permissible. The new law, for example, made it illegal for a married women to obtain an abortion without the consent of her husband. (The Supreme Court struck down this provision.) The new law also contained a simply worded provision requiring that before a physician may perform an abortion on an "unemancipated minor," one of the minor's parents must give his or her consent. (An "unemancipated minor" referred to an unmarried person under the age of eighteen.)

The new legislation was challenged as a violation of a minor's constitutional procreational rights before it even went into effect. In 1976, the case was decided by the Supreme Court. In that same year, the Alan Guttmacher Institute reported (albeit inaccurately) that there was a national "epidemic" of teen pregnancy. According to the report, there were 11 million pregnant teens in the United States. That figure was actually an estimate of the number of teens under eighteen who had intercourse at least once. "Teen pregnancies," writes Judith Levine, "actually numbered fewer than a million a year, and of those teen mothers, six in ten were legal adults."[14] In other words, in 1976, about 400,000 girls under the age of eighteen became pregnant.

The challengers to the Missouri law had remarkably little going for them in terms of legal precedent. There was nothing in the history of Supreme Court jurisprudence to suggest that children had a right to obtain nonemergency medical care over parental objection. Although critics of *Roe's* pronouncement that women have a constitutional right to terminate an unwanted pregnancy are famous for noting that an abortion right can be found nowhere in the Constitution, the argument is both misleading and simplistic. *Roe* did not declare that women have a constitutional right to an abortion, as such. Instead, it held that terminating an unwanted pregnancy is within a woman's broader constitutional right to privacy and self-identity, which are protected by the Due Process Clause of the Fourteenth Amendment. Although this distinction still leaves *Roe's* opponents critical of the result, the constitutional rights at stake are the rights to privacy and autonomy, components of the basic right to be let alone and to live one's life free from needless government interference.

Prior to 1976, however, no Supreme Court decision (or any decision from any other court, for that matter) had even hinted that minors had privacy or autonomy rights. Without these underlying rights, it is difficult to construct an argument that minors, like adults, have the constitutional right to terminate unwanted pregnancies.

Thus, *Planned Parenthood v. Danforth* became the first Supreme Court case ever to address the subject.[15] *Danforth's* holding straightforwardly declared the Missouri statute unconstitutional because it prohibited unmarried minors from obtaining abortions during the first trimester of their pregnancies without a parent's consent. Magisterially declaring that "[m]inors, as well as adults, are protected by the Constitution and possess constitutional rights," Justice Blackmun's opinion held that a state could not subject a minor's choice to terminate her pregnancy to a parent's absolute veto "without a sufficient justification for the restriction."

The case was decided by a vote of five-four. But even the closeness of that vote fails to reflect the real division within the Court. Although five members of the Court determined that a state could not subject a minor's choice to terminate her pregnancy to a parent's absolute veto "without a sufficient justification for the restriction," only two justices fully joined Blackmun's decision. Two others concurred separately on far narrower grounds.

One of the most striking aspects of the Court's decision is that its holding was reached with virtually no constitutional analysis. Blackmun quickly—one might say, facilely—reached the conclusion that "the State may not impose a blanket provision . . . requiring the consent of a parent or person in loco parentis as a condition for abortion of an unmarried minor during the first 12 weeks of her pregnancy."[16] The entire analysis is reduced to a single sentence: "Just as with the requirement of consent from the spouse, so here, the State does not have the constitutional authority to give a third party an absolute, and possibly arbitrary, veto over the decision of the physician and his patient to terminate the patient's pregnancy."[17]

This is nothing short of astonishing. The Court declared Missouri's law requiring parental consent before a minor could obtain a nonemergency abortion unconstitutional because the state delegated to parents a power it does not possess in the first place. But it should be immediately apparent that this reasoning is unsound. To begin with, by emphasizing that the Missouri legislature gave to parents a power it did not possess in the first place, the Court ignored the codifying function of the statute at issue. As we have seen, parents (in Missouri and everywhere else) have always had the authority to approve all nonemergency medical procedures for their children. Moreover, they had this authority without any benefit of a statute.[18] For this reason, it would have been more accurate to regard the challenged statute as clarifying extant law, rather than creating something new.

As we have also seen, a parent's right to control the details of a child's upbringing counts among the core substantive due process freedoms of Americans.[19] As the Court wrote in 1972, "The history and culture of Western civilization reflect a strong tradition of parental concern for the nurture and upbringing of their children. This primary role of the parents in the upbringing of their children is now established beyond debate as an enduring American tradition."[20]

Even more pertinent than the longevity of parental rights, however, the whole point of these rights is to permit the formation of a family unit free from government oversight. For this reason, Blackmun got it exactly backward even to regard parental rights as something the state gives to parents. Under any reasoning, these are not rights supplied to parents by the state. Instead, they are rights that parents possess as bulwarks against the exercise of state power.

The most problematic facet of Blackmun's logic, however, remains to be discussed: the *reason* parents have rights to raise children. According to the Court, Missouri's statute was illegal because the state may not give parents power that the state itself does not have in the first place.[21] But this is precisely what parental freedom is all about: the exercise of childrearing authority that the state does not have.

Another aspect of American constitutional principles is that, since the state may not prefer one religion over another, parents are free to train their children in a particular religion.[22] Can it plausibly be claimed that the state gave the power to parents to teach children religion? It is difficult to appreciate what is gained by describing the law in this way. The childrearing right reserved to parents is quintessentially one not given to them by the state.

Even assuming that it is valid to frame the claim in this manner, however, no one could plausibly assert that such a delegation is illegal because the state is prohibited from teaching children religion. Under the most fundamental of American constitutional principles, parents may do that which the state may not. This is the ineluctable implication of the well-known precept that the "custody, care and nurture of the child reside first in the parents, whose primary function and freedom include preparation for obligations the state can neither supply nor hinder."[23]

In all events, Blackmun's opinion was not enough to win the day. The votes of Justices Stewart and Powell were necessary to achieve the majority in *Danforth*. They concurred separately in an opinion written by Stewart which stressed that the "primary constitutional deficiency" of the parental consent requirement is "its imposition of an absolute limitation on the minor's right to obtain an abortion." Even this is somewhat difficult to comprehend. The only "absolute limitation" the law imposed was the long-accepted rule that parental consent be obtained before nonemergency surgery be performed on a child. If this is now to be regarded by the Supreme Court as an "absolute limitation" on a child's freedom, then children's freedom is always absolutely limited.

But Stewart's concurrence ultimately focused less on the limitation than on the valid reasons for granting children significantly fewer rights than adults. Quite different from Blackmun's majority opinion, Stewart emphasized that minors "may be ill-equipped" to decide for themselves whether to terminate a pregnancy. Because of this, he had "little doubt that the State furthers a constitutionally permissible end by encouraging an unmarried pregnant minor to seek the help and advice of her parents in making the very important decision whether or not to bear a child."[24] As a consequence, Stewart went on record stressing that "a materially different constitutional issue would be presented under a provision requiring parental consent or consultation in most cases but providing for prompt (i) judicial resolution of any disagreement between the parent and the minor, or (ii) judicial determination that the minor is mature enough to give an informed consent without parental concurrence or that abortion in any event is in the minor's best interest."[25]

In contrast, one of the dissenting opinions argued that the Missouri statute was constitutional because "Missouri is entitled to protect the minor unmarried woman from making the decision in a way which is not in her own best interests, and it seeks to achieve this goal by requiring parental consultation and consent." As Justice White explained, "This is the traditional way by which States have sought to protect children from their own immature and improvident decisions; and there is absolutely no reason expressed by the majority why the State may not utilize that method here."[26]

Justice Stevens also dissented. He concluded that Missouri was properly protecting the welfare of minors by requiring parental consent because a "state legislature may conclude that most parents will be primarily interested in the welfare of their children, and further, that the imposition of a parental-consent requirement is an appropriate method of giving the parents an opportunity to foster that welfare by helping a pregnant distressed child to make and to implement a correct decision."[27]

None of this means, nor is it my purpose to demonstrate, that the Court was wrong to hold that the Constitution is violated when parents have the power to prevent their pregnant minors from terminating an unwanted pregnancy. But as we shall see, the Court manipulated this result by purporting to declare that it had to do so because any other result would offend the Constitution. As is clear from a companion case decided the same day, there was never a majority of the Court who believed that children have the constitutional right to terminate unwanted pregnancies. *Danforth* was not simply incoherent; it was disingenuous. To see this, we need to examine *Bellotti v. Baird.*

The Bellotti Decision

In a companion case decided the same day as *Danforth,* the Court considered a challenge to a Massachusetts statute that also required parental consent for a minor to undergo an abortion. Because it was unclear whether Massachusetts's parental consent requirement was absolute or whether a minor had an opportunity to obtain a judicially authorized abortion in the absence of parental consent, the Supreme Court sent the case back to state court. In 1979, *Bellotti v. Baird* returned to the U.S. Supreme Court.[28]

As construed by the state high court, the statute retained a parental consent requirement like the one struck down in *Danforth,* but was supplemented by extraordinary new powers granted to judges. Under the Massachusetts law, pregnant minors were permitted to seek judicial authorization to terminate a pregnancy after unsuccessfully seeking permission from both parents. Judges were instructed to approve the abortion if they determined that the abortion would be in the minor's best interests.

Eight justices agreed that the Massachusetts statute as construed by the state court could not be sustained under *Danforth* because the law merely transferred to the judge the identical power to deny a minor an abortion that the *Danforth* Court voided when exercised by a parent. Although minors were given an option in Massachusetts unavailable to them in Missouri, the Massachusetts law required judges to disapprove an abortion if they believed it would disserve the child's best interests.

The Court declared the law unconstitutional in two plurality opinions, each of which was joined by four justices. The second of these opinions, written by Justice Stevens, would have declared the statute unconstitutional without much ceremony because "no minor in Massachusetts, no matter how mature and capable of informed decisionmaking, may receive an abortion without the consent of either both her parents or a superior court judge."[29] This opinion, had it carried the day, would have recognized minors to have adultlike rights to terminate a pregnancy. But the first opinion, authored by Justice Powell, was the one that ultimately prevailed.

Powell chose a very different route. His solution reveals that the Court was more interested in resolving a knotty public health problem than advancing children's constitutional rights. To accomplish this, however, Powell had no choice but to invoke the rhetoric of children's rights.

Powell's mission was to take away the states' power to make children obtain parental consent before obtaining abortions *without* establishing a precedent that would give children adultlike rights. This was, to say the least, a difficult task. Its difficulty lay in the need to appear to be acting on constitutional principle. The problem was that the only conceivable constitutional principle available for preventing states from requiring parental consent was children's rights.

No one familiar with Powell's voting record on the Supreme Court ever suspected him of being a supporter of children's rights.[30] But in *Danforth* he was faced with few good choices. He could allow states to require parental consent for their children's abortions or he could declare that such a requirement violated a minor's constitutional rights. Powell chose what for him was the lesser of two evils: he declared the Massachusetts law unconstitutional. In doing so, he used the language of children's rights to accomplish an otherwise improbable result. But it was the result Powell wanted, not the children's rights.

He accomplished his purpose by the highly unusual route of drafting an advisory opinion that included a model statute which he predicted a majority of the Court would uphold. He informed states that they may compel minors to seek judicial approval so long as judges are authorized to approve the abortion if they find the minor to be "mature."[31] Because the Massachusetts law lacked such a provision, he declared the law to be unconstitutional.

By writing an opinion that told states the kind of law the Court would likely uphold, he ensured that at least some states would draft such laws. When those laws, written in conformity with his opinion, were eventually reviewed by the Court, they were upheld.[32]

Although Powell worked hard to obfuscate the true meaning of his opinion, as he saw it, the Massachusetts law was unconstitutional for two reasons other than its authorization of an adult to veto the abortion. First, the law authorized *parents* to exercise the veto. Second, the law failed to impose a standard for determining when it would be impermissible to exercise the veto. Powell's solution was to turn the business of reviewing minors' abortion decisions over to the state.

Powell's opinion is among the most oddly argued in the Court's history. The opinion begins by discussing children's rights, reminding readers that "the Fourteenth Amendment . . . [is not] . . . for adults alone."[33] Since one of his purposes was to avoid establishing a precedent that children could use to advance their rights in other contexts, Powell quickly adds that "we are concerned here with a constitutional right to seek an abortion. The abortion decision differs in important ways from other decisions that may be made during minority."

Stressing the importance of the abortion decision to a pregnant minor, he observes that "considering her probable education, employment skills, financial resources, and emotional maturity, unwanted motherhood may be exceptionally burdensome for a minor . . . In sum, there are few situations in which denying a minor the right to make an important decision will have consequences so grave and indelible." This nicely sets the stage for justifying a rule that the Constitution may require allowing children a degree of autonomy in their lives usually denied them.

But Powell also sought to develop an argument for limiting children's rights. In famous language he next summarizes the reasons children lack the same constitutional rights as adults: "the peculiar vulnerability of children; their inability to make critical decisions in an informed, mature manner; and the importance of the parental role in child rearing." For these reasons, "the State is entitled to adjust its legal system to account for children's vulnerability and their needs for 'concern, . . . sympathy, and . . . paternal attention.'"[34]

Because children are often immature, Powell writes, "a State reasonably may determine that parental consultation often is desirable and in the best interest of the minor." Indeed, he quotes from Justice Stewart's *Danforth* concurrence (in which he had joined):

> There can be little doubt that the State furthers a constitutionally permissible end by encouraging an unmarried pregnant minor to seek the help and advice of her parents in making the very important decision whether or not to bear a child. That is a grave decision . . . It seems unlikely that she will obtain adequate counsel and support from the attending physician at an abortion clinic, where abortions for pregnant minors frequently take place.[35]

Ultimately, Powell justified the conclusion that Massachusetts's law violated the Constitution in a most unsatisfying manner. First, he declared that "the unique nature and consequences of the abortion decision [render it] inappropriate 'to give a third party an absolute, and possibly arbitrary, veto over the decision.'" But he also stressed that "an abortion may not be the best choice for the minor." This allowed him to search for a capable adult who could review the child's desire to terminate a pregnancy in a nonarbitrary way.

A recasting of his reasoning in the form of a sequence of arguments helps to highlight the circumlocution of the opinion. His argument in the analytical portion of his opinion is made in the following order: (1) children have constitutional rights; (2) ordinarily parents make all important decisions for their children because children are too immature to make decisions for themselves; (3) the abortion decision is distinctive because it cannot be postponed; (4) for this reason a child's choice to abort cannot be arbitrarily denied; (5) parents are prohibited from denying their children an abortion "arbitrarily"; (6) pregnant minors, like children generally, will not necessarily elect the option that best serves their interests.

The ordering of Powell's opinion served him well. By beginning his discussion about the constitutional rights of children, the case has come to be seen as vindicating children's rights. Had his opinion followed the logical reasoning of the holding, it would look very different: (1) Children presumptively lack constitutional rights to make important life decisions for themselves because they are too immature; (2) ordinarily we rely on parents to make decisions for their children; (3) when it comes to the abortion decision, however, we cannot rely on parents; (4) therefore the state is empowered to authorize children to terminate their pregnancy.

Ordinarily, transferring power over a child from one's parents to the state is the antithesis of recognizing rights in children. The net result of the Supreme Court's pronouncements in the abortion cases concerning minors is a denial of constitutional rights to parents, not a granting of rights to children. In *Danforth*, parents lost their previously recognized rights to decide all nonemergency medical decisions for their unemancipated children. *Bellotti* merely transferred guardianship of children from their parents to the state.

Even a casual review of the decision reveals how empty it is of meaningful constitutional reasoning. In order for Powell's opinion to make even modest sense in constitutional terms, he would have had to reach the startling conclusion that pregnant minors were oppressed by their parents. Of course, he concluded no such thing. His opinion, however, did more than divest parents of the power to prevent their children from terminating a pregnancy; it held that it is unconstitutional even to require minors to consult or notify their parents in the first place. In his words, "every minor must have the opportunity—if she so desires—to go directly to a court without first consulting or notifying her parents."[36]

It is highly telling how far the *Bellotti* rule strays from *Danforth's* holding. *Danforth* held that the constitutional infirmity of a parental consent statute was that parents are prohibited from exercising a "possibly arbitrary veto." The simple rule that would follow from this would permit the minor to go to court only if the parent fails to consent in a timely fashion. Moreover, once before the court, the proper question would be whether the parent's decision was "arbitrary." The logic of *Danforth* not only would leave parents with the power to exercise their parental authority in the first instance; the reviewing court would have to apply a presumption that the parent's decision was not arbitrary, with the child carrying the burden to show otherwise.

At the very least, a rule purporting to be faithful to *Danforth* surely would insist that parents be given a chance to participate in the judicial review and, at a minimum, to explain their reasons for opposing the abortion. Nothing in *Danforth* even hints that a parent's *non*arbitrary refusal to consent to a child's abortion is unconstitutional. How, following *Danforth's* reasoning, could the law do more than authorize judges to overrule the parent's refusal to consent to a child's abortion only after the court concluded that the parental decision should be overturned for a particular reason?

Moreover, when we reconsider the *Danforth* reasoning that led to striking the Missouri law, the *Bellotti* result becomes utterly insupportable. *Danforth*, it will be recalled, held that Missouri's parental consent law was unconstitutional because the state may not delegate a power it lacks in the first place. Yet, startlingly, *Bellotti* declared three years later that the state has this power after all. *Bellotti* declared that state judges may lawfully be empowered to deny ("veto") a minor's request to have an abortion. Although the state may not exercise this veto power in an arbitrary fashion, the Missouri law never afforded parents an arbitrary veto power either. The Missouri statute merely authorized parents to grant or withhold consent. That is the precise power *Bellotti* assigned to the state.

For this result even to begin to make constitutional sense, Justice Powell would have had to conclude that what differentiates judges from parents is the inevitable objectivity of a judicial officer. One searches in vain for even a sentence by Powell about what elevates judges over parents as better fit or more logically empowered to grant or deny a pregnant minor's request to terminate her pregnancy. It should be unsurprising that he stays far away from this subject. The closest he comes is to quote the Massachusetts court's opinion authoritatively interpreting the statute that judges "'must disregard all parental objections, and other considerations, which are not based exclusively on what would serve the minor's best interests.'"[37]

Stunningly, in *Bellotti,* parents were divested of their constitutional rights—not because of the child's rights, but because parents are less well suited than judges to make the correct decision for their children. Although Justice Powell never defends the substitution of judges for parents, his unstated premise could only have been that children's interests are better served by neutral and detached magistrates than by their parents, who may be too close to the situation to possess the appropriate perspective. It is difficult to believe that *anyone,* let alone Justice Powell, can seriously believe that the requirement of parental consent for an abortion exposes a minor to the risk of arbitrary exercise of power, but the requirement of a judge's consent does not.

(Mis)using Children's Rights to Fix a Crisis

For better or worse, politics has placed the Court at the center of the debate about pregnant teens. Legislators have proven themselves incapable of separating public health concerns from more ideological battles over the issue of abortion. In other areas than abortion—such as treatment for sexually transmitted diseases or drug and alcohol addiction—the American political process achieved sensible public health rules for minors without resorting to the Constitution or the courts. For more than forty years, legislatures have seen the wisdom of enacting laws in every state that permit children ready access to such treatment without any requirement of parental consent or even notice.

The reason states have been able to develop coherent and sound public health rules in these areas is because there is no counter-lobby to maximizing the treatment of addicted minors or minors infected with sexually transmitted diseases. In these areas, legislatures are aware that treating minors is the only appropriate result. As Franklin Zimring observes: "legislation dealing with venereal disease and drug and alcohol abuse is really state guidance of adolescents rather than any recognition of autonomy. In public policy terms, there is only one right answer to the question of whether alcoholism, drug misuse, or venereal disease should be treated rather than ignored."[38]

These laws were enacted even though many of the arguments in favor of notifying parents when children seek abortions are just as powerful as when they seek treatment for sexually transmitted diseases. There is, of course, an important distinction between *consent* and *notice*. Because there is a real choice to be made when considering whether to terminate a pregnancy, the arguments in favor of parental consent requirements for abortion are considerably more powerful than for the treatment of sexually transmitted diseases. This is especially true since the treatment for these diseases is relatively safe. Zimring correctly notes not only that parents really have no choice about whether to consent to their child being treated for a sexually transmitted disease, they have little choice even about what type of treatment to provide.

The arguments supporting parental notice requirements in the abortion context certainly have equal force when it comes to treatment for sexually transmitted diseases or addiction. Nonetheless, no legislature has been foolish enough to insist that parents are notified when their children seek antibiotics to treat chlamydia. Legislators simply don't think about this subject in terms of children's rights. These are intelligent rules for society. Legislators recognize the terrible consequences to society (in other words, to the world inhabited by adults) when children with sexually transmitted diseases go untreated. In the same way, a rule that dogs with rabies must be treated is less a rule about the rights of dogs than about the needs of people who might be bitten by them. The last thing rational adults want are rules that make it less likely that children with contagious infections will receive the treatment they want.

For most Americans, the same principle holds true with respect to pregnant minors. Although there are more adults who would rather that pregnant minors be prohibited from obtaining an abortion than there are adults against children obtaining medical treatment for sexually transmitted diseases, the overwhelming majority of adults support a minor's right to terminate a pregnancy.[39]

In contrast to the teen pregnancy cases, let us take brief note of the Court's treatment of legislative efforts to restrict minors' access to contraceptives. In 1977, the Supreme Court declared unconstitutional a New York statute that prohibited the sale or distribution of contraceptives to persons under sixteen years of age.[40] Four justices who thought the contraceptive law was unconstitutional expressly rejected the claim that minors under sixteen have constitutional procreational rights, even labeling as "frivolous" the "argument that a minor has the constitutional right to put contraceptives to their intended use, notwithstanding the combined objection of both parents and the State."[41] Nonetheless, these justices agreed that New York's law was unconstitutional because the law did not "measurably contribute[] to the deterrent purposes which the State advances as justification for the restriction." One justice was more direct, regarding the statute as a form of propaganda and characterizing the law as just as foolish as one in which "a State decided to dramatize its disapproval of motorcycles by forbidding the use of safety helmets."[42]

The abortion cases can only be properly understood as a public health challenge that the Court felt the responsibility to resolve, not an issue about the rights of children. Opponents of abortion have succeeded in many state legislatures in enacting laws restricting a minor's opportunity to terminate a pregnancy. They know that the Supreme Court may overturn them only by invoking the Constitution. The Court, in turn, agreed to write the rules under which pregnant minors may terminate their pregnancies.

The choices that faced the Court when hearing challenges to statutes interfering with a minor's opportunity to terminate a pregnancy, however, were few and unappealing. On the one hand, the choice to uphold laws that require parental consent before a non-emergency abortion may be performed on a minor—though quite coherent in terms of the Constitution—was unacceptable on public health grounds. Aware that many children would be reluctant to tell their parents, the Court was unwilling to risk that those children who wished to get an abortion would wait too long to act or, as before *Roe,* would secure an illegal one. On the other hand, by relying on the Constitution as the basis for striking statutes that require parental consent, the Court created incoherent doctrine in constitutional terms.

By 1979, the conservative justices had enough votes to control the outcome. The remarkable point is not that conservative justices would be opposed to expanding the constitutional rights of children. It is that they wanted a result that virtually ensured that pregnant minors could obtain an abortion. Nevertheless, they did not want to appear to the public to be pro-abortion. Nor did they wish to set any kind of precedent for the constitutional rights of adolescents that would impact other areas of the law.

The Court achieved its goals brilliantly. The result of the adolescent abortion cases is that pregnant minors who are unwilling to tell their parents of their condition but willing to appear before a judge in an anonymous proceeding are able to obtain an abortion; judges routinely rubber stamp the request (with some unfortunate exceptions), and minors remain under the control of an adult for precedential purposes.

This explanation will certainly be startling to some. Most writers on the subject point to the adolescent abortion cases as proof of the Court's antagonism to minors obtaining abortions. It is true that three current members of the Court, Chief Justices Rehnquist and Justices Scalia and Thomas, have always voted to limit women's opportunity to obtain an abortion, including minors. (Justice White also voted this way when he was on the Court.) But this is not true for anyone else on the Court. Nor have there ever been five members on the Court at the same time who sought to create obstacles that would reduce the incidence of abortions performed on minors.

Rather, it was the conservative justices, led by Powell, who had the common-sense understanding that requiring parental consent as a precondition to a child obtaining an abortion would result in too many teenagers becoming parents before they were prepared and before they would want to do so. They were barred by the rules of constitutional adjudication from acknowledging this. But their decisions are incoherent if read to mean anything else.

The leading biography on Justice Powell sheds some light on this speculation. Although there is little in his legal background to place Powell in the forefront of advancing a woman's right to terminate an unwanted pregnancy, his biographer reports that Powell "could not find an answer to the abortion issue in the Constitution" and "felt he would just have to vote his 'gut.'"[43] Powell is reported to have believed that, because the birth of unwanted children is a huge social cost, "the freedom to end unwanted pregnancy seemed consistent with the best interests of both women and children."[44]

In still one other way, the *Bellotti* decision reveals the Court's true intent. The Court has made quite clear on other occasions that it understands the huge social costs associated with unwanted teenage pregnancy. As it wrote in a 1981 opinion upholding a statutory rape law: "At the risk of stating the obvious, teenage pregnancies, which have increased dramatically over the last two decades, have significant social, medical, and economic consequences for both the mother and her child, and the State . . . Of those children who are born, their illegitimacy makes them likely candidates to become wards of the State."[45] It specifically observed, "The risk of maternal death is 60% higher for a teenager under the age of 15 than for a woman in her early twenties. The risk is 13% higher for 15-to-19-year-olds. The statistics further show that most teenage mothers drop out of school and face a bleak economic future."[46]

In a 1977 decision concerning the availability of contraceptives for minors, the Court noted that teenage motherhood involves a host of problems, including adverse physical and psychological effects upon the minor and her baby, the continuous stigma associated with unwed motherhood, the need to drop out of school with the accompanying impairment of educational opportunities, and other dislocations [including] forced marriage of immature couples and the often acute anxieties involved in deciding whether to secure an abortion.[47]

It is unsurprising that the Court is aware of these costs to society. What is revealing about the *Bellotti* decision, however, is that there is no reference to them anywhere. When the Court was directly involved in fixing a social problem it had no business addressing, it pretended the outcome had nothing to do with the social problem in the first place. Instead, the Court would have it, all it was doing was deciding an important constitutional question.

Bellotti compares most interestingly with *Parham v. J. R.*, decided only days earlier.[48] In *Parham*, children challenged the constitutionality of a statute that allows a parent to commit his or her child to a psychiatric institution for "observation and diagnosis" over the child's objection without providing a right to judicial review. The statute also authorized a child's indefinite commitment when the attending physician certifies that the child requires hospitalization. As applied to adults, the statute would certainly be unconstitutional. Unless an adult consents to such commitment, a patient may not be kept in a psychiatric hospital over objection except by court order.

In *Parham*, however, the child was considered a "voluntary patient" because the child's commitment was based on the parent's consent. Placing one's child in a psychiatric hospital over the child's objection is an extraordinary exercise of parental power, effecting a "massive curtailment of liberty." Moreover, the exercise of this power directly implicated a constitutional right of children which the Supreme Court already had held that children possess—the right to avoid loss of physical liberty.

Nonetheless, the Court upheld parental power in *Parham*, reasoning that parents usually make good childrearing choices, and, accordingly, their right to raise their children should not be lightly interfered with.[49] The Court also reasoned that because the parental decision was subject to review by the attending physician, doctors were able to protect children from wrongful institutionalization.[50]

The contrast between *Bellotti* and *Parham* could hardly be greater. *Parham* empowered parents to place their children in institutions without requiring judicial review in the face of evidence that "more than half of the State's institutionalized children were not in need of confinement if other forms of care were made available or used." It chose to rely on doctors, even though they "often lead to erroneous commitments since psychiatrists tend to err on the side of medical caution and therefore hospitalize patients for whom other dispositions would be more beneficial." *Parham* even stressed that judges were relatively ill-suited to determinate a minor's need for hospitalization, even though judges in every state regularly are asked to make such determinations. (This is especially remarkable given that the Court comfortably assigned to judges the unprecedented—and standardless—power to decide whether an abortion would further a pregnant minor's best interests.) Most amazingly of all, *Parham* rejected state oversight of parental decisionmaking. "The statist notion that governmental power should supersede parental authority in all cases because some parents abuse and neglect children is repugnant to American tradition."[51]

It is exceedingly rare to have two Court decisions substantively so far apart. That these decisions were announced twelve days apart makes clear the result-oriented base of children's rights. In the case of mental hospitalization, the Court could comfortably rely on physicians to review parental choice because the Court understood that physicians would tend to err on the side of admitting children into mental hospitals.[52] The political consequences of that error-proneness on the medical profession's part were quite tolerable. But in *Bellotti*, it was politically unacceptable to trust doctors because the doctors who perform abortions in the United States are already a self-selected group of physicians who believe in advancing the patient's choice. Here the concern is that the public understands that doctors would rubber stamp the minor's decision to have an abortion.[53]

Though rubber stamping by judges was politically acceptable, rubber stamping by physicians was not. Requiring nothing more than that a pregnant minor obtain the approval of the attending physician in order to have the abortion would be, in the eyes of the American public, tantamount to ceding the authority to the minor to decide for herself whether to terminate an abortion.

But surely the Court understood that the bypass procedure it created would result in almost every petition being granted. There is considerable evidence that this is precisely what happens. One writer reports, for example, "Between 1981 and 1983, ninety percent of the 1300 petitioning minors in Massachusetts courts were deemed 'mature.' In the rest (with one exception), abortion without parental consent was determined to be in the minors' best interest. That sole exception went to a neighboring state."[54] Similarly, evidence presented in federal litigation in the late 1980s showed that only fifteen out of 3,573 applications for abortions by minors in Minnesota were denied.[55]

This is not to suggest that the compromise the adolescent abortion cases effected imposes few costs on minors. Even though the outcome of the case is largely preordained, there are judges who permit their personal antipathy to abortions to control their behavior. Elizabeth Scott describes how a Utah judge hostile to minors having the right to terminate an abortion claimed to be faithfully applying the maturity test in concluding that a seventeen-year-old "good student" was immature because "she lived at home, engaged in sexual activity without contraceptives, sought counsel from friends rather than family members or church officials, and failed to recognize the long-term consequences of abortion."[56] For this judge, all minors who would use the bypass procedure are by definition immature.

Moreover, there are reports of some anti-abortion judges using the bypass process to harass the girls who come before them. One is chilled to read reports of judges who torment pregnant minors in their courtrooms, force them to go to anti-abortion clinics prior to granting a hearing, and assign anti-abortion lawyers to represent them in court. One writer describes an Alabama judge who appointed a guardian for a fetus in order to "assure that the fetus had 'an opportunity to have a voice, even a vicarious one, in the decision making.'"[57]

Among the terrible costs imposed on pregnant minors who appear before judges is the trauma of the experience. "'You see all the typical things that you would see with somebody under incredible amounts of stress, answering monosyllabically, tone of voice, tenor of voice, shaky, wringing of hands . . . one young lady had her—her hands were turning blue and it was warm in my office.'"[58]

Nonetheless, there can be little doubt that the Court fully understood it was creating a judicial bypass process that virtually guaranteed that the judge would ultimately approve the petition. The only two substantive questions before the court when a minor seeks judicial permission to terminate a pregnancy are whether the minor is mature and, if not, whether the abortion is in her best interests. The judge must approve the abortion if either question is answered in the affirmative. In Robert Mnookin's words: "how could the judge determine that it is in the interest of a minor to give birth to a child if she is too immature even to decide to have an abortion?"[59]

It is revealing that results in the adolescent abortion cases were achieved without providing any precedent for privacy or autonomy rights in any other context. *Danforth* proved not to be a ruling having to do with a child's privacy. The constitutional right to an abortion is, of course, based entirely on the more basic right of women to privacy. For adults, because they enjoy the constitutional right to privacy, they also possess the constitutional right to terminate unwanted pregnancies. With minors, the opposite was achieved. Minors are said to have the constitutional right to an abortion, but are denied the right to privacy. Instead of a minor's right to an abortion being a subcategory of the greater right to privacy, it becomes an end in itself.

The adolescent abortion cases are not really about children's rights. They are, instead, a well-disguised effort to settle a dispute among adults over the best rules for dealing with children who become pregnant unintentionally and do not want to become parents. But in telling the story of the dispute, Justice Powell strategically chose to rely on this defense: "the Constitution made me do it."

When the traditional means of creating sound public health policy—reliance on the common sense of the legislatures—failed to work, the Supreme Court became the only institution that could resolve the matter sensibly. Though the Court resorted to the language of constitutional rights, it had other goals in mind. It is useful to observe that those who support a minor's right to abortion do so in the name of children's rights. Even though the public health claim is more straightforward, the reproductive rights movement has attempted to sweep children into its sphere, despite the considerable difficulties raised by arguing that adolescents ought to have the same autonomy rights as adults.

It would be one thing if the Court actually held that minors really do have constitutional rights to decide whether to reproduce. That decision would have been considerably bolder than the one ultimately made by the Court. It also would have been considerably more controversial. But at least it would have freed pregnant minors from judicial oversight.

This is not to say minors gained nothing from the abortion decisions. Precisely speaking, the "right" pregnant minors gained from the abortion decisions is an option to seek approval from one of two adults. Before *Danforth,* minors were obliged to seek permission from their parents to terminate an unwanted pregnancy. After *Bellotti,* minors have a choice to seek permission from their parents or a judge.

Part of what is so remarkable about all of this is how successful the Court has been in promoting the notion that the abortion cases are about a child's rights. Just as amazingly, the Court was able to place in the state's hands the power to veto a minor's choice to terminate a pregnancy as the means of vindicating the minor's rights. Having first divested parents of a right they enjoyed through a line of Supreme Court cases stretching over fifty years, the Court endowed the state with the very same right.

The solution the Court created says a great deal about the degree to which the rights of children are malleable tools used to further the interests of adults.

8

How Children's Rights Impact Family Law and Juvenile Rights

THERE has never been a golden age for children's rights, nor does it seem likely that such an age is imminent. The modern era's emphasis on rights within families and on limiting parental authority over children has dramatically changed the American landscape. But whether the changes it has wrought serve children well is an entirely separate matter.

An overarching characteristic of the children's rights movement is a distrust of parental authority. The basis for some of this distrust is undeniably well grounded. Parents do not always act in their children's interests. But the modern solution for children's rights advocates has been to fuel a movement that encourages litigation to protect and enforce children's rights. Only a fraction of the causes of action regularly pursued against parents, however, have anything to do with protecting children from the extremes of parental misconduct.

The problem with how children's rights are used in modern family disputes is that they are used more often than not as an opportunity to "take it to the judge." One of the few palpable results of the children's rights movement over the last forty years is that more children are enmeshed in legal proceedings than would have been imaginable a generation ago.

Were a society's commitment to children measured by the number of law-related professionals paying attention to children, the

United States would easily rank first in the world.[1] But if, instead, this extraordinary means of demonstrating concern for children is a symptom of things gone awry, the United States has little of which to be proud.

More children than ever are the subject of legal proceedings whose purpose is to terminate their parents' rights. More children than ever are in state-supervised foster care, denied the opportunity to live with their parents and, even, to remain legally related to them. And more children than ever are embroiled in contentious custody and relocation cases. The enormous waste of resources engendered by this system should trouble us in itself, although there are far more grave consequences.

Over the past generation the fate of children has been steadily changed to an unprecedented degree from being left in their parents' hands to being left in a judge's. For some, this constitutes progress. But it is an odd form of progress that takes away parental control and gives it to the impersonal institution of state officials. The encouragement to protect children from their parents is fueled by those children's advocates who object to children being subject to the control of an adult. Yet the current solution only shifts the control from the parent to a different adult. The protections of due process of law do little to rein in the overreaching done by judges, caseworkers, and children's lawyers in the name of serving children well.

Some comfortably put their faith in a court's capacity to assess children's interests. They believe that judges are able objectively to evaluate a parent's capabilities to ascertain the children's best interests. But courts lack the expertise, time, and knowledge of human development to make the exquisitely individualized judgments about particular familial relationships that decisions involving children unavoidably involve.

For this and other reasons, the lives of both adults and children are advanced by limiting the situations in which either's fate is to be determined by state officials. "Rights" work best when they clearly delineate the power of a state official to act. In the topsy-turvy world of children's rights, "rights" have the opposite effect. Relying on them *expands* the power of state officials.

This unusual relationship between rights and state action is vastly underappreciated. A child's "right" to limit parental authority only to those decisions that further the child's best interests broadly authorizes state officials to oversee and control families. As we have seen, the principles upon which a free democracy rests are advanced by sharply constraining such authority. If the only way to reduce state control over the family were to oppose children's rights, I would stand as an opponent. But it is not the only way. If forced to say it, it is more than reasonable to assert that children have the right to limit the conditions in which their upbringing is subject to review by state officials.

If children's rights were understood to include limiting state officials from overreaching, huge numbers of cases currently litigated in the name of children's rights would be barred. Fights between adults over children would almost certainly continue to be waged. But courts would not be permitted to decide those disputes based on the child's best interests. That standard only ensures greater intervention through protracted litigation and an almost boundless authority by the judge to regulate the family.

Clear rules, quickly enforced, would do far more to protect children's rights than protracted litigation ever could. This is true whether the disputes are between parents and nonparents or between parents themselves. Legal disputes of the sort involving Baby Jessica should be avoided whenever possible and, when brought, should be resolved within a very short time.

This is best achieved when it is easiest to predict how the court will decide the dispute. Reliance on the best interests standard, however, is an open invitation to fight to the bitter end. That is why contested child custody and relocation cases have proliferated since that standard was adopted.

It is more than the basis for deciding cases that should be narrowed. So should the opportunity even to seek judicial review of parenting. Children's interests would be well served by reducing the opportunities for extended family members (such as grandparents) to sue the parents. Encouraging lawsuits among family members has an unfortunate byproduct of discouraging private resolution of disagreements. When grandparents have no rights over the upbringing of their grandchildren, they can get their way only by being nice. Among the unintended consequences of the children's rights movement is that adults are less kind with each other when engaged in familial disputes.

Child welfare cases should also be dismissed when agencies cannot make a plausible showing that the children are at risk of serious harm. Far too many cases currently prosecuted throughout the country fall considerably short of this showing. Child welfare cases have become the means by which we address the disturbing conditions that many poor children endure.

When high percentages of whole communities are raising children in disturbing conditions, however, the solution cannot be to label their parents unfit and turn the children over to the state. These disturbing conditions can be ameliorated. If we lack the political will to bolster the families of poor children, we should at least accept that fact and leave well enough alone. Coercively intruding into poor families simply because children are being raised in poverty ignores the insult and degradation this inflicts on parents. The disrespect the state shows for poor parents is deeply destructive to their children, who are denied the important developmental need of believing, and relying upon, their parents' omnipotence during crucial phases of their upbringing.

Children's rights are generally served best by restricting the conditions under which their lives are subject to review by state officials. The rule that pregnant minors must obtain judicial permission to obtain an abortion is a violation of that principle. We may disagree about the wisdom of a rule that a parent's approval is needed, but there should be no disagreement that it is not a judge's proper business.

Children are just as subject to the control of adults as they were before the 1960s. Only now, the adults who control their fate are less likely to be related to them or even to know them very well.

Judges, caseworkers, and lawyers are now deciding with whom children should live, whether they should be permitted to form or maintain relationships with particular adults, and even whether they should be permitted to terminate a pregnancy. It may be true that these professionals, unlike parents, lack any conflict of interest with the children whose future they are deciding. But neither do they have the concern for those children or the deep, individual knowledge of them upon which so much of parental rights is sensibly based.

Children do not need rights within the family. What they need are rules that work. Keeping families free from state oversight will do more for children than encouraging litigation and judicial intervention. Adults are the ones who need and want children to have rights. Regrettably, many children's advocates have unintentionally encouraged adults who wish to rearrange power relationships in families. If children's rights did not work for these adults, the movement would be of far less consequence.

It would be wonderful if children's rights advocates approached the world from the perspective of Supreme Court Justice Louis Brandeis. He famously warned that we need "to be most on our guard to protect liberty when the government's purposes are beneficent." This is true, he wrote, because "the greatest dangers to liberty lurk in insidious encroachment by men of zeal, well meaning but without understanding."[2]

The children's rights advocates have turned this warning on its head. They are content to turn all family disputes over to judges because they do not trust parents. It would be far preferable if they regarded children as needing rights against the overreaching of state officials, including judges. Only a perverse form of rights could invite such overreaching.

There is still one additional adverse consequence of the battle to give children rights. Children's rights advocacy has also had an insidious impact on an entire other field concerning children. As I mentioned at the very beginning of this book, children's rights can usefully be divided into two parts: the first—and the principal focus of this book—concerns the relationship of children and their parents. The second is the relationship between children and state officials.

There is little doubt that children need rights against the exercise of state power. Indeed, in many situations, such as when children are in state custody (including foster care), children even need lawyers. The agencies, institutions, and state parties who claim to speak on their behalf do a terrible job of meeting the basic needs of children. If children are at slightly less risk of being harmed by their parents since the modern movement began, they are at considerably greater risk of being harmed by the state.

Regrettably, children's rights advocates in family law have unintentionally disadvantaged children when challenging other interactions between children and the state. Because most of the contentious child-state clashes involve older children, advocates in this area of the law commonly are called "juvenile rights advocates." These advocates seek due process rights protections against suppression of speech, wrongful arrest and detention, and wrongful suspension from school, among many other important areas.

But the different messages delivered by children's rights advocates and juvenile rights advocates have become difficult to reconcile. It is surely possible to argue both that children deserve greater oversight by state officials and that they have the same rights as adults to thwart unwanted state intervention, but we should not be surprised when these messages get confused. In a little appreciated way, children's rights advocates have made it considerably more difficult for juvenile rights advocates to make much headway.

How the advocacy of children's rights could be turned against juveniles first became apparent to me in the early 1980s. At that time, I represented a mother of three boys whose parental rights were terminated solely because she was found by a Pennsylvania family court to be mentally retarded. No federal court had ever ruled that the U.S. Constitution permits destroying the parent-child relationship for this reason. As a result of the termination order, my client's children were in state-supervised foster homes as state wards.

We filed a writ of habeas corpus in federal court. To prevail, we needed to show that the children were in state custody in violation of the federal constitution. But habeas corpus law also requires showing that the challenged "custody" subjects the individual to "restraints not shared by the public generally." The case, *Lehman v. Lycoming County Children's Services,* reached the Supreme Court in 1982.[3]

The Court dismissed the case, ruling that children in state-supervised foster care are not in custody that is protectable by habeas corpus because children are always in some form of custody anyway. The Court held that foster care was not sufficiently distinguishable from the kind of custody to which children ordinarily are subjected when raised at home. This was a remarkable conclusion. As state wards, every decision about the children's lives, including with whom they would reside as well as all educational and medical choices, were to be made by state officials. The ruling was all the more remarkable because the Court had previously found persons on parole to be "in custody" within the meaning of the same statute and even held that persons who completed their sentences suffered a sufficient restraint on their freedom to fall within the statute because of the "collateral consequences" a former conviction might yield.[4]

You may forgive me for never quite agreeing with the Court's reasoning or conclusion. Even so, I acknowledge the plausibility of the Court's view. Two years later, however, I returned to the Court wearing my juvenile rights advocate hat. In *Schall v. Martin,* I sought another writ of habeas corpus, this time challenging the detention in New York of accused juvenile delinquents in jail-like facilities that included barbed wire, locked doors, and prison guards.[5] At the federal trial, the evidence supported the claim that state judges were sending juveniles to jail arbitrarily as a form of punishment even when they posed no danger to others and were likely to return to court for their trial. The legal question raised was whether or not the juveniles were lawfully in state custody in violation of the federal constitution.

Justice Rehnquist wrote the opinion for the Court. His decision used *Lehman* so brutally that I took it quite personally when I initially read his opinion. Relying on *Lehman,* he ruled that because children are always in some form of custody anyway, the Constitution permits a far wider range of justifications for jailing young people than is required for jailing adults. (In the early 2000s, the Court extended the metaphor of children always being in some form of custody to the public school arena, allowing school administrators to require suspicionless drug testing of all students engaged in any extracurricular activity, including the chess or debate club.)[6]

So here was a most unfortunate convergence of children's and juvenile's advocacy. If part of a child's right is to have the intimate details of their upbringing subject to supervision by the state, then older children may end up in jail without compliance with constitutional rules designed to protect the liberty of adults. It is not likely that many share Justice Rehnquist's deep cynicism, but it is clear that juveniles have fared relatively poorly over the past generation despite the resounding victory in *In re Gault* at the commencement of the modern era of children's rights.

I do not wish to be misunderstood. I do not blame children's rights advocates for the result in *Schall* or for the many setbacks in the juvenile rights movement ever since. But it is understandable if some confusion results when advocates for young people say simultaneously that a child's right is furthered by state oversight even of small details of their lives, and a child has the right to thwart state intervention to the same degree as does an adult. For better or worse, the juvenile rights advocate is well advised to try to find a different way of advancing children's interests than through the rhetoric of "rights."

Since the end of the 1980s, every state has revised its laws to facilitate the prosecution of more juveniles in adult criminal court.[7] It is now easier to prosecute a child in adult criminal court than it has been at any other point in the past seventy years. States have lowered the age for prosecution of children as adults and have expanded the list of crimes that permit prosecution in criminal court. Between 1992 and 1995 alone, forty jurisdictions enacted or expanded provisions for juvenile waiver to adult court.[8] Prosecutors in many states now have the authority to choose which court in which to bring criminal charges against young people.[9]

A generation ago, judges first had to conclude that there was something particularly egregious about the child's personality or the crime to determine that juvenile court was inappropriate. That is no longer a consideration in many cases today. A generation ago there was a strong presumption that children should be treated in juvenile court; the presumption was so strong that most children (simply by reason of being young) were ineligible under all circumstances for prosecution as an adult. For the others, judges had to hold a hearing to determine in each case whether the juvenile was "unamenable to treatment" in the juvenile system before being sent to criminal court. Today, many cases are automatically begun in criminal court based solely on the charges.

This punitive shift means that thousands of children are prosecuted as adults in adult criminal court and routinely receive sentences that would have been regarded as shockingly punitive—virtually unthinkable—a mere generation ago. Today more than forty states allow juveniles fourteen or younger to be prosecuted in adult court; at least twelve of these states set no minimum age for transfer.

As a result of these changes, the number of juveniles prosecuted in adult court over the last generation has risen by more than 80 percent. Our changing conception of a juvenile delinquent is so dramatic that, according to one report, the number of juveniles held in adult jails pending trial rose 366 percent between 1983 and 1998.[10] This rise has been encouraged even though we know that juveniles in adult facilities are eight times more likely to commit suicide, five times more likely to be sexually assaulted, and twice as likely to be attacked by inmates or staff.[11]

The United States stands alone as the only nation in the world that has refused to join international agreements prohibiting the execution of juvenile offenders. In 1989, the Supreme Court ruled that the Constitution does not protect sixteen- and seventeen-year-olds from being executed.[12] As of 2004, nineteen states expressly permit the execution of juveniles.[13] Even if, as many predict as of this writing, the Supreme Court in 2005 will overrule its 1989 decision and declare that imposing a capital sentence on persons under eighteen violates the Eighth Amendment's protection against the imposition of cruel and unusual punishments, 228 juvenile death penalties have been imposed in the United States between 1973 and 2004.[14]

Just as remarkably, very few states today expressly prohibit imposing a life sentence on a child. The overwhelming majority expose children to sentences of life in prison without the possibility of parole.[15] In Washington, D.C., for instance, offenders as young as eight are eligible to receive such sentences. Vermont permits ten-year-olds to suffer the same punishment.[16] These new laws have led to well-known cases such as that of Lionel Tate, the twelve-year-old boy from Florida who killed a younger playmate. In 2002, an adult criminal court judge in Florida sentenced Lionel to a mandatory term of life in prison before an appellate court set aside the conviction on grounds unrelated to children's rights.[17]

Nobody who is in favor of these changes takes the position that confining juveniles in adult facilities is good for them. Researchers who compared juvenile and adult correctional facilities agree that confining juveniles to adult facilities has a terrible impact on their long-term prospects when they are released. Juvenile facilities attempt to provide rehabilitation and education, whereas adult prisons do not even purport to help the inmates.

Not very long ago, the recognition that children lack the experience and maturity of adults served as the justification for treating children with understanding and leniency when they engaged in misconduct. The current trend in criminal justice is to regard children as morally blameworthy and sufficiently adultlike to receive adult punitive sentences of incarceration.

Another Way to Argue for Children's Rights

How are we to develop a cogent set of arguments that protect children against actions taken by state officials who wrongfully intrude in their lives? Perhaps the most important rule for children's advocates to remember is that their efforts can only be as successful as adults permit them to be. With this in mind, children's advocates may benefit from revisiting the way claims affecting children were addressed before the children's rights movement began.

Before the modern movement began, there was considerably less emphasis on rights than is common today. Two cases decided before the 1960s demonstrate this difference. In 1943, the Supreme Court decided *West Virginia Board of Education v. Barnette.*[18] In 1954, it decided *Brown v. Board of Education.*[19] Neither case mentions children's rights, yet both rank as landmark cases of constitutional law with results that are universally praised by advocates for children.

Barnette concerned the constitutionality of West Virginia's flag salute statute, which required all public school students to recite the Pledge of Allegiance each day. West Virginia's law, enacted in the midst of World War II, required all schools "to conduct courses of instruction in history, civics, and in the Constitutions of the United States and of the State 'for the purpose of teaching, fostering and perpetuating the ideals, principles and spirit of Americanism, and increasing the knowledge of the organization and machinery of the government.'" The school board defended the law, which included a provision that anyone who refused to salute would be expelled, on the grounds that the flag "signifies government resting on the consent of the governed, liberty regulated by law, protection of the weak against the strong, security against the exercise of arbitrary power, and absolute safety for free institutions against foreign aggression."

The question before the Court was whether school officials could *compel* students to utter the pledge. The Court declared the law unconstitutional because it impermissibly "requires affirmation of a belief and an attitude of mind," and insists that "the individual . . . communicate by word and sign his acceptance of the political ideas it thus bespeaks."

The Court held that under the First Amendment it does not matter whether what the government demands people say or believe is something "good, bad or merely innocuous." In the Court's words, "Validity of the asserted power to force an American citizen publicly to profess any statement of belief or to engage in any ceremony of assent to one presents questions of power that must be considered independently of any idea we may have as to the utility of the ceremony in question."[20]

The opinion was written by Justice Robert Jackson. In his hands, the case was told as a story about government, its role in educating youth, and its limitations. Rather remarkably, nowhere in the Court's opinion do we ever learn whether the persons challenging the law are children or their parents. The challengers are described thus: "Appellees, citizens of the United States and of West Virginia, brought suit in the United States District Court for themselves and others similarly situated asking its injunction to restrain enforcement of these laws and regulations against Jehovah's Witnesses."

The decision was written at a time when most of the world was engaged in a conflict between fascist and democratic governments. Jackson used *Barnette* as a platform to contrast the one from the other and to place the United States in a particular light by emphasizing both to Americans and others around the world that polities that honor the value of freedom of thought and expression must deny government the power to make its citizens speak.

In Jackson's hands, the case consisted of a "conflict . . . between authority and rights of the individual." Neither the Court's holding nor reasoning depended on an understanding that children possessed rights which the Constitution protected. Instead, the case stands for the closely related but materially different point that "individuals," whether they happen to be children, adherents of a particular religion, or whomever, are protected against improperly exercised state power.

The opinion emphasizes the potential ultimate cost to society, adults and children alike, if state officials are permitted to force any citizens, but particularly children, to express a particular view. "We set up government by consent of the governed, and the Bill of Rights denies those in power any legal opportunity to coerce that consent. Authority here is to be controlled by public opinion, not public opinion by authority."[21]

Even when Jackson discussed the impact of the challenged law on children, he did not indulge a "children's rights" perspective. Instead, his emphasis was on the cost to society as a whole that a rule requiring children to believe a particular thing would exact: "That they are educating the young for citizenship is reason for scrupulous protection of Constitutional freedoms of the individual, if we are not to strangle the free mind at its source and teach youth to discount important principles of our government as mere platitudes."

He ended his opinion with words that continue to ring as among the most eloquent expressed by the Court on the importance of freedom of expression: "If there is any fixed star in our constitutional constellation, it is that no official, high or petty, can prescribe what shall be orthodox in politics, nationalism, religion, or other matters of opinion or force citizens to confess by word or act their faith therein."[22]

In *Brown v. Board of Education,* among the best-known cases ever decided by the Supreme Court, the Court heard a challenge to the maintenance of racially segregated schools. *Brown* changed American law and the American way of life by overruling *Plessy v. Ferguson,* the 1896 Supreme Court case which declared that "separate but equal" was constitutional.[23]

In its decision, the Court stressed the significance of education in order to make clear why the question the Court had to decide was so important. But the Court emphasized education's significance *to society as a whole,* rather than to the children receiving it. In the Court's words, "education [wa]s perhaps the most important function of state and local governments." But this was not because of the potential value to children to lead a happy and fulfilled life. Rather, its import was to be found in its impact on "our democratic society." A good education is needed, the Court told us, to assist "in the performance of our most basic public responsibilities, even service in the armed forces. It is the very foundation of good citizenship."

The *Brown* opinion became a story about the commitment American society makes to equality. Even if a version of equality developed by the Court in 1896 seemed sufficient to some, the Court in *Brown* explained why separation ensured inequality. The precise holding is that "children of the minority group" are deprived of equal protection of the law "by the maintenance of segregated education even though the physical facilities and other 'tangible' factors may be equal," because segregation "generates a feeling of inferiority as to their status in the community that may affect their hearts and minds in a way unlikely ever to be undone."

In *Brown,* the Court sought to prevent the harm to society that is exacted as a result of maintaining racially segregated schools (not the harm to children per se). By assessing the damage, both to children and to society at large, from the continued maintenance of state-sponsored segregation, the Supreme Court reached the conclusion that separate but equal no longer comported with the needs and aspirations of American society. But *Brown* did not vindicate children's rights so much as it imposed a structural limit on the power of government officials.[24]

Brown declared that America's version of freedom denied state officials the power to discriminate against people on the basis of race. That children were the initial direct beneficiaries of this principle underscores the importance to the adults of the eradication of the prior discriminatory power. If state officials were permitted to discriminate against children on the basis of race, the legacy of slavery would inevitably continue into succeeding generations. This was the import of Kenneth Clark's famous testimony in the trial phase of the *Brown* litigation, which explained that the consequences of separate-but-equal policy negatively impacted the psyche of black children throughout their lives. This impact, in turn, negatively affected society as a whole. Thus, stopping this discrimination at the earliest possible time served important purposes for all of us.

By the 1960s, extensive writings extolling children's rights helped launch the children's rights movement.[25] The movement was inspired by several important Supreme Court decisions issued between 1966 and 1969. Among these was *Tinker v. Des Moines Independent Community School District,* decided in 1969.[26]

The decisions in *Barnette* and *Tinker* vividly demonstrate the different approaches available to a court considering a claim challenging government action as it affects children. In *Tinker,* the Court was asked to determine whether the suspension of students from school because they wore black armbands in protest of the Vietnam War offended the Constitution. The school officials justified their decision to suspend the students because of concerns that the protest would interfere with classes and disrupt the educational mission of the school.

There was evidence in the record to suggest that the school officials disagreed with the particular message the suspended students wished to deliver, that the school commonly allowed students to wear a wide range of symbols, and that no actual disruption resulted from the protest.[27] As the Court wrote, "the school authorities did not purport to prohibit the wearing of all symbols of political or controversial significance. The record shows that students in some of the schools wore buttons relating to national political campaigns, and some even wore the Iron Cross, traditionally a symbol of Nazism. The order prohibiting the wearing of armbands did not extend to these."[28]

Thus, *Tinker* could have been written in very traditional First Amendment terms that prohibited state officials from engaging in "viewpoint" discrimination. A victory for the schoolchildren merely on the ground that school authorities must maintain viewpoint neutrality would not have necessitated a change in existing laws.

The opinion was written by Justice Abe Fortas. Fortas sat on the Court only from 1965 to 1969, yet he was the justice most focused on children's rights in the Court's history. For Fortas, it was the students and their rights that deserved center stage. He began thus: "Students in school as well as out of school are 'persons' under our Constitution. They are possessed of fundamental rights which the State must respect . . . [and] may not be regarded as closed-circuit recipients of only that which the State chooses to communicate." He also chose to emphasize that a "student's rights . . . do not embrace merely the classroom hours. When he is in the cafeteria, or on the playing field, or on the campus during the authorized hours, he may express his opinions, even on controversial subjects like the conflict in Vietnam, if he does so without 'materially and substantially interfer[ing] with the requirements of appropriate discipline in the operation of the school.'"[29]

A *Barnette*-like opinion would have emphasized the duties of state officials not to prefer one political view over another and not to discriminate against a speaker merely because of a disagreement with the content of the suppressed speech. The point of such an opinion would have been that state officials must respect the First Amendment even when it is applied to students not because children have constitutional rights but because the Constitution constrains the government in particular ways.

Indeed, although *Tinker* was widely hailed as a children's rights victory, the *reason* for the result actually had little to do with the aggrieved citizens being children. It may be that what made the decision difficult, and precedential, was that the Supreme Court ruled that the First Amendment was to be applied in that case *even though* the plaintiffs were children. To this extent, the fact that children were involved becomes relevant. One of the ways in which the subject of juvenile rights differs from that of the rights of adults is that often a court must engage in an additional analytical step before ruling that government action is unconstitutionally applied. The first step (taken in all cases) is whether the governmental conduct can be said to have violated a norm of the Constitution. If the answer is "no," the inquiry ends. In cases involving juveniles, there is often a second step to determine whether there are special reasons not to apply the ordinary rule to them.

But very often the decision to apply the ordinary rule even to children is not because of some quality about children or their rights. More often it is because adults do not want to establish a precedent for tolerating governmental conduct that is ordinarily prohibited. In this understanding of the case, *Tinker* stands for the important but uncontroversial principle that government may not take sides in political debates. When government actors discriminate against citizens based on the content of the citizens' expression, courts will declare the government action to be out of bounds.

It is true that, as reconstructed, we are hard pressed to identify any reason not to apply this important principle to children. At the same time, adults who care deeply about limiting the government's power to censor certain viewpoints would want the rule to be applied to children precisely to be able to establish for the future just how important the principle is. In this sense, many issues affecting children are of deep interest to adults, but in not the sense that most usually appreciate.

Justice Fortas instead avidly pursued the children's rights agenda. His opinion for the Court became a story about the children in the case and their rights. The opinion begins by telling the reader the names and ages of the petitioners. This contrasts sharply with *Brown*, which describes the plaintiffs only as "minors of the Negro race." Fortas instead made the suspended teens the protagonists in his story. "Neither students or teachers shed their constitutional rights to freedom of speech or expression at the schoolhouse gate," he proclaimed. "Students in school as well as out of school are 'persons' under our Constitution. They are possessed of fundamental rights which the State must respect, just as they themselves must respect their obligations to the State."

For Fortas, because students have constitutional rights, school officials may not suppress speech of which they disapprove. This may seem reasonably close to the reasoning of the Court in the 1940s and 1950s; but on careful inspection, it turns out to be radically different. For Justice Jackson in *Barnette* and the entire Court in *Brown*, students are protected from certain challenged state action because the Constitution constrains state officials in their official duties.

A federal court of appeals decision in 2000 nicely captures this distinction and suggests that it may make a great difference to a judge to consider whether restricting government authority advances a child's right or advances an important principle of American society. In *American Amusement Machine Assoc. v. Kendrick*, Judge Richard Posner wrote a decision declaring unconstitutional an Indianapolis ordinance limiting the access of children to video games that depict violence.[30] The city enacted the law because of its belief that exposure to violent video games has a negative impact on children (and, ultimately, on society). The court's technical holding was that the ordinance violated a child's First Amendment right to access to nonobscene materials.

Perhaps in an effort to assure readers he was no bleeding-heart children's rights supporter, Posner explained that the law's real threat was not to a child's right to be exposed to various materials but the danger to society if the right is denied. Fearful that his opinion be seen as "merely a matter of pressing the First Amendment to a dryly logical extreme," Posner stressed that restrictions on government officials' capacity to regulate the content of material read by children is crucial: "People are unlikely to become well-functioning, independent-minded adults and responsible citizens if they are raised in an intellectual bubble." Posner felt comfortable warning that the Indianapolis ordinance could lead to the "murderous fanaticism displayed by young German soldiers in World War II" because the history of the Hitler *Jugend* "illustrates the danger of allowing government to control the access of children to information and opinion."[31]

This distinction has other useful qualities. It eliminates what may for some decision makers be an unnecessary obstacle to deciding a case sensibly. To make this point, it is instructive to consider the views expressed by Justice Powell in a 1975 decision in which he obviously was still quite upset over the children's rights emphasis in *Tinker.*

In *Goss v. Lopez,*[32] the Supreme Court held that public school officials could not, consistent with the Due Process Clause of the Fourteenth Amendment, expel students from school without first providing some kind of hearing and an opportunity to be heard. The record in *Goss* amply demonstrated that students were commonly suspended from schools for alleged violations of rules without providing them with any chance to show they did nothing wrong. The ruling was relatively straightforward, continuing the expansion of procedural due process that requires some kind of hearing whenever state officials deprive someone of "property" based on alleged behavior of the individual. *Goss* held that if a student denies the charges, he must be given "an explanation of the evidence the authorities have and an opportunity to present his side of the story."

Nonetheless, the ruling triggered a vigorous dissent from Justice Powell. Yet Powell seemed more disturbed by Fortas's rhetoric in *Tinker*, which had been decided six years earlier, than with the actual result reached in *Goss*. Powell was not yet a member of the Court when *Tinker* was decided and perhaps he used the occasion of his dissent in *Goss* to register his strong disagreement with the concept of students' rights.

Powell saw fit to complain that "school authorities must have broad discretionary authority in the daily operation of public schools."[33] Of course they must; but what does that have to do with a rule insisting that school officials have all the facts before they act? *Goss* does not limit the discretionary authority of school officials to make decisions beyond requiring them to obtain the facts about a situation before they act.

But Powell regarded the combination of *Tinker* and *Goss* as inviting "'an entirely new era in which the power to control pupils by the elected officials of state supported public schools' . . . is in ultimate effect transferred to the Supreme Court." What plainly bothered Powell the most was the prospect that limiting educational authorities in their power to impose discipline would harm children's true interests: "One who does not comprehend the meaning and necessity of discipline," he emphasized, "is handicapped not merely in his education but throughout his subsequent life."

There is no legal doctrine requiring courts to regard cases like *Goss* as being about children or furthering their rights. Saying that students must be given "an explanation of the evidence the authorities have and an opportunity to present" their version of the facts is a child-centered way of looking at things. But the corollary is just as powerful. State officials are prohibited from making important decisions without undertaking the minimal steps to ensure they have all the facts.

Moreover, this alternative proposition is palatable to more people. It defends an important principle to which many adults are

committed: Whenever state officials make decisions that affect another person's legally protected interest, a fair society should insist
that the official conduct a minimal inquiry into the facts before taking action. Even more, when we change our orientation from students' rights to basic fairness—from protecting a student's interest
to guarding against arbitrary state action—it becomes almost inconceivable that someone would regard such a requirement as a
travesty.

This alternative way of seeking to protect children from state action has much to commend it. As we have seen, the Supreme Court
in *In re Gault* held that juveniles accused in juvenile court must be
afforded the essentials of due process because they are people with
protected constitutional rights. What if we placed the accent elsewhere? What if we were to say that state officials may not deprive
people (including children) of their liberty without due process of
law. By placing the stress on the limitations of state officials, there is
no need to persuade decision makers that children deserve adult
rights because they are like adults.[34]

The history of the modern children's rights movement proves,
if nothing else, that reliance on children's rights is no guarantee
against the enactment of policies that serve children poorly. Even
more to the point, nothing within the rights lexicon can protect
children from adults' insistence on treating children like adults.

Some will counter that this is but a variation on the now familiar
claim that the civil rights movement has not proven sufficient to advance the plight of minorities in the United States. Many note, for
example, that racism and discrimination continue in the United
States despite the formal outlawing of discrimination. This suggests
that rights invariably have a limited utility and that much more is
needed to transform a society than the recognition that individuals
or a class of people have rights.[35] But it would be wrong to think of
these phenomena as being basically the same. They are radically
different.

Even if it is true that *Brown v. Board of Education*'s requirement
that *de jure* racial discrimination be eliminated did not prevent
white flight and that, as a consequence, the vast majority of black

schoolchildren continue to attend segregated public schools, there is a categorical difference between this sort of limitation on the power of rights to make a difference and the barrenness of children's rights. Equal protection rights are a powerful means of preventing government from officially privileging one group over another. They provide minorities with the ability to demand equal treatment under the law. An ever-growing number of blacks are real beneficiaries of civil rights laws and live a materially better life because of these laws. That these laws do not reach far enough is not to say they do not reach far.

But equal protection rights are outside of most formulations of children's rights. Very often, however, children deserve to have rights that adults already have. For those interested in doing better for children, we should recognize that some arguments will be more persuasive than others. At least in the United States, the strongest arguments for treating children better, in almost every context, will stress their needs or interests. It is considerably more straightforward to argue against an adultlike sentence for children based on children's interests and needs. Much is gained by this. Just as important, little is lost.

The principal advantage to relying on rights in the first place is their capacity to require particular outcomes in legal disputes. Thus, courts and judges are said to be compelled to rule a certain way once particular rights are established. But, for reasons having nothing to do with children in the first place, we should expect courts to protect children only against the most egregious state acts.

Sentences for young people who are found guilty of criminal violations provide one such example. When legislatures authorize sentences of up to twenty years for fifteen-year-olds, courts may strike the law only if it violates the Eighth Amendment's proscription against cruel and unusual punishment. Under standards of American constitutional law, it is extremely difficult to get the Supreme Court to declare any sentence authorized by a legislature unconstitutional. It is worth recalling in this context that in 1987 the Court even ruled that executing sixteen-year-olds was consistent with constitutional principles.

In this and countless other areas, children's advocates are obliged to turn to the legislature if they want to advance children's lives. In the legislative arena, stressing rights has no particular clout. Even more, it has some clear costs.

When rights come to mean little more than what adults should do to treat children appropriately, we really mean something different from rights in the first place. Rights are most coherent when enforcing legally recognized norms. Thus, rights are commonly pressed when one seeks to get something someone else already has. For this reason, it is often sensible to rely on them when arguing claims for treating children like adults. But when the claim is that children deserve to be treated *un*like adults, they need something other than rights upon which to depend.

If children's rights advocates could recast claims on behalf of children from rights to what is fair and just for children, perhaps we could recapture a time when adults would better accept their responsibilities toward children. However inadvertently, our current emphasis on children's rights reduces the pressure on adults to do right by children.

We have reached the point in our history where perhaps the greatest goal for advancing children's rights should be a return to a time when we treated children like children; when the mistakes they made were understood to be part of the natural process of growing up; and when adults understood their obligations.

There is little doubt that a caring society would insist on carefully considering the needs and interests of its children when debating knotty social choices. What is doubtful is whether there is much use for considering children's rights, at least to the extent the term means anything beyond their needs and interests. One thing, however, is certain: unless children's rights include society's obligations to deal with children well, children don't need them.

Notes | Acknowledgments | Index

Notes

1. A Brief History of Children's Rights in the United States

1. Joseph M. Hawes, *The Children's Rights Movement, A History of Advocacy and Protection* (Boston, Mass.: Twayne Publishers, 1991), p. xi.

2. Viviana A. Zelizer, *Pricing the Priceless Child, The Changing Social Value of Children* (Princeton, N.J.: Princeton University Press, 1994), p. 69, quoting "Child Labor, the Home and Liberty," *The New Republic* 32 (Dec. 3, 1924): 41.

3. Zelizer, *Pricing the Priceless Child*, p. 69, quoting *New York Times*, (Dec. 7, 1924), p. 19.

4. Zelizer, *Pricing the Priceless Child*, p. 71, quoting Marion Delcomyn, "Why Children Work," *Forum* 57 (Mar. 1917): 324–325.

5. Zelizer, *Pricing the Priceless Child*, p. 67, quoting Mrs. William Lowell Putnam, "Why the Amendment is Dangerous," *The Woman Citizen,* 9 (Dec. 27, 1924): 12.

6. Zelizer, *Pricing the Priceless Child*, p. 63. "Children were 'pushed out of industry' not only by the declining demand for unskilled labor but also by a simultaneous increase in its supply." This has led some to remark that "compulsory school legislation was the result, not the cause, of a changing youth labor market: 'Since firms no longer required the labor of children and adolescents, those pressing for longer compulsory schooling were able to succeed.'" (Zelizer quotes Paul Osterman, *Getting Started: The Youth Labor Market* (Cambridge, Mass.: MIT Press, 1980).

7. Beatrice Gross and Ronald Gross, eds., *The Children's Rights Movement: Overcoming the Oppression of Young People* (Garden City, N.Y.: Anchor Books, 1977).

8. Richard Farson, *Birthrights* (New York: Macmillan Publishing Co., 1974).

9. John Holt, *Escape From Childhood* (New York: E. P. Dutton & Co., 1974).

10. Anthony M. Platt, *The Child Savers: The Invention of Delinquency* (Chicago: University of Chicago Press, 2d ed., 1977), pp. 88–93.

11. Rochelle Beck, "White House Conferences on Children: An Historical Perspective," *Harvard Educational Review* 43 (1973): 653, 662.

12. Kathleen Federle, "Children, Curfews, and the Constitution," *Washington University Law Quarterly* 73 (1995): 1315, 1344.

13. See, e.g., Akhil Reed Amar and Daniel Widawsky, "Child Abuse as Slavery: A Thirteenth Amendment Response to Deshaney," *Harvard Law Review* 105 (1992): 1359 (comparing the status of children to slaves); James G. Dwyer, "Parents' Religion and Children's Welfare: Debunking the Doctrine of Parents' Rights," *California Law Review* 82 (1994): 1371, 1412–1415 (comparing children's status to slaves and more generally to property); Barbara Bennett Woodhouse, "'Out of Children's Needs, Children's Rights': The Child's Voice in Defining the Family," *Brigham Young University Journal of Public Law* 8 (1994): 321, 326 (comparing parent-child relationships to slavery).

14. Stephen Scales, "Intergenerational Justice and Care in Parenting," *Social Theory & Practice* 28 (2002): 667, 668.

15. Onora O'Neill, "Children's Rights and Children's Lives," *Ethics* 98 (1988): 447.

16. Ibid., p. 462.

17. Bruce C. Hafen, "Children's Liberation and the New Egalitarianism: Some Reservations about Abandoning Youth to Their Rights," *Brigham Young University Law Review* (1976): 605, 656.

18. Ex parte Crouse, 4 Whart. 9 (Pa. 1839).

19. O'Neill, "Children's Rights," p. 463.

20. See, e.g., *American Amusement Machine Association v. Kendrick*, 244 F.3d 572 (7th Cir. 2001).

21. Henry H. Foster and Doris Jonas Freed, "A Bill of Rights for Children," *Family Law Quarterly* 6 (1972): 343, 347.

22. Hillary Rodham, "Children under the Law," *Harvard Educational Review* 43 (1973): 487.

23. Hawes, *Children's Rights Movement*, p. x.

24. Martha Minow, "Whatever Happened to Children's Rights?," *Minnesota Law Review* 80 (1995): 267, 287. Two relatively early efforts to make sense of modern children's rights were Michael S. Wald, "Children's Rights: A Framework for Analysis," *University of California Davis Law Review* 12 (1979): 255, 260 and Frances Barry McCarthy, "The Confused Constitutional Status and Meaning of Parental Rights," *Georgia Law Review* 22 (1988): 975, 1013.

25. *United Nations Convention on the Rights of the Child*, G. A. Res. 44/25, 44 U. N. GAOR Supp. No. 49, U. N. Doc. A/44/736 (Nov. 28, 1989).

26. See, e.g., Barbara Bennett Woodhouse, "Talking About Children's Rights in Judicial Custody and Visitation Decision-making," *Family Law Quarterly* 36 (2002): 105, 108, n.6.

2. The Rights of Parents

1. The first of these quotes is from *Stanley v. Illinois*, 405 U.S. 645, 651 (quoting *Skinner v. Oklahoma*, 316 U.S. 535, 541 (1942) (quoting *May v. Anderson*, 345 U.S. 528, 533 (1953); the second, from *Troxel v. Granville*, 530 U.S. 57, 65 (2000); the third, from *Wisconsin v. Yoder*, 406 U.S. 205, 232 (1972).

2. Several writers have actually proposed a parenting licensing requirement. See Hugh LaFollette, "Licensing Parents," *Philosophy & Public Affairs* 9 (1980): 183; Howard B. Eisenberg, "A 'Modest Proposal': State Licensing of Parents," *Connecticut Law Review* 26 (1994): 1416.

3. See *Li v. Ashcroft*, 356 F.3d 1153 (9th Cir. 2004).

4. See William Blackstone, *Commentaries*, ed. Wayne J. Morrison (Buffalo, N.Y.: William S. Hein, 1992), vol. 1, p. 447.

5. *Smith v. Organization of Foster Families for Equality and Reform*, 431 U.S. 816, 845 (1977). See also *Meyer v. Nebraska*, 262 U.S. 390, 399 (1923). But see Bruce A. Ackerman, *Social Justice in the Liberal State* (New Haven, Conn.: Yale University Press, 1980), pp. 5–6.

6. Jean-Jacques Rousseau, *Social Contract* (New York: Penguin Group, 1979).

7. John Locke, *The Second Treatise of Government in Political Writings of John Locke*, ed. David Wooton (Cambridge, Mass.: Hackett Publishing Co., 1993).

8. See, e.g., Mark Tushnet, "An Essay on Rights," *Texas Law Review* 62 (1984): 1363; Peter Westen, "The Rueful Rhetoric of Rights,"

U.C.L.A. Law Review 33 (1986): 977. But see *Meachum v. Fano*, 427 U.S. 215, 230 (1976) (Stevens, J., dissenting).

9. See, e.g., Frances E. Olsen, "The Myth of State Intervention in the Family," *University of Michigan Journal of Law Reform* 18 (1985): 835, 838.

10. See Laurence D. Houlgate, "What Is Legal Intervention in the Family? Family Law and Family Privacy," *Law and Philosophy* 17 (1998): 141.

11. See, e.g., *R.A.V. v. St. Paul*, 505 U.S. 377 (1992).

12. *Prince v. Massachusetts*, 321 U.S. 158, 166 (1944).

13. *Meyer v. Nebraska*, 262 U.S. 390 (1923).

14. Ibid., p. 401.

15. *Pierce v. Society of Sisters*, 268 U.S. 510 (1925).

16. Ibid., p. 535.

17. See "Developments in the Law: Family Law," *Harvard Law Review* 93 (1980): 1156, 1354.

18. See *Pierce v. Society of Sisters*, 268 U.S. . . . 510, 535 (1925); *Bellotti v. Baird*, 443 U.S. . . . 622, 637–639 (1979); *Wisconsin v. Yoder*, 406 U.S. 205, 218 (1972).

19. Stephen Jay Gould analyzed the facts of the case in the 1980s and concluded that Carrie Buck would not "be considered mentally deficient by today's standards." Stephen Jay Gould, *The Mismeasure of Man* (New York: Norton, 1981), p. 336.

20. *Buck v. Bell*, 274 U.S. 200 (1927).

21. *Skinner v. Oklahoma*, 316 U.S. 535 (1942).

22. 381 U.S. 479 (1965).

23. *Griswold v. Connecticut*, 381 U.S. 479, 495 (1965) (quoting *Poe v. Ullman*, 367 U.S. 497, 551–52 (1961) (Harlan, J., dissenting)).

24. 410 U.S. 113 (1973). See also *Eisenstadt v. Baird*, 405 U.S. 438 (1972).

25. 410 U.S. at 152–153 (citations omitted).

26. *Cleveland Board of Education v. LaFleur*, 414 U.S. 632, 639–640 (1974).

27. *Stanley v. Illinois*, 405 U.S. 645 (1972).

28. *Troxel v. Granville*, 530 U.S. 57 (2000).

29. *Lawrence v. Texas*, 539 U.S. 558, 562 (2003).

30. David A. J. Richards, "The Individual, the Family, and the Constitution: A Jurisprudential Perspective," *New York University Law Review* 55 (1980): 1, 28.

31. Peggy Cooper Davis, "Contested Images of Family Values: The Role

of the State," *Harvard Law Review* 107 (1994): 1348, 1371–1373; Peggy Cooper Davis, *Neglected Stories: The Constitution and Family Values* (New York: Hill and Wang, 1997), p. 168.

32. Kenneth L. Karst, "The Freedom of Intimate Association," *Yale Law Journal* 89 (1980): 624, 636. In this regard, it is useful to recall Aristotle's criticism of Plato's vision of children being raised by guardians. "[E]ach citizen would have a thousand sons: they will not be the sons of each citizen individually: any and every son will be equally the son of any and every father, and the result will be that every son will be equally neglected by every father." See *Bowen v. Gilliard,* 483 U.S. 587, 633 (1987) (Brennan, J., dissenting). Artistotle's objection was that both children and parents would be losers. Parents, he reasoned, have the need to raise and love their children and any policy that denies them that opportunity is suspect. Aristotle, *Politics, Book I,* trans. Ernest Baker (New York: Oxford University Press, 1962), chap. 13, pp. 33–34.

33. "Children are valued not only for themselves, but as living expressions of their parents' love for each other." Karst, "Freedom," p. 640 n.88.

34. Davis, "Contested Images of Family Values," p. 1363.

35. Ibid., p. 1363.

36. Ibid., p. 1371.

37. Barbara Bennett Woodhouse, "Who Owns the Child? Meyer and Pierce and the Child as Property," *William and Mary Law Review* 33 (1992): 996, 1042.

38. Barbara Bennett Woodhouse, "The Constitutionalization of Children's Rights: Incorporating Emerging Human Rights into Constitutional Doctrine," *University of Pennsylvania Journal of Constitutional Law* 2 (1999): 1, 27.

39. Locke, *Second Treatise,* 85.

40. See, e.g., Gary S. Becker, *A Treatise on the Family* (Cambridge, Mass.: Harvard University Press, 1991), pp. 37–38; John H. Beckstrom, *Sociobiology and the Law: The Biology of Altruism in the Courtroom of the Future* (Champaign, Ill.: University of Illinois Press, 1985), pp. 81–102, 130–134. See also Elizabeth S. Scott and Robert E. Scott, "Parents as Fiduciaries," *Virginia Law Review* 81 (1995): 2401, 2433–2436.

41. *Parham v. J. R.,* 442 U.S. 548, 602 (1979).

42. See Annette R. Appell, "Blending Families through Adoption: Implications for Collaborative Adoption Law and Practice," *Boston University Law Review* 75 (1995): 997, 1013–1020 (arguing that the impor-

tance of biological relationships to adults and children supports open adoption).

43. See Ronald Dworkin, "Liberal Community," *California Law Review* 77(1989): 479, 487.

44. Joseph Goldstein, Anna Freud, and Albert Solnit, *Before the Best Interests of the Child* (New York, Free Press, 1979), p. 25. See also Robert A. Burt, "Developing Constitutional Rights Of, In, and For Children," *Law & Contemporary Problems* 39 (1975): 118.

45. See "Developments in the Law," p. 1214; Goldstein, Freud, and Solnit, *Before The Best Interests of the Child,* p. 13.

46. See Neil Binder, "Taking Relationships Seriously: Children, Autonomy, and the Right to a Relationship," *New York University Law Review* 69 (1994): 1150, 1154.

47. See, e.g., Goldstein, Freud, and Solnit, *Beyond the Best Interests of the Child,* pp. 49–52; Robert Mnookin, "Foster Care—In Whose Best Interests?" *Harvard Educational Review* 43 (1973): 599, 613–622.

48. 140 N. W.2d 152 (Iowa 1966).

49. Robert H. Mnookin, "Child-Custody Adjudication: Judicial Functions in the Face of Indeterminacy," *Law and Contemporary Problems* 39 (Summer 1975): 226, 260.

50. Richard W. Garnett, "Taking Pierce Seriously: The Family, Religious Education, and Harm to Children," *Notre Dame Law Review* 76 (2000): 109, 132.

51. See Ira Bloom, "The New Parental Rights Challenge to School Control: Has the Supreme Court Mandated School Choice?" *Journal of Law & Education* 23 (2003): 139, 141, n.8. See also Stacey Bielick, Kathryn Chandler, and Stephen P. Broughman,*Homeschooling in the United States: 1999* (U.S. Department of Education, 2001), p. 4 (this report estimates that 850,000 students nationwide were being homeschooled in 1999), available at nces.ed.gov/pubsearch/pubsinfo.

52. Garnett, "Taking Pierce Seriously," p. 132.

53. John H. Garvey, *What Are Freedoms For?* (Cambridge, Mass.: Harvard University Press, 1996), p. 122.

54. 406 U.S. 205 (1972).

55. A number of scholars have criticized *Yoder* as failing to protect Frieda's independent rights. See generally Joel Feinberg, "The Child's Right to an Open Future," in William Aiken and Hugh LaFollette eds., *Whose Child? Children's Rights, Parental Authority, and State Power* (Lanham, Md.: Rowman & Littlefield, 1980), p. 124; Lawrence D.

Houlgate, "Three Concepts of Children's Constitutional Rights: Reflections on the Enjoyment Theory," *University of Pennsylvania Journal of Constitutional Law* 2 (1999): 77.

56. *Wisconsin v. Yoder,* 406 U.S. 205, 245–246 (Douglas, J., dissenting).

57. *Bowen v. Gilliard,* 483 U.S. 587, 632 (1987) (Brennan, J., dissenting).

3. Getting and Losing Parental Rights

1. See, e.g., Lucinda Franks, "The War for Baby Clausen," *The New Yorker* (March 22, 1993), p. 56; Nancy Gibbs, "In Whose Best Interest?" *Time* (July 19, 1993), p. 44; Don Terry, "Tug-of-War Ends as Child Is Moved," *The New York Times* (August 3, 1993), p. A13.

2. Before the case was over, Cara and Dan married (in April 1992) and the court eventually ruled that Cara's original surrender was void under Iowa law because it was signed too soon after Jessica's birth. Cara's parental rights to Jessica were also restored.

3. In re BGC, 496 N. W.2d 239 (Iowa, 1992).

4. William Blackstone, *Commentaries,* ed. Wayne Morrison and Wayne J. Morrison, vol. 1 (Buffalo, N.Y.: William S. Hein, 1992), p. 459 ("[H]e cannot be heir to any one, neither can he have heirs, but of his own body; for, being nullius filius. . ."). American law softened this rule over time. In 1824, for example, Connecticut changed its law to permit a child born out of wedlock to inherit from his or her mother. *Heath v. White,* 5 Conn. 228 (1824).

5. Mary Ann Mason, *From Father's Property to Children's Rights, The History of Child Custody in the United States* (New York: Columbia University Press, 1994), p. 68.

6. Mary E. Becker, "The Rights of Unwed Parents: Feminist Approaches," *Social Service Review* 63 (1989): 496, 497.

7. Harry D. Krause and David D. Meyer, "What Family for the 21st Century?" *American Journal of Comparative Law* 50 (2002): 101.

8. See Harry D. Krause, "Child Support Reassessed: Limits of Private Responsibility and the Public Interest," *Family Law Quarterly* 24 (1990): 1, 4.

9. See Roger Levesque, "Targeting 'Deadbeat': The Problem with the Direction of Welfare Reform," *Hamline Journal of Public Law & Policy* 15 (1994): 1, 6.

10. Bureau of the Census, U.S. Dept. of Commerce, *Statistical Abstract of the United States* (118th ed. 1998) p. 1347, tbl 156.

11. See Mary L. Shanley, "Unwed Fathers' Rights, Adoption, and Sex Equality: Gender-Neutrality and the Perpetuation of Patriarchy," *Columbia Law Review* 95 (1995): 60, 66.

12. 405 U.S. 645 (1972).

13. 434 U.S. 246 (1978).

14. 441 U.S. 380 (1979).

15. He also could have challenged New York's differential treatment of unwed fathers and wed fathers. Had Mr. Caban married the mother, there would be no question that the adoption would be denied over his objection.

16. 463 U.S. 248 (1983).

17. Ibid. at 262.

18. In some states, including Alabama, Illinois, Ohio, Pennsylvania, and Texas, the unwed father has a set time after the child's birth to register. In others, including Arkansas, New Hampshire, and Wisconsin, registration is allowed up to the time an adoption petition is filed. Some states combine these two approaches. Other states require unwed fathers to bring a paternity action. Nebraska requires that fathers register within five days of birth. See *Friehe v. Schaad,* 545 N. W.2d 740, 747 (Neb. 1996).

19. Among the jurisdictions that issued court rulings seemingly permitting a similar defense to be raised are the District of Columbia, Illinois, Mississippi, New York, South Dakota, Tennessee, and West Virginia.

20. 496 N. W.2d at 241 & n.1.

21. See, e.g., 750 Ill. Comp. Stat. 50/12.1(g) (West 2003).

22. See Tex. Fam. Code Ann. §160.254 (Vernon Supp. 2002); *Robert O. v. Russell K.,* 604 N. E.2d 99 (N.Y. 1992).

23. For a proposal that she should be required to inform the father, see Rebeca Aizpuru, Note, "Protecting the Unwed Father's Opportunity to Parent: A Survey of Paternity Registry Statutes," *Review of Litigation* 18 (1999): 703.

24. Children's Bureau, U.S. Department of Health and Human Services, *Adoption and Foster Care Analysis System Report* (Washington, D.C.: 2000), available online at www.acf.dhhs.gov/programs/cb.

25. See, e.g., *Iowa Code* §600A.2(16) (2002); In re Goettsche, 311 N. W.2d 104, 105 (Iowa 1981).

26. United States Constitution, Art. IV, §1.

27. See, e.g., *Donovan v. Donovan,* 212 N. W.2d 451 (Iowa 1973).

28. Uniform Child Custody Jurisdiction Act, §9 *U.L.A.,* pt. I, 261 (1999).

29. 28 *U.S.C.* §1738A (West 2002).
30. See *May v. Anderson,* 345 U.S. 528, 539 (1953) (Jackson, J., dissent-ing): "A state of the law such as this, where possession is not merely nine points of the law but all of them and self-help the ultimate author-ity, has little to commend it in legal logic or as a principle of order in a federal system."
31. *Thompson v. Thompson,* 484 U.S. 174 (1988).
32. The Equal Protection Clause only protects similarly situated persons. If the first claim fails, Jessica is not similarly situated to those children whose custody matters are decided under a different substantive stan-dard.
33. *Clausen v. Schmidt,* 502 N. W.2d 649, 652, 666 (Mich. 1993).
34. See *E. E. B. v. D. A.,* 446 A.2d 871 (New Jersey, 1982), cert. denied sub nom., *Angle v. Bowen,* 459 U.S. 1210 (1983).
35. Elizabeth Bartholet, *Nobody's Children, Abuse and Neglect, Foster Drift, and the Adoption Alternative* (Boston, Mass.: Beacon Press, 2000), p. 22.
36. Michael D. A. Freeman, "The Limits of Children's Rights" in Michael Freeman and Philip Veerman eds., *The Ideologies of Children's Rights* (Dordrecht, The Netherlands: Kluwer Academic Press, 1992).
37. *Dauber v. Dauber v. Schmidt,* 509 U.S. 1301, 1302 (1993) (Stevens, J., Circuit Justice) (Chambers).

4. Who Gets to Be the Parent?

1. See *Boland v. Boland,* 588 N.Y.S.2d 485 (App. Div. 1992).
2. See *Matter of Janis C. v. Christine T.,* 742 N.Y.S.2d 381 (App. Div. 2002) (reversing *Matter of J. C. v. C. T.,* 711 N.Y.S.2d 295, (Fam. Ct. 2000)). In *Matter of Alison D. v. Virginia M.,* 572 N.E.2d 27 (1990) the Court of Appeals held that same-sex partners who are "biological strangers" to the children are not "parents" for purposes of New York's Domestic Relations Law and, thus, have no standing to petition for visitation when the children at issue are properly within the cus-tody of a fit legal or biological parent.
3. See *King v. King,* 828 S.W.2d 630 (Ky. 1992).
4. Readers interested in a more in-depth legal analysis of the issues raised in this chapter should consult Katherine Bartlett, "Rethinking Parent-hood as an Exclusive Status: The Need for Legal Alternatives when the Premise of the Nuclear Family Has Failed," *Virginia Law Review* 70

(1984): 879; Gilbert A. Holmes, "The Tie that Binds: The Constitutional Right of Children to Maintain Relationships with Parent-like Individuals," *Maryland Law Review* 53 (1994): 358, 410–411; John DeWitt Gregory, "Blood Ties: A Rationale for Child Visitation by Legal Strangers," *Washington & Lee Law Review* 55 (1998): 351; David D. Meyer, "Lochner Redeemed: Family Privacy After Troxel and Carhart," *UCLA Law Review* 48 (2001): 1125, 1183–1184; Gregory A. Loken, "The New 'Extended Family'—'De Facto' Parenthood and Standing under Chapter 2,"*Brigham Young University Law Review* (2001): 1045; Aleissa Bell, Note, "Public and Private Child: Troxel v. Granville and the Constitutional Rights of Family Members," *Harvard Civil Rights & Civil Liberties Law Review* 36 (2001): 225.

5. U.S. Department of Commerce, Bureau of Census, *Current Population Reports, 1997 Population Profile of the United States* (1998), p. 27.

6. A recent study by the American Association of Retired Persons found that one in ten grandparents acts as a primary caretaker or a regular caregiver for a grandchild. Tamar Lewin, "Grandparents Play Big Part in Grandchildren's Lives, Survey Finds," *New York Times* (Jan. 6, 2000), p. A16.

7. Some estimates are even higher. See Catherine DeLair, "Ethical, Moral, Economic and Legal Barriers to Assisted Reproductive Technologies Employed by Gay and Lesbian Women," *Depaul Journal of Health Care Law* 42 (2000): 147.

8. Melisa G. Thompson, "In Re Interest of Z. J. H.: Are Two Moms Too Many?" *Depaul Law Review* 42 (1993): 1125.

9. Frank Furstenberg, "The New Extended Family: The Experience of Parents and Children After Remarriage," in K. Pasley & M. Ihinger-Tallman eds., *Remarriage and Stepparenting: Current Research and Theory* (New York: Guilford Publications, 1987).

10. U.S. Department of Commerce, *Current Population Reports, 1997 Population Profile of the United States* (1998), p. 50.

11. U.S. Department of Commerce, Bureau of Census, *Current Population Reports, 2000 Population Profile of the United States* (2001). Available at www.census.gov/main/www/cen2000.html.

12. See, e.g., Barbara Bennett Woodhouse, "'Out of the Children's Needs': The Child's Voice in Defining the Family," *Brigham Young University Journal of Public Law* 8 (1994): 321, 325–326.

13. See, e.g., Catherine Bostock, "Does the Expansion of Grandparent

Visitation Rights Promote the Best Interests of the Child?: A Survey of Grandparent Visitation Laws in the Fifty States," *Columbia Journal of Law & Social Problems* 27 (1994): 319, 331–341.

14. See generally John DeWitt Gregory, "Blood Ties: A Rationale for Child Visitation by Legal Strangers," *Washington & Lee Law Review* 55 (1998): 351.

15. See *Rubano v. DiCenzo*, 759 A.2d 959 (R. I. 2000); *E.N.O. v. L.M.M.*, 711 N.E.2d 886 (Mass. 1999); *V. C. v. M.J.B.*, 748 A.2d 539 (N.J. 2000), cert. denied, 531 U.S. 926 (2000); *T.B v. L.R.M.* 786 A.2d 913 (Pa. 2001); *Holtzman v. Knott* (In re Custody of H.S.H.K.), 533 N.W.2d 419 (Wis. 1995).

16. Martha Albertson Fineman, *The Neutered Mother, the Sexual Family, and Other Twentieth Century Tragedies* (New York: Routledge, 1995), pp. 177–178.

17. *Troxel v. Granville*, 530 U.S. 57, 90 (2000) (Stevens, J. dissenting).

18. Defense of Marriage Act, Pub. L. No. 104–199, 110 Stat. 2419 (codified at 1 *U.S.C.* §7, 28 *U.S.C.* §1738C (2000)).

19. The *Times* explained its decision as choosing to recognize "a growing and visible trend in society toward public celebrations of commitment by gay and lesbian couples." "*Times* Will Begin Reporting Gay Couples' Ceremonies," *New York Times* (Aug. 18, 2002), p. A30. Other papers have followed suit since. See James M. Donovan, "Same-Sex Union Announcements: Whether Newspapers Must Publish Them, and Why We Should Care," *Brooklyn Law Review* 68 (2003): 721, 725 n.6.

20. *Goodridge v. Department of Public Health,* 440 Mass. 309 (2003).

21. See   www.usatoday.com/news/nation/2003-06-30-gaypoll-usat_x.htm (over 60 percent of Americans eighteen to twenty-nine years old favor legalizing same-sex marriages).

22. See Holmes, "Tie that Binds," p. 358.

23. See Joseph Goldstein, Anna Freud, and Albert Solnit, *Beyond the Best Interests of the Child* (New York: Free Press, 1973), pp. 97–101.

24. *Troxel v. Granville,* 530 U.S. 57 (2000).

25. Among the groups that filed friend-of-the-court briefs were the American Civil Liberties Union, the Christian Legal Society, the National Association of Counsel for Children, the National Center for Lesbian Rights, the Lambda Legal Defense and Education Fund, Grandparents United for Children's Rights, Inc., and the American Association of Retired Persons.

26. *Troxel v. Granville,* 530 U.S. 57, 99 (2000) (Kennedy, J., dissenting).

27. Janet L. Dolgin, "The Constitution as Family Arbiter: A Moral in the Mess?" *Columbia Law Review* 102 (2002): 337, 388.

28. For a rare, remarkable acknowledgment that grandparent visitation statutes really are for the grandparents, see the Kentucky Supreme Court's opinion in the case upholding the constitutionality of its grandparent statute:

> [T]he General Assembly determined that, in modern day society, it was essential that some semblance of family and generational contact be preserved. If a grandparent is physically, mentally and morally fit, then a grandchild will ordinarily benefit from contact with the grandparent . . . Each benefits from contact with the other. The child can learn respect, a sense of responsibility and love. The grandparent can be invigorated by exposure to youth, can gain an insight into our changing society, and can avoid the loneliness which is so often a part of an aging parent's life. These considerations by the state do not go too far in intruding into the fundamental rights of the parents. Thus, we find that [the Kentucky grandparent visitation statute] is constitutional.

King v. King, 828 S. W.2d 630, 632 (Ky. 1992).

29. *Smith v. Org. Foster Families for Equal. & Reform,* 431 U.S. 816, 845 (1977).

30. Ibid., p. 847.

31. *In re Custody of H.S.H.-K.,* 533 N. W.2d 419 (Wis. 1995).

32. The American Law Institute's "Principles of the Law of Family Dissolution" developed two categories for parental figures who are able to secure legal rights: "parents by estoppel" and "de facto parents." Under the ALI definition, a de facto parent is a person who shares (at least) equally in primary childcare responsibilities while residing with a child for reasons other than money. The de facto parent's assumption of childcare responsibility must either be with the agreement of the natural parent or result from a parent's inability to care for the child. In addition, an individual must have lived with a child for at least two years in order to be considered that child's de facto parent. American Law Institute, *Principles of the Law of Family Dissolution: Analysis and Recommendations,* §§2.03(1)(c)(i) (ii) (2000).

33. *Holtzman v. Knott* (In re Custody of H.S.H.-K), 533 N.W.2d 419, 442 (Wis. 1995) (Steinmetz, J., dissenting).

34. This may be an unspoken factor relied upon by the Supreme Court in rejecting the application of a biological father to visit with his daughter over the objection of the birth mother and her husband in *Michael H. v. Gerald D.,* 491 U.S. 110 (1989).

5. Divorce, Custody, and Visitation

1. Bureau of the Census, United States Department of Commerce, *Statistical Abstract of the United States, Vital Statistics* (1999), p. 75.
2. Bureau of the Census, United States Department of Commerce, *Statistical Abstract* (1996), p. 106. As of 1990, 36 percent of women in the age group 40–44 were divorced after a first marriage. Ibid.
3. U.S. Commission on Interstate Child Support, *Supporting Our Children: A Blueprint for Reform* (1992), p. 5.
4. June R. Carbone and Margaret F. Brinig, "Rethinking Marriage: Feminist Ideology, Economic Change, and Divorce Reform," *Tulane Law Review* 65 (1991): 953, 985.
5. See Robert Emery, *Marriage, Divorce, and Children's Adjustment* (Thousand Oaks, Calif.: Sage Publications, 2000).
6. Steven L. Nock, "Is the Current Concern About American Marriage Warranted?" Virginia Journal of Social Policy & Law 9 (2001): 48.
7. See Arland Thornton, "Changing Attitudes toward Family Issues in the United States," *Journal of Marriage & the Family* 51 (1989): 873, 880.
8. Elizabeth S. Scott, "Divorce, Children's Welfare, and the Culture Wars," *Virginia Journal of Social Policy & Law* 9 (2001): 95.
9. Ibid., pp. 111–113.
10. Judith S. Wallerstein, Julie Lewis, and Sandra Blakeslee, *The Unexpected Legacy of Divorce: The 25 Year Landmark Study* (New York: Hyperion, 2000).
11. Katha Pollitt, "Is Divorce Getting a Bum Rap?" *Time* (Sept. 25, 2000), p. 82.
12. Paul Amato and Alan Booth, *A Generation at Risk: Growing Up in an Era of Family Upheaval* (Cambridge, Mass.: Harvard University Press, 1997), p. 237.
13. Ibid., p. 84.
14. See Scott, "Culture Wars," p. 96.
15. Ira M. Ellman, Katherine T. Bartlett, and Paul M. Kurtz, *Family Law* (Charlottesville, Va.: LEXIS Law Publishing, 1991), p. 492. By the mid 1800s, Michael Grossberg reports that a treatise on the law of child custody suggested that "children are not born for the benefit of the parents alone, but for the country; and, therefore, that the interest of the public in their morals and education should be protected." The treatise continued by noting that "children, though younger in years have themselves an interest more sacred than their parents, and more

deserving of protection." Michael Grossberg, *Governing the Hearth: Law and the Family in Nineteenth Century America* (Chapel Hill, N.C.: University of North Carolina Press, 1985), p. 32.

16. Grossberg, *Governing the Hearth*, p. 225.
17. Ibid.
18. Ibid.
19. Ibid., pp. 244–245.
20. See Mary Ann Mason, *From Father's Property to Children's Rights: The History of Child Custody in the United States* (New York: Columbia University Press, 1994), pp. 94–95.
21. Such as the Atlanta-based Fathers Are Parents Too, www.fapt.org.
22. See, e.g., *Pusey v. Pusey*, 728 P.2d 177 (Utah 1986) (finding that the tender years presumption is based on outdated stereotypes); *Ex parte Devine*, 398 So. 2d 686 (Ala. 1981) (holding the doctrine unconstitutional); *Bazemore v. Davis*, 394 A.2d 1377 (D.C. 1977) (holding that the doctrine violates best interest standard).
23. Grossberg, *Governing the Hearth*, p. 243.
24. *Bradwell v. Illinois*, 83 U.S. (16 Wall.) 130, 141 (1873) (Bradley, J., concurring).
25. See, e.g., Mary Becker, "Maternal Feelings: Myth, Taboo, and Child Custody," *Southern California Review of Law & Women's Studies* 1 (1992): 133.
26. But see Rena K. Uviller, "Fathers' Rights and Feminism: The Maternal Presumption Revisited," *Harvard Women's Law Journal* 1 (1978): 107, 109.
27. Martin Guggenheim, Alexandra Lowe, and Diane Curtis, *The Rights of Families* (Carbondale, Ill.: University of Southern Illinois Press, 1996).
28. See, e.g., Martha Albertson Fineman, *The Illusion of Equality, The Rhetoric and Reality of Divorce Reform* (Chicago: University of Chicago Press, 1991); Karen Czapanskiy, "Interdependencies, Families, and Children," *Santa Clara Law Review* 39 (1999): 957.
29. See Herma Hill Kay, "No-Fault Divorce and Child Custody: Chilling Out the Gender Wars," *Family Law Quarterly* 36 (2002): 27.
30. See Mel Roman, Susan Manso, and William Haddad, *The Disposable Parent: The Case for Joint Custody* (New York: Henry Holt & Company, 1978); James A. Cook, "California's Joint Custody Statute," in Jay Folberg, ed., *Joint Custody and Shared Parenting* (Washington, D.C.: B.N.A. Books, 1984).

31. See, e.g., *Cal. Fam. Code* §3170 (West Supp. 2002).

32. See generally Jana B. Singer and William L. Reynolds, "A Dissent on Joint Custody," *Maryland Law Review* 47 (1988): 497.

33. See Katharine T. Bartlett and Carol B. Stack, "Joint Custody, Feminism, and the Dependency Dilemma," *Berkeley Women's Law Journal* 2 (1986): 9, 32. See also Mary Ann Mason, *The Custody Wars: Why Children Are Losing the Legal Battle and What We Can Do About It* (New York: Basic Books, 1999), p. 2.

34. *Malone v. Malone,* 842 S. W. 2d 621 (Tenn. App. 1992). See Judith S. Wallerstein and Sandra Blakeslee, *Second Chances: Men, Women, and Children a Decade after Divorce* (Boston, Mass.: Houghton Mifflin, 1989), pp. 256–273.

35. *Cal. Fam Code* §3080 (West Supp. 2002).

36. Linda D. Elrod and Timothy B. Walker, "Family Law in the Fifty States," *Family Law Quarterly* 28 (Winter 1994): 515, 568, 586–588.

37. See Nancy D. Polikoff, "Why Are Mothers Losing: A Brief Analysis of Criteria Used in Child Custody Determinations," *Women's Rights Law Reporter* 7 (1982): 235, 237; Martha Fineman, "Dominant Discourse, Professional Language, and Legal Change in Child Custody Decisionmaking," *Harvard Law Review* 101 (1988): 727, 770–774.

38. Judith T. Younger, "Responsible Parents and Good Children," *Law & Inequality* 14 (1996): 489.

39. See Elizabeth S. Scott, "Pluralism, Parental Preference, and Child Custody," *California Law Review* 80 (1992): 615, 617.

40. See American Law Institute, *Principles of the Law of Family Dissolution: Analysis and Recommendations* (Philadelphia, Pa.: American Law Institute, 2001).

41. See Katharine T. Bartlett, "Child Custody in the 21st Century: How The American Law Institute Proposes to Achieve Predictability and Still Protect the Individual Child's Best Interests," *Willamette Law Review* 35 (1999): 467, 477–478 (explaining why the American Law Institute did not adopt the primary caretaking parent rule).

42. *Palmore v. Sidoti,* 466 U.S. 429 (1984).

43. Although some courts have rules that authorize judges to review and set aside agreements they regard as unacceptable, in the overwhelming majority of cases such supervention is unthinkable. But see *McClain v. McClain,* 716 P.2d 381, 385 (Alaska 1986) (parents' agreement is not binding on the court, and court must independently determine what arrangement is in the best interests of the child); *In re Marriage of*

Fesolowitz, 852 P.2d 658, 662 (Mont. 1993) (court is not bound by parents' agreement and has power to order a custody arrangement in accordance with the best interests of the child).

44. Some commentators have suggested limitations on divorce during children's minority. See, e.g., Judith T. Younger, "Marital Regimes: A Story of Compromise and Demoralization, Together with Criticism and Suggestions for Reform," *Cornell Law Review* 67 (1981): 45, 90; Debra Friedman, *Towards a Structure of Indifference, The Social Origins of Maternal Custody* (Berlin: Aldine de Gruyter, 1995), pp. 133–135.

45. *Meldron v. Novotny,* 640 N. W.2d 460, 466 (N. D. 2002). Even more remarkably, one of the "KeyCites" used by Weslaw to aid in speedy legal research actually begins by announcing "Because child custody issues are some of the most difficult and agonizing decisions a trial judge must make . . ." West KeyCite 76D.

46. Roger M. Baron, "Child Custody Determinations in South Dakota: How South Dakota Courts Decide Child Custody Cases," *South Dakota Law Review* 40 (1995): 411. See *Matter of O'Shea v. Brennan,* 387 N.Y.S.2d 212, 216 (N.Y. App. Div. 1976). *Horton v. Horton,* 519 P.2d 11312, 1132 (Alaska 1974).

47. Lee E. Teitlebaum, "Divorce, Custody, Gender and the Limits of Law: On Dividing the Child," *Michigan Law Review* 92: 1808, 1816.

48. Jon Elster, *Solomonic Judgements: Studies in the Limitations of Rationality* (New York: Cambridge University Press, 1989), p. 124.

49. David Chambers, "Rethinking the Substantive Rules for Custody Disputes in Divorce," *Michigan Law Review* 83 (1984): 477, 499.

50. Judith S. Wallerstein and Joan B. Kelly, "Children and Divorce: A Review," *Social Work* 24 (1979): 468.

51. Catherine J. Ross, "From Vulnerability to Voice: Appointing Counsel for Children in Civil Litigation," *Fordham Law Review* 64 (1996): 1571; Howard A. Davidson, "The Child's Right to Be Heard and Represented in Judicial Proceedings," *Pepperdine Law Review* 18 (1991): 255.

52. See, e.g., Katherine Hunt Federle, "Looking Ahead: An Empowerment Perspective on the Rights of Children," *Temple Law Review* 68 (1995): 1585, 1594–1596. See also Randy Frances Kandel, "Just Ask the Kid! Towards a Rule of Children's Choice in Custody Determinations," *University of Miami Law Review* 49 (1994): 299, 347.

53. Art. 3(2), 28 I. L. M. 1448 (Nov. 20, 1989).

54. Barbara Bennett Woodhouse, "Talking About Children's Rights in Judicial Custody and Visitation Decision-Making," *Family Law Quarterly* 36 (2002): 105.

55. See Younger, "Marital Regimes," p. 90.

56. Emery, *"Marriage, Divorce,"* pp. 132–133. "If being caught in the middle of the parents' conflict is one of the greatest sources of distress for children then soliciting their opinion as to who is their preferred custodian is hardly a solution. The articulation of a preference can be tantamount to asking children to choose between their parents."

57. See, e.g., Kim J. Landsman and Martha L. Minow, Note, "Lawyering for the Child: Principles of Representation in Custody and Visitation Disputes Arising from Divorce," *Yale Law Journal* 87 (1978): 1126, 1165.

58. Landsman and Minow, "Lawyering," pp. 1133–1134.

59. Judith S. Wallerstein and Sandra Blakeslee, *Second Chances*, p. 238; Judith S. Wallerstein and Tony J. Tanke, "To Move or Not to Move: Psychological and Legal Considerations in the Relocation of Children Following Divorce," *Family Law Quarterly* 30 (1996): 305, 312.

60. *Knock v. Knock*, 621 A.2d 267, 276 (Conn. 1993).

61. Landsman and Minow, "Lawyering."

62. See, e.g., Shannan L. Wilber, "Independent Counsel for Children," *Family Law Quarterly* 27 (1993): 349, 362; Linda D. Elrod, "Reforming the System to Protect Children in High Conflict Custody Cases," *William Mitchell Law Review* 28 (2001): 495. Most children's rights advocates, however, particularly those interested in empowering children, would not be satisfied by limiting the children's lawyer's role to protecting children.

63. See, e.g., *Ballard v. Wold*, 486 N. W.2d 161 (Minn. App. 1992); *In re Marriage of Smith*, 491 N. W.2d 538 (Iowa App. 1992).

64. *Burgess v. Burgess*, 913 P.2d 473 (Cal. 1996); *Tropea v. Tropea*, 665 N. E.2d 145, 150 (N.Y. 1996).

65. Compare *Jaramillo v. Jaramillo*, 823 P.2d 299, 304 (N. Mex. 1991) with *Paulson v. Bauske*, 574 N. W.2d 801, 803 (N. D. 1998).

66. *Ireland v. Ireland*, 717 A.2d 676 (Conn. 1998).

67. *Lamb v. Wenning*, 600 N. E.2d 96, 99 (Ind. 1992).

68. Janet Leach Richards, "Children's Rights v. Parents' Rights: A Proposed Solution to the Custodial Relocation Conundrum," *New Mexico Law Review* 29 (1999): 245, 255.

69. See, e.g., *Maeda v. Maeda*, 794 P.2d 268, 270 (Haw. Ct. App. 1990)

(custodial parent is free to move, but not free to relocate the child absent a showing that relocation serves the child's best interest). See also *Lozinak v. Lozinak*, 569 A.2d 353, 354 (Pa. Super. Ct. 1990).

70. American Law Institute, *Principles of the Law of Family Dissolution*, §2.17 (2000).

71. "[G]ranting [relocation] would likely benefit the child by making the custodian a happier, better adjusted parent than would be the case if the custodian's freedom of movement was more restrained." *In re Marriage of Burgham*, 408 N. E.2d 37, 40 (Ill. App. Ct. 1980).

72. Joseph Goldstein, Anna Freud, and Albert Solnit, *Beyond the Best Interests of the Child* (New York: Free Press, 1979), p. 175 n.12; Joseph Goldstein, Anna Freud, and Albert Solnit, *In the Best Interests of the Child* (New York: Free Press, 1986), p. 24; Robert Mnookin, *Child-Custody Adjudication: Judicial Functions in the Face of Indeterminacy, Law & Contemporary Problems* 39 (Summer 1975): 289–292; Elster, *Solomonic Judgements*, pp. 123–174.

73. See Chambers, "Rethinking," 538 n.230.

74. Elster, *Solomonic Judgements*, pp. 147–148.

6. Child Protection, Foster Care, and Termination of Parental Rights

1. This modification of a folk parable is reported in *American Bar Association Presidential Working Group on the Unmet Legal Needs of Children and Their Families* (Chicago, Ill.: American Bar Association, 1993). My thanks to Frank Cervone for first bringing it to my attention.

2. Joseph Goldstein, Anna Freud, and Albert Solnit, *Beyond the Best Interests of the Child* (New York: Free Press, 1973), pp. 14–15.

3. 431 U.S. 816 (1977).

4. Eventually, it became impossible for the lawyers in the Children's Rights Project to work with the lawyers in the Juvenile Rights Project, even though we were each supposed to be operating under the same banner. I was asked to work on this case when it reached the Supreme Court of the United States, my first case before that august court. The section of the brief I was responsible for was a relatively minor procedural point (on which we prevailed). I could not, then or now, personally agree with the position the NYCLU advocated—a common predicament among lawyers—and I was pleased when the Court ruled unanimously in favor of the birth parent.

5. Linda Gordon, *The Great Arizona Orphan Abduction* (Cambridge,

Mass: Harvard University Press, 1999), pp. 3–19. See also Stephen O'Connor, *Orphan Trains: The Story of Charles Loring Brace and the Children He Saved and Failed* (New York: Houghton Mifflin Co., 2001).

6. See C. Henry Kempe et al., "The Battered Child Syndrome," *Journal of the American Medical Association* 181 (1962): 17.

7. Gilbert Y. Steiner, *The Children's Cause* (Washington, D.C.: Brookings Inst., 1976), p. 10.

8. See William Julius Wilson, *The Truly Disadvantaged* (Chicago: University of Chicago Press, 1987), pp. 119–131.

9. See Michael B. Katz, *The Undeserving Poor: From the War on Poverty to the War on Welfare* (New York: Knopf Publishing Co., 1989).

10. See Barbara Nelson, *Making an Issue of Child Abuse, Political Agenda Setting for Social Problems* (Chicago: University of Chicago Press, 1984), p. 135.

11. *Smith v. Org. Foster Families for Equal. & Reform*, 431 U.S. 816, 845–847 (1977). Fifteen years later, New York's highest court reaffirmed the importance of not permitting the time a child spends in foster care to count toward a legal recognition of the foster parent-child relationship because it would undermine the underlying purpose of the foster care system.

    To use the period during which a child lives with a foster family, and emotional ties that naturally eventuate, as a ground for comparing the biological parent with the foster parent undermines the very objective of voluntary foster care as a resource for parents in temporary crisis, who are then at risk of losing their children once a bond arises with the foster families.

    In re Michael B., 604 N. E.2d 122, 130 (N.Y. 1992).

12. George H. Russ, "Through the Eyes of a Child, 'Gregory K.': A Child's Right to be Heard," *Family Law Quarterly* 27 (1993): 365, 388.

13. Marsha Garrison, "Parents' Rights vs. Children's Interests: The Case of the Foster Child," *New York University Review of Law and Social Change* 22 (1996): 371, 373.

14. Pub. L. No. 96–272, 94 Stat. 500 (codified at 42 U.S.C. §602 (1982)).

15. Duncan Lindsey, *The Welfare of Children* (New York: Oxford University Press, 1994), pp. 65–66. See also U.S. General Accounting Office, *Child Welfare: States' Progress in Implementing Family Preservation and Support Services* (1997), p. 3.

16. See Mark E. Courtney, *The Foster Care Crisis* (University of Wiscon-

sin Madison Institute for Research on Poverty Discussion Paper No. 1048–1094, 1994), p. 8. The rate of removal from families after reunification generally runs between 20 and 25 percent. See also Daan Braveman and Sarah Ramsey, "When Welfare Ends: Removing Children from the Home for Poverty Alone," *Temple Law Review* 70 (1997): 447, 458.

17. See Toshio Tatara, "Some Additional Explanations for the Recent Rise in the U.S. Child Substitute Care Population: An Analysis of National Child Substitute Care Flow Data and Future Research Questions," in Richard Barth, Jill Duerr Berrick, and Neil Gilbert, eds., *Child Welfare Research Review* 1 (1994): 126, 130 table 6.1.

18. See Mary Ann Jones, *Parental Lack of Supervision: Nature and Consequence of a Major Child Neglect Problem* (Washington, D.C.: Child Welfare League of America, 1987), pp. 29, 64; National Council of Juvenile and Family Court Judges, Child Welfare League of America, Youth Law Center & National Center for Youth Law, *Making Reasonable Efforts: Steps for Keeping Families Together* (New York: Edna McConnell Clark Foundation, 1987), p. 8; Richard Wexler, *Spies in the Living Room (and Other Problems with the Recommendations in "Nobody's Children: Abuse and Neglect, Foster Drift, and the Adoption Alternative")* (Alexandria, Va.: National Coalition for Child Protection Reform, 1999), p. 4.

19. Lindsey, *Welfare of Children,* p. 97.

20. Douglas J. Besharov, "The Misuse of Foster Care: When the Desire to Help Children Outruns the Ability to Improve Parental Functioning," in Douglas J. Besharov, ed., *Protecting Children from Abuse and Neglect: Policy and Practice* (Springfield, Ill.: Charles C. Thomas, Ltd., 1988), p. 198; National Commission on Children, *Beyond Rhetoric: A New American Agenda for Children and Families* (1991), p. 290.

21. Martin Guggenheim, Book Review, "Somebody's Children: Sustaining the Family's Place in Child Welfare," *Harvard Law Review* 113 (2000): 1716, 1730.

22. Pub. L. No. 105–189, 111 Stat. 2115 (codified as amended in scattered sections of 42 *U.S.C.A.* (West Supp. 2002)). See Kathleen Haggard, Note, "Treating Prior Terminations of Parental Rights as Grounds for Present Terminations," *Washington Law Review* 73 (1998): 1051, 1057–1058 (discussing relevant ASFA provisions).

23. Lindsey, *Welfare of Children,* pp. 141, 155.

24. Mark E. Courtney, "The Costs of Child Protection in the Context of Welfare Reform," in *The Future of Children, Protecting Children from*

Abuse and Neglect (Los Altos, Calif.: David and Lucile Packard Foundation, 1998), pp. 88, 95.

25. Lindsey, *Welfare of Children,* p. 153.
26. See Tamar Lewin, "Child Welfare Is Slow to Improve Despite Court Order," *New York Times* (Dec. 30, 1995), p. A6.
27. Lindsey, *Welfare of Children,* p. 157.
28. Jane Waldfogel, *The Future of Child Protection: How to Break the Cycle of Abuse and Neglect* (Cambridge, Mass.: Harvard University Press, 1998), pp. 124–125.
29. National Center on Child Abuse and Neglect, *Study Findings: Study of National Incidence and Prevalence of Child Abuse and Neglect* (Washington, D.C.: U.S. Department of Health and Human Services, 1988), pp. 5–6.
30. Waldfogel, *Future of Child Protection,* p. 68.
31. 325 Ill. Comp. Stat. 5/8.1 (West Supp. 2002).
32. See Wexler, "Spies," 16 (citing Conna Craig and Derek Herbert, *The State of Children: An Examination of Government-Run Foster Care* (1997), p. 9.
33. See Nina Bernstein and Frank Bruni, "She Suffered in Plain Sight but Alarms Were Ignored," *New York Times* (Dec. 24, 1995), p. A1. See also "Aggressive Prosecutions Flooding the System," *Child Welfare Watch* (Winter 1999): 4.
34. *Nicholson v. Williams,* 203 F.Supp. 2d 153 (E.D.N.Y., 2002).
35. See National Council of Juvenile and Family Court Judges et al., *Making Reasonable Efforts,* p. 8.
36. See, e.g., Mary B. Larner, Carol S. Stevenson, and Richard E. Behrman, "Protecting Children from Abuse and Neglect: Analysis and Recommendations," *The Future of Children* (Spring 1998): 15; Leroy H. Pelton, "Resolving the Crisis in Child Welfare: Simply Expanding the Present System Is Not Enough," *Public Welfare* 48 (Fall 1990): 19; Patricia A. Schene, "Past, Present, and Future Roles of Child Protective Services," *The Future of Children* (Spring 1998): 29. See also Daan Braveman and Sarah Ramsey, "When Welfare Ends: Removing Children from the Home for Poverty Alone," *Temple Law Review* 70 (1997): 447, and Jim Moye and Roberta Rinker, "It's a Hard Knock Life: Does the Adoption and Safe Families Act of 1997 Adequately Address Problems in the Child Welfare System?" *Harvard Journal on Legislation* 39 (2002): 375, 390. Richard Gelles is one of the few scholars who regards the gravest problem of child welfare from 1980 through 1997 as being that states tried too hard to keep children with

families. See Richard J. Gelles, *The Book of David: How Preserving Families Can Cost Children's Lives* (New York: Basic Books, 1996), pp. 115–143.

37. Dorothy E. Roberts, "Is There Justice in Children's Rights?: The Critique of Federal Family Preservation Policy," *University of Pennsylvania Journal of Constitutional Law* 2 (1999): 112, 133.

38. Leroy Pelton, "Welfare Discrimination and Child Welfare," *Ohio State Law Journal* 60 (1999): 1479, 1489 ("Child removal is a way to serve 'innocent' children without 'rewarding' their 'undeserving' parents"). See also Marsha Garrison, "Child Welfare Decisionmaking: In Search of the Least Detrimental Alternative," *Georgetown Law Journal* 75 (1987): 1745, 1810.

39. See Renny Golden, *Disposable Children: America's Child Welfare System* (Belmont, Ca.: Wadsworth Pub., 1997), p. 55, table 1.

40. Ibid., p. 68. Poverty statistics were retrieved from www.childrens defense.org/familyincome/childpoverty/basicfacts.asp

41. Joel F. Handler, "'Ending Welfare As We Know It'": The Win/Win Spin or the Stench of Victory," *Gender, Race & Justice* 5 (2001): 13, 14. Christine Paxson and Jane Waldfogel, *Welfare Reform and Child Maltreatment* (Chicago, Ill.: Joint Center for Poverty Research, 2000). Leroy H. Pelton, "Child Welfare Policy and Practice: The Myth of Family Preservation," *American Journal of Orthopsychiatry* 67 (1997). Leroy H. Pelton, "Commentary," in *Future of Children* (Spring 1998): 126, 128.

42. See Robert D. Bullard, "Leveling the Playing Field Through Environmental Justice," *Vermont Law Review* 23 (1999): 453, 468.

43. See Megan Sandel, Joshua Sharfstein, and Randy Shaw, eds., *There's No Place Like Home: How America's Housing Crisis Threatens Our Children* (Collingdale, Pa.: DIANE Publishing Co., 1999), p. 6.

44. Arloc Sherman, Cheryl Amey, Barbara Duffield, Nancy Ebb, and Deborah Weinstein, *Welfare to What: Early Findings on Family Hardship and Well-Being* (Collingdale, Pa.: DIANE Publishing Co., 1997), p. 30.

45. See Jocelyn Guyer, Matthew Broaddus, and Michelle Cochran, *Missed Opportunities: Declining Medicaid Enrollment Undermines the Nation's Progress in Insuring Low-Income Children* (Washington, D.C.: Center on Budget and Policy Priorities, 1999), available at www.cbpp .org/10-20-99health.htm.

46. See R. Christopher Barden et al., "Emergency Medical Care and In-

jury/Illness Prevention Systems for Children," *Harvard Journal on Legislation* 30 (1993): 461, 462.

47. See Jill M. Ward, *Children and Guns: A Children's Defense Fund Report on Children Dying from Gunfire in America* (Washington, D.C.: Children's Defense Fund, 1999), p. 2, also available at www.childrens defense.org.

48. Lindsey, *Welfare of Children*, p. 93 table 5.2.

49. Richard Wexler, *The Lengthening Shadow* (Alexandria, Va.: National Coalition for Child Protection Reform, 2001), also available at www.nccpr.org/reports/lengtheningshadow.htm.

50. The best national standards are *Child Welfare League of America Standards of Excellence for Family Foster Care Services* (Washington, D.C.: Child Welfare League, rev. ed., 1995). See generally Bill Grimm, "Foster Parent Training: What the CFS Reviews Do and Don't Tell Us," *Youth Law News* 24, 2 (April-June 2003).

51. Dorothy Roberts, *Shattered Bonds* (New York: Basic Civitas, 2002), p. 151.

52. *Selected Child Welfare Trends* (New York: New York City Administration for Children's Services, 1998), p. 81.

53. Leroy H. Pelton, *For Reasons of Poverty: A Critical Analysis of the Public Child Welfare System in the United States* (Westport, Conn.: Greenwood Publishing Group, 1989).

54. "In Bushwick, Brooklyn 20 out of every 1,000 children have been removed from their homes and placed in protective custody. In Central Harlem, the rate is 1 out of every 10 children is in foster care. In the Upper East Side of Manhattan, less than one in 200 children are in care." Roberts, *Shattered Bonds*, p. 45. New York City has a total population in excess of 7.3 million people, of whom approximately 52 percent are "white." Thus, in a city of nearly 4 million people (speaking only of "whites"), New York has managed to maintain a foster care population of only 1,300 (again, speaking only of "whites"). See *Community Data Profiles* (New York: New York City Administration for Children's Services, 1998), p. 24.

55. Nanette Schorr, "Foster Care and the Politics of Compassion," *Tikkun* 7, 3 (May/June 1992).

56. Annette R. Appell, "Protecting Children or Punishing Mothers: Gender, Race, and Class in the Child Protection System," *South Carolina Law Review* 48 (1997): 577, 595–596.

57. Ibid., p. 598.

58. Jeff Katz, "Finally the Law Puts These Kids' Interests First," *Milwaukee Journal Sentinel* (Dec. 28, 1997), p. 1 (quoted in Robert M. Gordon, "Drifting through Byzantium: The Promise and Failure of the Adoption and Safe Families Act of 1997," *Minnesota Law Review* 83 (1999): 637, 638).

59. Gordon, "Drifting through Byzantium," p. 638, n.6 (quoting statement of Sen. DeWine and Rep. Hoyer, respectively).

60. Nina Bernstein, *The Lost Children of Wilder: The Epic Struggle to Change Foster Care* (New York: Pantheon, 2001), p. xiii.

7. Children's Rights that Serve Adults' Needs

1. Since the Court decided *Roe v. Wade,* 410 U.S. 113 (1973), it has decided the following cases involving minors and abortion: *Lambert v. Wicklund,* 520 U.S. 292, 293 (1997) (per curiam) (upholding constitutionality of a statute that required one-parent notification but allowed for judicial bypass when the judge finds that notice would not serve a child's best interests); *Planned Parenthood v. Casey,* 505 U.S. 833, 899 (1992) (joint opinion of O'Connor, Kennedy & Souter, JJ.) (upholding a statute requiring one parent's consent for an unwed minor's abortion because of its bypass option permitting the minor to seek judicial consent based on a finding that the minor is mature or that abortion is in her best interests); *Ohio v. Akron Ctr. for Reprod. Health,* 497 U.S. 502, 508, 519–520 (1990) (deciding that there is no undue burden in requiring judicial bypass whereby the minor either could show maturity, that she is a victim of abuse, or that notice is not in her best interests); *Hodgson v. Minnesota,* 497 U.S. 417, 455 (1990) (holding that a two-parent notification requirement is constitutional as long as the minor has an option to seek judicial review); *Planned Parenthood v. Ashcroft,* 462 U.S. 476, 493 (1983) (upholding a parental and judicial consent scheme which permitted unwed minors to obtain an abortion when a judge determined that the minor was mature or that the abortion was in her best interests); *City of Akron v. Akron Ctr. for Reprod. Health, Inc.,* 462 U.S. 416, 440 (1983) (holding that a parental and judicial consent scheme for unwed minors which contained a blanket determination that all minors under the age of fifteen were too immature to make a decision and that abortion could never be in minor's best interests in the absence of parental consent is unconstitutional), overruled in part by *Planned Parenthood v. Casey,* 505 U.S. 833 (1992)

(joint opinion of O'Connor, Kennedy & Souter, JJ.); H. L. v. Matheson, 450 U.S. 398, 413 (1981) (holding that a statute requiring a physician to notify the parent "if possible" of an unemancipated, immature minor when performing an abortion is facially constitutional); *Bellotti v. Baird*, 443 U.S. 622, 647, 650 (1979) (plurality opinion) (holding that even when judicial bypass is available, a state law requiring parental notification in all cases is unconstitutional); *Bellotti v. Baird*, 428 U.S. 132, 146–47, 151 (1976) (abstaining from deciding the constitutionality of a statute restricting an unwed minor's abortion and certifying questions to the state supreme court to obtain authoritative construction of law); *Planned Parenthood v. Danforth*, 428 U.S. 52, 74 (1976) (holding that a state statute prohibiting unmarried minors from procuring abortions during the first trimester of their pregnancies without a parent's consent is unconstitutional).

2. *Am. Acad. of Pediatrics v. Lungren*, 940 P.2d 797, 800 (Cal. 1997) (striking California's law because it offended the minor's right to the state constitution's right to privacy); *Planned Parenthood v. Farmer*, 762 A.2d 620, 621 (N.J. 2000) (striking, on equal protection grounds, New Jersey's judicial bypass statute because it impermissibly treats different classes of young women—those who seek an abortion and those who seek medical and/or surgical care related to pregnancy and childbirth).

3. Approximately half a million children are born to teenage mothers in the United States. *State of the World's Mothers* (Westport, Conn.: Save the Children, 2001), available at www.pela.fi/STC_fact_sheet_%20 Final.pdf.

4. Teenage pregnancy, however, declined markedly in the 1990s. Alan Guttmacher Institute, *Why Is Teenage Pregnancy Declining? The Roles of Abstinence, Sexual Activity and Contraceptive Use* (1999), available at www.guttmacher.org/pubs/or_teen_preg_decline.html.

5. See Jonathan Zimmerman, *Whose America? Culture Wars in the Public Schools* (Cambridge, Mass.: Harvard University Press, 2002), pp. 188–189.

6. Reported by the Center for Disease Control at www.cdc.gov/reproductivehealth/up_adolpreg.htm.

7. National Committee for Adoption Staff, *Adoption Factbook* (Alexandria, Va.: National Council for Adoption, 1985).

8. These are Alaska, California, Colorado, Connecticut, Florida, Hawaii, Illinois, Maryland, Montana, New Hampshire, New Jersey, New

Mexico, New York, Oklahoma, Oregon, Vermont, Washington, and Washington, D.C. See "A Patchwork of U.S. Laws on Abortion," *New York Times* (Jan. 20, 2003), p. A16.

9. Judith Levine, *Harmful to Minors: The Perils of Protecting Children from Sex* (Minneapolis, Minn.: University of Minnesota Press, 2002), p. 117.

10. See Abigail English and Madlyn Morreale, "A Legal and Policy Framework for Adolescent Health Care: Past, Present & Future," *Houston Journal of Health Law & Policy* 1 (2001): 63. See also Jennifer L. Rosato, "Let's Get Real: Quilting A Principled Approach to Adolescent Empowerment in Health Care Decision-Making," *DePaul Law Review* 51 (2002): 769.

11. *Alaska Stat.* §25.20.025(2) (Michie 2002); *Ark Code Ann.* §20–9–602(7) (Michie 2002); *Idaho Code* §39–4302 (Michie 2001); *New. Rev. Stat. Ann.* §129.030(2) (Michie 2001).

12. See Elizabeth S. Scott, "The Legal Construction of Adolescence," *Hofstra Law Review* 29 (2000): 547, 572, n.97 (citing a number of states that enacted laws expressly deeming pregnant minors adults for purposes of deciding whether to carry a fetus to term).

13. See *Hodgson v. Minnesota*, 497 U.S. 417, 466–467 (Marshall, J., dissenting).

14. Levine, *Harmful to Minors*, p. 96.

15. 428 U.S. 52 (1976).

16. 428 U.S. at 74.

17. Ibid.

18. See, e.g., *Morrison v. State*, 252 S. W.2d 97, 102 (Mo. Ct. App. 1952). See also *Mo. Ann. Stat.* §§431.061(1), 431.063 (West 2002). Both of these statutes were enacted in 1971 before the decision in *Roe v. Wade*, 410 U.S. 113 (1973).

19. See, e.g., *Meyer v. Nebraska*, 262 U.S. 390, 403 (1923).

20. *Wisconsin v. Yoder*, 406 U.S. 205, 232 (1972).

21. *Danforth*, 428 U.S. at 69.

22. See, e.g., *Abington Sch. Dist. v. Schempp*, 374 U.S. 203, 215–226 (1963).

23. *Prince v. Massachusetts*, 321 U.S. 158, 166 (1944).

24. See Danforth, 428 U.S. at 91 (Stewart, J., concurring).

25. Ibid. at 90–91 (Stewart, J., concurring) (footnote omitted).

26. See Danforth, 428 U.S. at 95 (White, J., dissenting).

27. Ibid. at 104 (Stevens, J., concurring in part and dissenting in part).

28. *Bellotti v. Baird*, 443 U.S. 622 (1979).

29. Ibid. at 653–654 (Stevens, J., concurring in the judgment).

30. I have elsewhere discussed Powell's voting record in many children's rights cases. Time and again, he voted against the children's rights position. In a number of these cases he expressed his views forcefully. From these statements, it is reasonable to conclude that Powell was among the Court's most anti–children's rights justices in the modern era. See Martin Guggenheim, "Minor Rights: The Adolescent Abortion Cases," *Hofstra Law Review* 30 (2002): 589.

31. See *Bellotti*, 443 U.S. at 650 (plurality opinion).

32. See, e.g., *Planned Parenthood v. Casey*, 505 U.S. 833, 899 (1992) (joint opinion of O'Connor, Kennedy & Souter, JJ.).

33. *Bellotti*, 443 U.S. at 633.

34. Ibid. at 634–635 (plurality opinion).

35. Ibid. at 640–641 (plurality opinion).

36. Ibid. at 647.

37. Ibid. at 644 (plurality opinion).

38. Franklin E. Zimring, *The Changing Legal World of Adolescence* (New York: Free Press, 1982), p. 64.

39. See Kate Zernike, "30 Years After *Roe v. Wade*, New Trends but the Old Debate," *New York Times* (Jan. 20, 2003), p. A1. The success of the anti-abortion stance in the legislative arena must also be considered against surveys that consistently show that about 80 percent of Americans support the right to an abortion and that this figure has remained basically the same since 1989.

40. *Carey v. Population Services International*, 431 U.S. 678 (1977).

41. Ibid. at 702–703 (White, J., concurring in part and concurring in the result).

42. See ibid. at 715 (Stevens, J., concurring in part and concurring in the judgment).

43. John C. Jeffries, Jr., *Justice Lewis F. Powell, Jr.* (New York: Charles Scribner, 1994), p. 346.

44. Ibid., p. 347.

45. See *Michael M. v. Superior Court*, 450 U.S. 464, 470–471 (1981) (plurality opinion).

46. Ibid. at 471, n4.

47. *Carey v. Population Servs. Int'l*, 431 U.S. 678, 696 n.21 (1977).

48. 442 U.S. 584 (1979).

49. Ibid. at 603–604.

50. Ibid. at 604–605.

51. Ibid. at 603.

52. Ibid. at 612–613.
53. This concern is made explicitly by Justice Stewart in his concurring opinion in *Danforth*, which was joined by Justice Powell. See *Danforth*, 428 U.S. at 91 n.2 (1976).
54. See Scott, "Legal Construction," 574 & n.111 (citations omitted).
55. See *Hodgson v. Minnesota*, 497 U.S. 417, 441 (1990).
56. Scott, "Legal Construction," p. 574, n.110 (discussing H. B. v. Wilkenson, 639 F.Supp. 952, 955–956 (D. Utah 1986)).
57. See Amy Bach, "No Choice for Teens," *The Nation* (Oct. 11, 1999), pp. 6–7 (quoting Juvenile Judge Mark Anderson of Montgomery, Alabama). See also Steven A. Holmes, "Courts Put Girls on the Stand in Alabama," *New York Times* (January 20, 2003), p. A16.
58. *Hodgson v. Minnesota*, 648 F.Supp. 756, 766 (D. Minn. 1986) (quoting testimony of Judge William Sweeney).
59. Robert H. Mnookin, *In the Interest of Children: Advocacy, Law Reform, and Public Policy* (New York: W. H. Freeman Company, 1985), p. 263. See also *Hodgson v. Minnesota*, 497 U.S. 417, 475 (1990) (Marshall, J., concurring in part and dissenting in part).

8. How Children's Rights Impact Family Law and Juvenile Rights

1. Even so, leaders of the children's rights movement lament the degree to which children remain under-represented in legal proceedings affecting their interests. "America's Children at Risk: A National Agenda for Legal Action, Executive Summary of the American Bar Association Presidential Working Group on the Unmet Legal Needs of Children and Their Families," *Family Law Quarterly* 27 (1993): 433, 442.
2. *Olmstead v. United States*, 277 U.S. 438, 479 (1928) (Brandeis, J., dissenting).
3. 458 U.S. 502 (1982).
4. See *Jones v. Cunningham*, 371 U.S. 236 (1963); *Carafas v. LaVallee*, 391 U.S. 234 (1968).
5. 467 U.S. 263 (1984).
6. *Board of Education v. Earls*, 536 U.S. 822 (2002).
7. See, e.g., Barry C. Feld, "Violent Youth and Public Policy: A Case Study of Juvenile Justice Law Reform," *Minnesota Law Review* 79 (1995): 965.
8. Office of Juvenile Justice and Delinquency Prevention, *Juvenile Offenders and Victims: 1999 National Report*, p. 89, at www.ncjrs.org/html/ojjdp/nationalreport99/chapter4.pdf.

9. See Jeffrey Fagan and Franklin E. Zimring, eds., *The Changing Borders of Juvenile Justice: Transfer of Adolescents to the Criminal Court* (Chicago, Ill.: University of Chicago Press, 2000).

10. Richard E. Redding, "The Effects of Adjudicating and Sentencing Juveniles as Adults," *Youth Violence and Juvenile Justice* 1 (2003): 128, 129.

11. Marty Beyer, "Experts for Juveniles at Risk of Adult Sentences," in Patricia Puritz, A. Capozello, and W. Shange, eds., *More Than Meets the Eye: Rethinking Assessment, Competency and Sentencing for a Harsher Era of Juvenile Justice* (Washington, D.C.: American Bar Association Juvenile Justice Center, 1997), pp. 1–22. A different study found that juveniles were ten times more likely to be sexually assaulted than if kept in a juvenile facility. J. Zeidenberg and V. Schiraldi, *The Risks Juveniles Face When They Are Incarcerated with Adults* (1997). Retrieved from www.cjcj.org/jpi/risks.html.

12. Available from www.law.onu.edu (search for "faculty," "Streib," and "juvenile offenders on death row").

13. Ibid.

14. Ibid.

15. Walter A. Logan, "Proportionality and Punishment: Imposing Life Without Parole on Juveniles," *Wake Forest Law Review* 33 (1988): 681, 690–691.

16. See *State v. Furman*, 858 P.2d 1092, 1102 (Wash. 1993); Vt. Stat. Ann. tit. 13, § 2303; id. tit. 33, §5506.

17. Dana Canedy, "As Florida Boy Serves Life Term, Even Prosecutor Wonders Why," *New York Times* (Jan. 5, 2003), p. A1.

18. 319 U.S. 624 (1943).

19. 347 U.S. 483 (1954).

20. *Barnette*, 319 U.S. at 634.

21. Ibid. at 641.

22. Ibid. at 642.

23. 163 U.S. 537 (1896).

24. But see Theresa Glennon and Robert G. Schwartz, "Foreword: Looking Back, Looking Ahead: The Evolution of Children's Rights," *Temple Law Review* 68 (1995): 1557, 1559 (citing *Brown* and *In re Gault* as laying the foundation for the modern children's rights movement).

25. See, e.g., Paul Goodman, *Growing Up Absurd* (New York: Random House, 1960); Edgar Z. Friedenberg, *The Dignity of Youth and Other Atavisms* (Boston, Mass.: Beacon Press, 1965).

26. See, e.g., *In re Gault*, 387 U.S. 1, 13 (1967) ("Neither the Fourteenth Amendment nor the Bill of Rights is for adults alone") and *Tinker v. Des Moines Indep. Comm. School Dist.*, 393 U.S. 503 (1969).
27. *Tinker*, 393 U.S. at 509, 510–511.
28. Ibid. at 510.
29. Ibid. at 511, 512–513.
30. 244 F.3d 572 (7th Cir. 2000).
31. Ibid. at 577.
32. 419 U.S. 565 (1975).
33. Ibid. at 589–590.
34. A parallel set of claims can be made on behalf of illegal aliens and others who are denied rights possessed by Americans. Thus, the challenge by detainees in Guantánamo Bay that they are impermissibly being held yields a first response that they have no rights. But if the challenge focused on the limits of government officials to arrest and detain individuals (whether or not they are Americans and even if they do not have rights protected by American law), American law might be found by the Court to place restraints on these officials.
35. See, e.g., Richard Delgado, ed., *Critical Race Theory: The Cutting Edge* (Philadelphia: Temple University Press, 1995).

Acknowledgments

As I hope is apparent from the subject and content of this book, children are a very important part of my life. I am blessed because I have been able to combine my personal and professional lives by focusing children and families. This has, of course, come at some expense to my own family. A lot of the time I spent thinking about and writing this book prevented me from paying as close attention to my family as I should have been paying. I am especially grateful to my wife, Denise Guggenheim, who not only encouraged me to write this book but proved to be a wonderful and careful reader of early drafts.

I'm blessed in still other ways. I have the privilege of working at a great university with remarkable colleagues who happily make themselves available to others. This book was especially important for me personally because I began to write it after I recovered from an illness in 2002. At the time, I needed a sustained project to help heal me. But I don't think I would ever have written this book without enthusiastic encouragement from friends and colleagues. I owe special thanks to Jerome Bruner, David Garland, Jennifer Gordon, and Linda Mills for helping me believe that I should write this book. I am very grateful to Anthony Amsterdam for helping me think through some knotty questions. I am amazed at the generosity of friends who took the time to carefully read and react to various earlier drafts and am particularly grateful to Annette Appell,

Christine Gottlieb, Elizabeth Scott, and Lydia Tugendrajch for their fabulous contributions.

This book is an amalgam of my experiences as a lawyer and law teacher for more than thirty years. I've learned so much about children's and parents' rights from working with my colleagues Paula Fendall, Randy Hertz, and Madeleine Kurtz it's sometimes difficult for me to really know where my ideas begin and theirs end. The same thing can be said for my countless students.

I also want to acknowledge the generosity and support of the New York University School of Law, particularly Deans Ricky Revesz and John Sexton, who allowed me a sabbatical in academic year 2002–03 during which I wrote the bulk of this book. The law school has also provided generous research support through its Filomen D'Agostino and Max E. Greenberg Research Fund. In addition, I am grateful to the law school for allowing me to present a chapter at a faculty workshop luncheon. The law library was extremely helpful, and I especially thank Gretchen Feltes, who unfailingly complied with any and all requests for assistance.

Thanks to the *Arizona Law Review,* which published "Maximizing Strategies for Pressuring Adults to Do Right by Children," *Arizona Law Review* 45 (2003): 765; the *Harvard Law Review,* which published "Somebody's Children: Sustaining the Family's Place in Child Welfare Policy," *Harvard Law Review* 113 (2002): 1716; and the *Hofstra Law Review,* which published "Minor Rights: The Adolescent Abortion Cases," *Hofstra Law Review* 30 (2002): 589 for permitting me to draw upon those articles.

Finally, a very special thanks is due to Elizabeth Knoll at Harvard University Press, who encouraged me every step of the way (even before I wrote a first sentence) and who carefully read the manuscript as it went through various drafts. Her feedback was invaluable, but her support is worth even more.

Index

DATE DUE

June			